Law and Politics

FELIX FRANKFURTER

Law and Politics

OCCASIONAL PAPERS OF

FELIX FRANKFURTER

1913-1938

EDITED BY ARCHIBALD MAC LEISH

AND E. F. PRICHARD, JR., WITH

A FOREWORD BY MR. MAC LEISH

Harcourt, Brace and Company, New York

Designed by Robert Josephy

PRINTED IN THE UNITED STATES OF AMERICA

BY QUINN & BODEN COMPANY, INC., RAHWAY, N. J.

CONTENTS

Contents

Contents

Foreword

AUTHORS who stop writing usually go where they can't watch their editors at work. The author of this book has gone instead to the Supreme Court of the United States. He has stopped writing in the usual journalistic sense of the word as certainly as though he had retired from the planet. But he has not gone far enough to be oblivious to the use made of his papers nor has he left testamentary instructions for their disposition. The consequence is that their publication presents certain difficulties. Other editors can retire behind the general responsibility of their authors, for an author who dies is presumed to intend the consequences of his act, one of which is certainly the publication of his scattered writings. We have no such refuge. Elevation to the Supreme Court, however it may remove a man from the journalistic world, is scarcely the equivalent of death, and similar literary conclusions cannot be drawn. The responsibility for publication is therefore ours. And though we shoulder that responsibility with pride so far as our readers are concerned, we bear the burden a little more heavily in the face of our author. Both Mr. Prichard and I have been law students of Felix Frankfurter, though at periods twenty years apart. We remember very well a blue ironic eye behind a brightly polished eye-glass. We remember also a voice which can crackle under a fool's complacence like dry wood under an empty kettle.

There are, nevertheless, two reasons why we believe the magazine articles and occasional papers of Mr. Frankfurter should be published at this time. The first is a very simple reason. They are good articles. The second is hardly more complex. They are an index to the American future.

The first reason will be apparent to anyone who will sample this book. I do not refer to its manner and style alone, though

ix

its manner and style are remarkable. Few scholars, and fewer scholars of the law, have written a more natural, more lucid or more readable English than Mr. Frankfurter writes at his best—his Sacco-Vanzetti article, for example. When it is considered that Mr. Frankfurter's first tongue was German and his second Hungarian, that he had not heard the sound of English until he came to this country at the age of twelve, his mastery of English becomes astonishing. But even more remarkable than the English in which he writes are the penetration and the sense of history with which he has written. Not only has he mastered a tongue other than the tongue he was born to: he has mastered a profession other than his own.

If the test of a good journalist is his ability to discern the historic issues under the political pother and the apparent divisions of his time, then Felix Frankfurter is one of the few, the very few, really good journalists of his generation. For twenty-five years he has been writing on the principal controversial questions occupying the American mind. He has written on these questions not in the terms in which they presented themselves but in the terms, as it now seems, in which they will be remembered. The result is that a great part of what he has written journalistically and for the moment is as interesting today as it was when it was written. Some of it, indeed, is more interesting today, for time has underlined its justness.

The first article here reprinted, which is also Mr. Frankfurter's first contribution to a general magazine, is as good an example as any. Mr. Frankfurter is discussing what was then the controversial issue of "judicial recall"—the recall of judicial decisions by popular vote. Theodore Roosevelt had supported judicial recall in his 1912 campaign. The American Bar Association had adopted a resolution (of which Mr. Frankfurter approved) condemning it. General newspaper discussion of the issue was in terms either of the campaign or the resolution. But Mr. Frankfurter did not discuss it in these terms. To Mr. Frankfurter the question was "the cause of the ferment that partly expresses itself in the ill-conceived proposal of the judicial recall." Why were the

Foreword

with decisions of the Supreme Court that people seriously proposed their recall by popular referendum?

Of that question Mr. Frankfurter writes in words which have a
peculiar pertinence today when a second proposal for the correction of the judiciary, supported by a second Roosevelt, has been
buried under the indignant resolutions of another generation of
self-righteous lawyers and newspaper publishers. It was no answer
then, and it is no answer now, to condemn the cure. What must
be studied is the disease. "Until social and economic legislation
came before the courts," writes Mr. Frankfurter, "they did not
touch the people at large. But dealing with such legislation, involving as it does the vital interests of life of a vast body of the
community, the courts necessarily are brought in direct contact
with the public needs, and their work has intimate public significance. Hence, the importance of recognizing the true character of
the questions which come before them." "In so far as these questions are necessarily questions of fact, dealing with actual conditions of life and current dominant public opinion, it is essential
that the stream of the Zeitgeist be allowed to flood the sympathies
and the intelligence of our judges. This is necessary, not only for
the well-being of the state and the social order, but for the unimpaired continuance of our judicial system." This language must
have shocked the resolutions committee of the American Bar Association in 1912. To us it reveals the true nature of one of the
principal issues of that time, and thereby the true nature of one
of the principal issues of our own. To make past history presently
significant is a trick any good historian can turn. To make the
present significant to an unknown future is a much more difficult
achievement. It is an achievement few journalists ever touch. Mr.
Frankfurter has touched it several times.

For that reason alone the papers here collected would be well
worth publishing. But there is another and a more convincing
reason why they should appear. They chart the social and economic and political thinking of a man who may well sit on the
Supreme Court for the next quarter of a century. And the social

and economic and political thinking of a Justice of the Supreme
Court who may serve for many years is an index to the probable
future of the republic.

Down to a relatively recent past, or so long as the social beliefs
of the Justices of the Supreme Court were the same as the social
beliefs of the leaders of the bar and the owners of the newspapers,
it was not considered good form to acknowledge this fact. Eminent
attorneys and eminent journalists of the period would no more
admit in public that Justices of the Supreme Court had opinions
of their own, or that those opinions were important, than they
would admit in public that ladies had legs. The Supreme Court
was presented to laymen and law students as a draped impersonal
figure which moved from one point to another like a vast Victorian
female, without the aid of human limbs. But with the passage of
time and the emergence of a Court minority which expressed conclusions different from the conclusions of the leaders of the bar,
even the leaders of the bar began to admit that some, at least,
of the Justices had opinions of their own and that those opinions
counted.

It is now possible in all social circles, the most conservative as
well as the most radical, to lift the skirts of the Court and see the
boots of the Justices. And seeing the boots of the Justices, it is
possible to foretell with considerable accuracy the direction in which
the republic is *not* about to move. For the power of the Court to
shape the American future is neither more nor less than the power
of a majority of its members to refuse to permit the American
future to be legislated in a given sense.

The Court exerts this power negatively by digging in with its
heels rather than affirmatively by pushing forward with its toes.
The direction of its heels is therefore the direction in which the
future is impenetrable. The papers which follow show the orientation of Mr. Justice Frankfurter's boots. They show this orientation,
moreover, not accidentally or by implication or in spite of themselves, but with the full consent and blessing of their author. Mr.
Frankfurter, though he may have left the more sanctified radicals
in some doubt as to the precise features of the things he is for,

has never left room for question in any man's mind as to the precise nature of the things he is against. His political utopia may be less visible than some but not so his political Gehenna. One proof of that was his willingness to face the mass hysteria of Boston's Back Bay in the Sacco and Vanzetti case and his choice of Boston's *Atlantic Monthly* as the place in which to face it.

Furthermore, Mr. Frankfurter's consent goes not merely to the content of his opinions on social and political questions but to the relation of those opinions to his present functions on the Supreme Court. He has been for years one of the most convinced advocates of realism in dealing with the Justices of the Court. Writing in the *New Republic* eighteen years ago, he said: "Granted this power of judicial review is to be retained, its true nature should be frankly recognized by the public and frankly avowed by the courts. The simple fact of the matter is that in a decision like *Truax* v. *Corrigan* the Court, under the guise of legal form, exercises political control. That the courts are especially fitted to be the ultimate arbiters of policy is an intelligent and tenable doctrine. But let them and us face the fact that five Justices of the Supreme Court *are* conscious molders of policy instead of the impersonal vehicles of revealed truth."

Mr. Frankfurter's position, whether expressed in criticism of the pretense of impersonality or in some other connection, has always been that the Court "exercises political control" and that the functions of its members are functions of statesmanship. Writing two years ago of Mr. Justice Holmes he quoted with approval from Theodore Roosevelt's letter to Senator Lodge on the occasion of Holmes's appointment. "In the ordinary and low sense which we attach to the words 'partisan' and 'politician' a judge of the Supreme Court should be neither. But in the higher sense, in the proper sense, he is not in my judgment fitted for the position unless he is a party man, a constructive statesman, constantly keeping in mind his adherence to the principles and policies under which this nation has been built up and in accordance with which it must go on; keeping in mind also his relations with his fellow statesmen who, in other branches of the government, are striving in co-operation with him to advance the ends of government."

Mr. Frankfurter, it may safely be assumed, agrees with Mr. Roosevelt, and agrees therefore that the political and social views of a Justice of the Court are proper matters of inquiry. To Mr. Frankfurter also a man is not fitted for a place on the Supreme Court unless he is a constructive statesman and, in the higher sense, in the proper sense, a politician. Suggestions are made from time to time that the political activities of the Supreme Court are the creations of nothing more than its own willingness to entertain objections to social and economic legislation under the Due Process clauses, and that the need for statesmanship and political sagacity would disappear if the Court should refuse to entertain such pleas. There is some weight in the suggestion. The phrase "due process of law" is a technical legal phrase which can no more fix the proper limits of social and economic legislation than a mathematical formula can fix the proper limits of the sea. It is therefore true that the attempt of the Court to use the phrase for that inappropriate purpose has had the effect of remitting the Justices to their private notions of the kind of legislation an American legislature ought to pass. But it is not true that the refusal of the Court to hear objections of this kind would take the Court out of politics or its Justices out of affairs of state. "The Supreme Court," as Mr. Frankfurter writes in the *Encyclopedia of the Social Sciences*, has "ceased to be a common law court. The stuff of its business is what on the continent is formally known as public law. . . . The construction of important federal legislation and of the Constitution is now [its] staple business. . . ." So long as that remains true the Justices of the Supreme Court will continue to be what Theodore Roosevelt said they were, and their personal opinions on political and social and economic matters will be opinions of the greatest importance to citizens of the republic.

"The history of the Supreme Court," Mr. Frankfurter has written, "is not the history of an abstraction but the analysis of individuals acting as a Court who make decisions and lay down

doctrines. . . ." "It would deny all meaning to history to believe
that the course of events would have been the same if Thomas
Jefferson had had the naming of Spencer Roane to the place to
which John Adams called John Marshall or if Roscoe Conkling
rather than Morrison R. Waite had headed the Court before
which came the Granger legislation. The evolution of finance
capitalism in the United States, and, therefore, of American
history after the Reconstruction period, would hardly have been
the same if the views of men like Mr. Justice Miller and Mr.
Justice Harlan had dominated the Court from the Civil War to
Theodore Roosevelt's administration."

All this is even truer today than it was of the generation of
which Mr. Frankfurter writes. The American system is faced with
a more urgent necessity of adapting itself to changed conditions
now than ever before in its history. The critical question is the
question whether it will be able to make the required changes by
legislation under the Constitution, preserving the democratic
forms which are the only guarantees of democratic substance, or
whether the required changes will be made outside the Constitution, destroying democratic forms and establishing in their place
a form of government which solves economic problems by sacri-
ficing human liberty. The answer to that question is an answer to
be made first by the framers of state and federal legislation and
by the electorate which gives them power. But in that answer the
Justices who will sit on the Supreme Court over the next several
years have also a great and equal responsibility. For it is in the
power of these Justices to say in what direction change is possible
within the Constitution and in what direction change is possible
only without the Constitution. What they say on this question will
be determined in the last analysis by their convictions as to the
kind of nation this nation, under the Constitution, is and must
remain—or should become.

The convictions of a Justice of the Supreme Court, like the convictions of any other man, are the products of his experience. Mr.
Frankfurter's experience of the kind of nation this nation is began

with an immigrant's landing in New York in 1896. One thing he was certain of then, and has been certain of ever since, is the democracy of the country to which he came. What other men inherited and therefore took for granted he discovered for himself and therefore earned. There may have been other Justices of the Court who have held American democracy in as great respect as Mr. Frankfurter holds it: none has respected it more, or more earnestly resented its disrepute. What he said in April, 1938, he meant—"I can express with very limited adequacy the passionate devotion to this land that possesses millions of our people, born like myself under other skies, for the privilege this country has bestowed in allowing them to partake of its fellowship."

But American democracy, as he soon learned, had its problems also, and two months after his graduation from the Harvard Law School in 1906 he was dealing with one of the most pressing. That problem was the problem of the application of the laws, including the criminal laws, to the great property interests which had acquired a control not only of the national economy but of a considerable part of the national government as well. Theodore Roosevelt's attempt to bring within the law the "malefactors of great wealth" of lower Manhattan had enlisted the aid of Colonel Henry L. Stimson who took over the job of District Attorney for the Southern District of New York. Colonel Stimson had hired Felix Frankfurter as an assistant. And Felix Frankfurter spent the first five years of his career as a lawyer in the struggle to teach Big Business that it also owed obedience to the people's laws.

That experience was illuminating. The young lawyer who won the appeals in the Sugar Fraud cases was a young lawyer who had learned unforgettable things. But what followed was even more instructive. By a curious twist of history Felix Frankfurter was dropped, in 1911, into the center of one of the first American attempts at a regulation of industry not for police purposes only but for an affirmative, social end. Colonel Stimson was again the god in the machine. Colonel Stimson had become Secretary of War Stimson under Taft, and Felix Frankfurter had gone to Washington as Law Officer of the Bureau of Insular Affairs, and counsel to the Secretary in the exercise of his jurisdiction over rivers and harbors. It was in this last capacity that Mr. Frankfurter found himself again on the Government-Big Business front. President Taft had announced at the beginning of his administration that no permits were to be issued for the construction of dams on navigable streams without some *quid pro quo* to the government. That principle, once enunciated, produced in the logic of time the Federal Power Commission and the yard-stick theories developed by the TVA. And Mr. Frankfurter, as counsel to the Secretary, was the guardian of the principle. Through the last two years of Mr. Taft's administration and the first year of Mr. Wilson's, Mr. Frankfurter was thus concerned with the conflict between democratic government and industrial imperialism at the point where that conflict was sharpest and most sharply felt.

But it was not merely his professional work which turned his mind in this period to the place of the law and of lawyers in the economic problems of a democratic society. It was also his friends. The two men who most influenced the thinking of Mr. Frankfurter at this time, and throughout his life, were Mr. Justice Brandeis, then a practicing lawyer in Boston, and Mr. Justice Holmes.

Mr. Justice Holmes was a man of the world, who was also a philosopher, who was incidentally a lawyer. The result was that he was a very great judge—so great a judge indeed that his quality as a man and as a mind was often hidden behind his judicial eminence. But his influence on his friends, which was itself one of the great forces of his time, was always the influence of a personality and a way of thinking. It was not in all cases—however heretical it may be to say so—a fortunate influence. The skepticism and the philosophic detachment which sat so easily with Mr. Justice Holmes himself, giving flavor and taste to his strong humanity as salt gives flavor and taste to fresh meat, had a caustic and pickling effect on lesser vitalities, so that many of the great Justice's disciples were left only with the skepticism and the detachment and without the human and believing force.

But with Mr. Frankfurter, and with others of equal exuberance of mind and of emotion, the influence of Mr. Justice Holmes was a sovereign prescription. For Mr. Justice Holmes saw the law, as few great jurists have ever seen it, in a decent relation to a world which contains also men and women and poetry and work and wars. He saw the pretensions of the law to final precision as skeptically as he saw the pretensions of philosophers to ultimate truth or the pretensions of politicians to disinterested service. And he, therefore, perceived and taught and said that the law—even the law of the Constitution—must make its own adjustments to its time. What he gave his fortunate friends was not a complete philosophy: it is more than doubtful that he had one. What he gave them, and Mr. Frankfurter among them, was an understanding of the relation of the law to life which made impossible a conception of the law as anything but a means to an end. To most great lawyers the law sooner or later becomes a substantive, a noun. To Mr. Justice Holmes it was always a verb having a predicate to follow.

The influence of Mr. Justice Brandeis was more immediate, more specific, more controlling, and perhaps less deep. To Mr. Justice Brandeis also the law was a means to social ends, but a specific means to specific social ends. Though no philosopher in the humanistic sense, Mr. Justice Brandeis held more precise philosophic beliefs than Mr. Justice Holmes and his trace in Mr. Frankfurter's thinking is easier to follow. He is directly responsible, for example, for an early interest in scientific management and the Taylor Society which Mr. Frankfurter developed before the War. He is directly responsible, also, for Mr. Frankfurter's concern with labor legislation after Mr. Frankfurter's appointment to the faculty of the Harvard Law School in 1914 and thus indirectly responsible for Mr. Frankfurter's war-time career first on the President's Mediation Commission and eventually as Chairman of the War Labor Policies Board. And echoes of his views about the evils of industrial "bigness" and the advantages of Federalism may be caught in much of what Mr. Frankfurter has since written.

But Mr. Justice Brandeis's principal contribution to the shaping of Mr. Frankfurter's mind was his development, in association with

Mr. Frankfurter and Miss Josephine Goldmark, of a new technique for the argument of cases involving social and economic issues—a technique which was to have radical effects not only on the pleading of such cases but on the attitude toward them of the profession and even of the general public. It was Mr. Brandeis's view that appellate briefs in cases involving social and economic legislation should argue not only the principles of law involved, but the factual background of relevant social and economic considerations which had influenced the legislature. The statute, in other words, should be looked at, not through the cracks in the constitutional fence, but out in the open lot where its place in a total social organization of people actually alive in an actual world might be seen. The Oregon ten-hour law was thus presented in a Brandeis-Frankfurter-Goldmark brief in the case of *Bunting* v. *Oregon* and Mr. Frankfurter, after the appointment of Mr. Brandeis to the Bench, successfully argued that brief in the Supreme Court. From that time forward, in subsequent magazine articles as well as in subsequent briefs, Mr. Frankfurter's thinking was deeply affected by the implications of this method. In a 1916 article in the *New Republic,* of which magazine he was a contributing editor from the beginning, he cites with approval Mr. Brandeis's remark to the Chicago Bar Association that he hoped to be able to extend the domain of law by absorbing into it the facts of life, as Lord Mansfield, in his day, extended the common law by absorbing into it the law merchant.

Further examples of the influence of one or the other of these two greatest of modern judges, Holmes and Brandeis, will be found throughout the papers which follow. The influence of the two together is to be seen in Mr. Frankfurter's reluctance to accept for himself any of the definable political positions of his time; a matter of vivid concern to many of his friends upon the Left. Writing in 1937 (*A Rigid Outlook in a Dynamic World*), Mr. Frankfurter expresses his conviction that dogmatic positions and universal theories must yield to fact. ". . . In the resistance to these practical, empiric, *ad hoc* interventions of organized society by doctrines which either have become obsolete or only partially valid because qualified by counter-doctrines, we find the clue not only to the history of the last fifty years but to the tensions of the future. Once there is adequate recognition of the intrinsic complexity of the problems that confront us and the extremely limited range of issues that can be settled out of hand by invoking general formulas, however hallowed, the whole mental climate in which these problems are thought out and worked out will be changed. For then it will become manifest that the science of government is really the most difficult of all the arts, that it is, in the language of one of the great Justices of the Supreme Court, uttered more than a hundred years ago, 'the science of experiment.' " Those who believe that there is very little time for democratic experiment left and that blundering action is preferable to advised inaction may object to so detached a view. They must admit, however, that it is the natural child of the philosophic skepticism of Holmes and of Brandeis's passion for the facts.

But if Mr. Frankfurter's masters taught him to bring his laboratory methods into politics they also taught him to take his political conscience into the laboratory. In 1914, after three years of Washington, Mr. Frankfurter was called to the Harvard Law School as a member of the faculty. The Harvard Law School, in 1914, was what it had long been, the greatest school of law and one of the greatest educational institutions in the country. It made young men who had never used their minds before use their minds until they forgot to eat and sleep. But even the Harvard Law School had its failings, the chief of which was its attitude toward "the law." "The law" at Harvard at that time was an intellectual pattern which young men, armed with a dialectical tool called the Socratic Method, were expected to excavate, like some beautiful and buried city which needed only digging to be known. The relating of cases to their occasions or of legal principles to their human effects was not encouraged. There was no nonsense about justice in the Harvard Law School of the years before the War.

To this school Mr. Frankfurter came as a young man of thirty-two with ten years of public service and many evenings of exciting talk in the back of his mind. The law to him was a very different thing from the law as it appeared to many of his older colleagues. "I look forward," he quotes Holmes as saying, "to a time when the part played by history in the explanation of dogma shall be very small and instead of ingenious research we shall spend our energy on a study of the ends sought to be attained and the reasons for desiring them." What concerned Mr. Frankfurter from the beginning of his teaching was the study of "the ends sought to be attained and the reasons for desiring them." The law to him was not a buried antique city lying perfect underground, but a means by which the city of the future might perhaps be built.

That there were differences of opinion between Mr. Frankfurter and his older colleagues will surprise no one. Neither should it be surprising that the bright young men who were adept at sapping and mining in the traditional manner should find Mr. Frankfurter frivolous. Passionate golfers and chess players take the same attitude toward those who ask them why they play. But what *is* perhaps surprising is the fact that Mr. Frankfurter was able to survive that opposition and eventually to leave an ineffaceable mark not only on the instruction of the School but on the lives of many of the best men who attended it. For years—long before the New Deal—he was diverting to a brief experience of public service men who, in the old days, would have sniffed at anything but a warm berth in a big New York office. The Federal Trade Commission, the Interstate Commerce Commission, the chambers of Justices of the Court, and the many federal bureaus and commissions of the War, were peppered with Harvard Law School men. Most went back to private practice. A few stayed. But all had formed a different picture of the law. From the days of the War on there were fewer graduates of the Harvard Law School who could look forward complacently to a lifetime spent in a down-town law office with the hope perhaps of rising to the presidency of a bank.

Mr. Frankfurter's own experience of the relation of law to the life of his time did not end with his appointment to the School. In 1917 he left Cambridge for a Washington week-end with Secretary of War Newton D. Baker, which lasted for two years.

Mr. Frankfurter's previous experience of the adaptation of the law to social necessities had familiarized him with two aspects of the struggle of government to control Big Business. Now he was to see the legal implications of the struggle of labor to gain economic freedom. First as Secretary and Counsel to the President's Mediation Commission, investigating labor difficulties, and later as Chairman of the War Labor Policies Board, framing a labor policy for the country as a whole, Mr. Frankfurter had extraordinary opportunities to study the American labor situation at first hand and in national terms.

What he there observed influenced his actions over the next ten years and gave him the intellectual preoccupations which, more than anything else, have determined the public estimate of his character. The Labor issue, in the years of the Great War and the years immediately following, was not so much an economic issue or a social issue as an issue involving fundamental questions of civil rights. Mr. Frankfurter's War Labor Policies Board worked out collective bargaining standards which were extremely useful to the framers of the NIRA and the Wagner Act. But it was Mr. Frankfurter's experience on the President's Mediation Commission which most deeply influenced his thinking. His service on that Commission took him to California to study and report on the Mooney Case, and to Bisbee, Arizona, to inquire into the deportation by vigilantes of a thousand IWW miners who were marooned without adequate food or water in a desert town. Having seen industrial terrorism at first hand, it was natural that he should take action when Attorney-General Palmer began his Red Raids in the Boston Area in 1919, and natural that he should take part in the formation of the American Civil Liberties Union which shortly followed. Having committed himself thus to the defense of civil rights, it was natural also that he should join forces with those who attempted to save Sacco and Vanzetti from legal lynching in the capital of Massachusetts.

Mr. Frankfurter's 1927 article on that case is important not only because it is the best single statement of the facts and not only because it established Mr. Frankfurter's general reputation as a defender of constitutional liberties but because it shows his peculiar sensitivity to attacks on civil rights and his deep and passionate devotion to their defense. It would be impossible to overestimate the importance of that sensitivity and that devotion in the present constitutional crisis. The question which history presents to us is the question whether our present industrial and economic system can be changed over to an efficient, workable and socially effective system without the substitution of authoritarian forms of government for the democratic forms of government to which we are devoted. Translated into constitutional terms that question becomes the question whether the Court can and will permit the legislatures the widest latitude in framing economic measures altering property relations while sharply rejecting all attempts to curtail or restrict civil liberties. On that issue the position of Mr. Frankfurter is clear. He has stated his views on both halves of the question separately. And, in writing of Mr. Justice Holmes, he has by inference stated his view of the two together. In the case of economic measures, as Mr. Frankfurter puts it, Holmes was "hesitant to oppose his own opinion to the economic views of the legislature." The legislatures clearly having power to interfere with property rights in certain cases, Mr. Justice Holmes was willing, in cases involving economic and social legislation alleged to violate the Due Process clauses, to make the legislative discretion as broad as possible. But not so in cases where laws and other acts encroached on guaranteed rights and liberties such, for first example, as freedom of speech. There he was far more ready to declare acts of legislation unconstitutional because history had taught him that "since social development is a process of trial and error, the fullest possible opportunity for the free play of the human mind was an indefeasible prerequisite. . . ."

It is difficult to avoid the conclusion that Mr. Frankfurter will take his stand upon the same distinction. But there is more than a persuasive distinction persuasively drawn to reassure those who believe in American democracy and hope for its successful issue from the crisis of our time. There are also Mr. Frankfurter's proven qualities of head and heart—his great courage, his brilliant scholarship, his magnanimity of mind. Not only his friends but those who are not his friends may well believe that liberal democracy will be defended on the Supreme Court in the next generation as it has rarely been defended in the history of this country.

No one who reads this book can doubt that Mr. Frankfurter, in his capacity as a Justice of the Supreme Court, will think of the labor of that Court as a labor of statesmanship. No one can doubt either that he will see that labor in contemporary terms: in the terms in which history has posed it. Twenty-seven years ago he supported the Square Deal of Theodore Roosevelt. Seven years ago he supported the New Deal of Franklin Roosevelt. Their common characteristic as he sees it is this: that they were both efforts "to reconcile modern economic forces with the demands of a popular democracy."

This book will indicate how, and in what terms, the necessities of such a reconciliation appeared to Felix Frankfurter, lawyer and teacher of law. How and in what terms they will appear to Mr. Justice Frankfurter we shall read hereafter in the history of our times.

ARCHIBALD MacLEISH

Conway, Mass.

The Supreme Court: Its Political and Judicial Functions

The Zeitgeist and the Judiciary

This selection is an address delivered by Mr. Frankfurter, then Law Officer of the Bureau of Insular Affairs, at the twenty-fifth anniversary dinner of the Harvard Law Review, *in 1912 and published, in substantially the same form, in the* Survey *for January, 1913. In his 1912 campaign, Theodore Roosevelt had proposed the recall by popular vote of judicial decisions invalidating state social and economic legislation under the "due process" clause of the Constitution; and other political leaders had proposed the recall of judges themselves.*

I AM sure that none of us will ever again enjoy the divine feeling of being one of the potentates of the profession that the editorship of the *Review* afforded; no, not even were we to sit on the Supreme Bench, for it was our frequent and joyous duty to reverse even that tribunal in an infallible judgment of one hundred and sixty-five words. Representing those to whom that luxury is still a green memory, I suppose I am to give expression to the ardor of youth, still untempered by responsibility, and not yet disillusioned by experience.

Last August, the American Bar Association with solemnity adopted vigorous resolutions condemning the recall of judges. I was one of those who favored the resolution, and I should vote for it again. But as I left the meeting, I had a conviction that the action was inadequate, that the American Bar Association fell short of its responsibility in not going beyond negative criticism and inquiring into the cause of the ferment that partly expresses itself in the ill-conceived proposal of the judicial recall. The fallacy of a specific remedy may be crushingly exposed, but we cannot whistle down the wind a widespread, insistent, and well-vouched feeling of dissatisfaction.

The tremendous economic and social changes of the last fifty years have inevitably reacted upon the functions of the state. More and more government is conceived as the biggest organized social effort for dealing with social problems. Our whole evolutionary thinking leads to the conclusion that economic independence lies at the very foundation of social and moral well-being. Growing democratic sympathies, justified by the social message of modern scientists, demand to be translated into legislation for economic betterment, based upon the conviction that laws can make men better by affecting the conditions of living. We are persuaded that evils are not inevitable, and that it is the business of statesmanship to tackle them step by step, tentatively, experimentally, not demanding perfection from social reforms any more than from any other human efforts.

This movement, this hopeful experiment, is world-wide, but in this country it encounters a unique factor—in the United States, a social legislation must pass challenge in the courts, it must have the visé of our judiciary. Having regard to things and not words, the fate of social legislation in this country rests ultimately with our judges.

The existence of this power is so elementary a feature of our constitutional system that until recently we little considered the true nature of the problems involved in the exercise of the power. Social legislation concerns itself with economic and social conditions, and aims at their conscious readjustments, for social legislation deals with the stuff of life. And, in so far as they have the last word on this legislation, our courts, of necessity, are concerned with economic and social questions, which can be rightfully solved only by a due regard to the facts which induced the legislation. For instance, in passing upon the constitutionality of an eight-hour law for bakers, just what principles of jurisprudence are to be resorted to for guidance? Questions of hygiene, of health, of the present conditions of the industry, the occasion for protecting this particular class against its employers, and the public against both employer and employee—these are the considerations, it would seem, which ought to be vitally in the minds of the judges. Is it really to be doubted that in passing upon the validity of a workmen's compensation act, a court cannot get at the heart of the question without concerning itself, whether avowedly or implicitly, with economic and social questions? It involves a consideration of the vital changes produced by modern industrialism, the bearing of such legislation to the fairer adjustments of the inevitable risks of modern industry, the promotion of harmonious relations between capital and labor and the resulting peace to the community—in a word, its promotion of the social welfare. When the Supreme Court sustained the validity of legislation restricting the hours of work for women, it invoked no legal principles, it resorted to no lawbooks for guidance, but considered the facts of life, marshaled with overwhelming force by Mr. Brandeis, drawn from medical data, industrial reports, and the experience of the world. And so, when the minimum wage bills, the first of which is now before the Massachusetts Legislature, will, without doubt, soon come up for judicial determination, will not the decisive consideration that will inevitably confront the courts be the facts of the particular industries and the right of the community to insist upon a social wage as the first condition of human welfare over against the claim of the individual unrestricted industrial enterprise? Must not of necessity facts, not general principles or well-worn phrases, be the determinants?

This, which may now have the sound of heterodoxy, will, one is warranted in hoping, before long enjoy the respectability of the commonplace. For the viewpoint here urged has, fortunately, during the last few years, received the tremendous authority of, and increasing application from, the Supreme Court of the United States. Far in advance of any state court, our Supreme Bench recently has come to realize Time's change of emphasis, that new conditions bring new problems and press for new solutions. Social legislation, under our constitutional system, must rest upon the exercise of the police power. Only the other day the Supreme Court told us that "in a sense the police power is but another name for the power of government," and "that it extends to so dealing with the conditions which exist in the state as to bring out of them the greatest welfare of the people." But "the power of the government is a living power, constantly changing and developing to meet new conditions and accomplish new purposes." And the conception of the people's welfare varies, according to the dominant opinion, with time and place. Of necessity, therefore, the police power, as the power of government, is no more stable than the conditions which induce its exercise. If facts are changing, law cannot be static. So-called immutable principles must accommodate themselves to facts of life, for facts are stubborn and will not yield. In truth, what are now deemed immutable principles once, themselves, grew out of living conditions. Thus, the notion of unrestrained liberty of contract arose at a time when industrial conditions were shackled by restrictive legislation and the slogan of the hour was unrestricted industrial enterprise. The conditions of life have changed; the shibboleths remain. There is an increasing conviction of the need of collective responsibility and a demand of governmental intervention for fairer social adjustment. More and more we realize that there is no greater inequality than the equality of unequals. And, happily, the Supreme Court, unlike some of the state courts, realizes, in the words of Justice Holmes, that "the Fourteenth Amendment does not interfere [with legislation] by creating fictitious equality where there is a real difference." In a word, may not one venture the suggestion that constitutional law, in its relation to social legislation, is not at all a science, but applied politics, using the word in its noble sense?

It is important to recognize this not only abstractly, as an intellectual proposition, but to make it a dynamic part of our professional equipment of the legal habits of thought.

The felt necessities of the time, the prevalent moral and political theories, institutions of public policy, avowed or unconscious, even the prejudices which judges share with their fellow men, have had a good deal more to do than the syllogism in determining the rules by which men should be governed.

Thus wrote Mr. Holmes more than thirty years ago. And because he has so vitally felt this, Justice Holmes has been a powerful influence in the changed attitude of the Supreme Court. Again and again we find him yielding to the social expression of the day, with which, if one should make a guess, as an individual, he was probably not in sympathy. Speaking of the English bench, Professor Dicey, a distinguished Conservative, says while the judges

are swayed by the prevailing beliefs of a particular time, they are also guided by professional opinions and ways of thinking which are, to a certain extent, independent of, and possibly opposed to, the general tone of public opinion. The judges are the heads of the legal profession. They have acquired the intellectual and moral tone of English lawyers. They are men advanced in life. They are for the most part persons of a conservative disposition.

It is because of this natural tendency of our profession, and because of the far-reaching power enjoyed by the bench in this country, that it is essential that a correct appreciation of the problems raised by social legislation should become a vital part of our professional thinking. It is not only a delicate but an infinitely difficult human function that our courts discharge in passing upon the limits of their own power. In so far as these questions are necessarily questions of fact, dealing with actual conditions of life and current dominant public opinion, it is essential that the stream of the Zeitgeist must be allowed to flood the sympathies and the intelligence of our judges. This is necessary, not only for the well-being of the state and the social order, but for the unimpaired continuance of our judicial system. Until social and economic legislation came before the courts, they did not touch the people at large. But dealing with such legislation, involving as they do the vital interests of life of a vast body of the community, the courts necessarily are brought in direct contact with the public needs, and their work has intimate public significance. Hence the importance of recognizing the true character of the questions that come before them. If this is done, it is safe to say that courts generally will reach the conclusion which one may gather from the recent Supreme Court decisions: namely, that which is reasonably defensible on economic or social grounds, whether or not it accords with our individual notion of economics, cannot be offensive on constitutional grounds. Otherwise, it necessarily follows that the Constitution definitively incorporated an economic theory prevalent over a hundred years ago that may well be inadequate and unsuited to modern conditions, whereas, in truth, "a constitution is not intended to embody a particular economic theory . . . it is made for people of fundamentally differing views."

One of the great leaders of the bar, and a distinguished statesman, seeking for a deeper explanation for the present widespread unrest than one generally hears, attributes it to our failure, as yet, to make through our legislation and constitutions the readjustments demanded by the new conditions incident to the extraordinary industrial development of the last half century. One ventures the suggestion that it is demonstrable, as Professor Roscoe Pound has shown, that one of the prime factors contributing to the dissatisfaction is the fact that judges have thwarted legislative efforts at such readjustments, not because of any coercion of the Constitution, but by reason of their constitutional conservatism. Therefore, as to legislation of this character, the suggestion of constitutional amendments does not meet the situation, for back of the constitutional amendment is the construing power of the courts. Unless our profession, from whose ranks the courts are recruited, has the right attitude of approach to these questions, human ingenuity cannot frame language specific enough, even if desirable, to meet the situation. Mere words cannot induce insight and right sympathies or appreciative interpretation. On the other hand, if our courts, generally, will have the attitude that the Supreme Court now has, it is safe to say that all social legislation which has the commanding facts of life behind it will be allowed to justify itself by experience.

The standards here suggested in dealing with the constitutionality of this class of legislation are broad, but not indefinite.

The limits of the life of a people cannot be charted by easy rules of thumb. We are dealing with considerations as flexible and complex as the public welfare. The constitutional limitation upon the law-making power is as definite, but not more so, as a reasonably possible view of the public welfare. This leaves us still unimpaired the benefits of the reviewing power of the judiciary in our governmental system, for the reflex action of the *existence* of this power on the part of the courts to set aside legislation restrains unwise legislative action and induces the scientific attitude of basing legislation only upon adequately ascertained facts. On the other hand, it does not make of the Constitution a mere charter of negation upon the power of the state. The courts should be a restraining, but not a hampering, force. Doubtless, grave mistakes in legislation will thus go unchallenged through the courts, but legislation is essentially empirical, experimental, and the Constitution was not intended to limit this field of experimentation. Think of the gain of having experience demonstrate the fallacy of a law after the Supreme Court has sustained its constitutionality. For, as a wise man has truly said, to fail and learn by failure is one of the sacred rights of a democracy.

The Red Terror of Judicial Reform

The following selection appeared as an unsigned editorial in the
New Republic *for October 1, 1924. Senator Robert M. La Fol-*
lette, of Wisconsin, Progressive candidate for the presidency in
the 1924 election, had proposed a constitutional amendment em-
powering Congress, by a two-thirds vote, to override any Supreme
Court decision holding a statute invalid. President Coolidge, the
Republican candidate, and John W. Davis, the candidate of the
Democratic party, both opposed Senator La Follette's proposal.

REPUBLICAN papers are entitled to point out the identity of
views between the Republican and Democratic candidates on the issues raised by judicial control over legislation. It is a mere coincidence that the President and Mr. Davis
spoke on this subject at the same time; but it is of the deepest
significance that they expressed the same beliefs. The two speeches
reflected a common mind, and they might have been written by
the same pen. What meaning would they convey to a foreign student of our affairs who aimed at a disinterested understanding of
vital American problems? If such an inquirer were confined for
understanding to the Coolidge and Davis utterances, he would
only be told that some precious aspects of human liberty were formulated by the American Constitution and that the Supreme
Court of the United States is their vigilant and effective guardian.
Nothing more appearing in the explanations of the President of
the United States and his contender for the presidency, speaking
with the added apparent authority of eminence at the bar, our foreign seeker for truth would be wholly baffled to understand why
traditional liberties, or the means of rendering them effective,
should find opposition. Naturally he would assume that only ma-

levolence compounded with ignorance can be the enemy. This is, of course, precisely the aim of the Coolidge and Davis speeches.

One expects nothing better on this profoundly important issue from Mr. Coolidge. He doubtless honestly entertains all his fears and phantasies about constitutional law in action. The famous author of "The Reds in Our Colleges" knows no better. But what is one to say of John W. Davis? He cannot be unfamiliar with the judicial record which has kept this issue in American politics, with vigorous insistence, during the last thirty years. Surely he must know that neither William J. Bryan nor Theodore Roosevelt was a malevolent foreigner bent on destroying Americanism; he must know that these two leaders expressed deep grievances in their attacks upon judicial abuses, whatever one may think of the remedies which they proposed. Does Mr. Davis's conscience really permit him to miseducate his hearers, as he did in his Dubuque speech, on a subject so vital to the maintenance of confidence in the essentials of the American Constitution? For it is inconceivable that Mr. Davis is unaware of the fact that by grave omissions in his treatment of the courts and the Constitution he conveyed a mutilated and, therefore, untrue picture.

Of course, our constitutional mechanism requires an independent Supreme Court. In all governments there must be organs for finality of decision. In a federated government like ours, with powers distributed in necessarily broad terms under a written constitution, a free court is the most dependable instrument for adjusting controversies between the constituent states and the nation, and between individual states. It does not, however, follow that the Supreme Court should be the arbiter for all controversies in state and nation. At once, therefore, distinctions must be taken as to the power of the Supreme Court, and the wisdom of the grant of power, in the different classes of cases over which the Court has jurisdiction. Under the Commerce Clause the Supreme Court maintains the equilibrium between states and nation by determining when a state has sought to project its authority beyond its state lines and when, on the other hand, Congress has interfered with the purely domestic concerns of the individual states. Here is a power that must be left with the Supreme Court although its exercise is not at all a necessary deduction from "principles" hidden in the Constitution, to which only the Supreme Court has the code. The simple truth of the matter is that decisions of the Court denying or sanctioning the exercise of federal power, as in the first child labor case, largely involve a judgment about practical matters, and not at all any esoteric knowledge of the Constitution. Therefore it is that the decisions of the Court must be subjected to relentless scrutiny to save them from pedantry and sterility, as the unconscious rationalizations of the economic and social biases of individual justices. . . .

The next broad class of constitutional provisions which comes before the Court involves specific prohibitions upon the legislative power both of the states and of Congress and is intended to protect individual rights. These guarantees are based upon the history of a specific political grievance, or they embody a specific limitation of power in the formulation of governmental powers which came out of the Philadelphia convention. These are the features of the Constitution that Messrs. Coolidge and Davis disingenuously dwell upon, because, in their judicial construction, they give rise to relatively little difficulty. The definiteness of the terms of these specific provisions, the definiteness of their history, the definiteness of their aims, all combine to limit narrowly the scope of judicial review in the rare instances when their meaning is called into question. Only occasionally is doubt raised as to whether "a fact tried by a jury" has been "re-examined in any court of the United States" otherwise than "according to the rules of the common law"; or whether a tax is "laid upon articles exported from any state"; or whether a crime is "infamous"; or whether the prohibition against "unreasonable searches and seizures" is violated. Here, in other words, is a part of constitutional law relatively easy of application because it allows comparatively meager play for individual judgment as to policy. In this field, economic and social conflicts play little or no part. Even here, however, the record of the Supreme Court in interpreting the guarantee of "freedom of speech" shows how, with rare exceptions, passions lay prey even to the courts.

But there are two clauses of the Constitution which present very different problems of statecraft—the "due process" clause of the Fifth Amendment, a limitation upon the federal government and the "due process of law," and the denial of the "equal protection of the laws" of the Fourteenth Amendment, limiting state action and subjecting every local act of every state to the scrutiny of the Supreme Court at Washington. President Coolidge in his innocence assumes that there are settled "principles" and fixed rules by which these provisions are specifically applied, all, as he thinks, "with the sole purpose of protecting the freedom of the individual, of guarding his earnings, his home, his life." Doubtless Mr. Coolidge would say that courts in declaring unconstitutional workmen's compensation laws, the ten-hour law for bakers, laws prohibiting discrimination against trade union workers, the minimum wage law for women, as violative of due process, did so "with the sole purpose of protecting the freedom of the individual, of guarding his earnings, his home, his life." Mr. Davis evidently knows better, for he is significantly silent about the "due process" and the "equal protection of the laws" clauses and the actual results of their judicial interpretation. Mr. Davis must know that these broad "guarantees" in favor of the individual are expressed in words so undefined, either by their intrinsic meaning, or by history, or by tradition, that they leave the individual Justice free, if indeed they do not actually compel him, to fill in the vacuum with his own controlling notions of economic, social, and industrial facts with reference to which they are invoked. These judicial judgments are thus bound to be determined by the experience, the environment, the fears, the imagination, of the different Justices. For it cannot be too often made clear that the meaning of phrases like "due process of law," and of simple terms like "liberty" and "property," is not revealed within the Constitution; their meaning is derived from without. As a great legal scholar has put it, social legislation of the twentieth century is declared unconstitutional by putting eighteenth-century Adam Smith into the Constitution. As an outstanding and candid member of the federal bench, Judge Charles M. Hough, reminds us, due process of law is a phrase of "convenient vagueness." "Convenient" for whom or to what end?

. . . .

The sophisticated suggestion is sometimes made that the Supreme Court has invalidated only a few laws, compared with the total which has passed muster. It isn't true! A numerical tally of the cases does not tell the tale. In the first place, all laws are not of the same importance. We are here concerned with matters that involve qualitative judgment. Secondly, a single decision may decide the fate of a great body of legislation, as was true of *Coppage* v. *Kansas,* declaring invalid a Kansas law prohibiting discrimination against trade unionists and, more recently, in the District of Columbia minimum wage case. Moreover, the discouragement of legislative efforts in fields related to that involved in a particular adjudication and the general weakening of the sense of legislative responsibility have wrought incalculable harm to the fruitful development of American political life. These are the themes upon which the electorate is entitled to hear from a presidential candidate who professes, as does Mr. Davis, progressivism as well as candor in public discussion, and whose past peculiarly charges him with the responsibility of educating the American people to an understanding of the actual workings of our constitutional system. Unfortunately, Mr. Davis on the stump only repeats the conservative platitudes which last year he expressed as president of the American Bar Association.

Angling for Progressive votes Mr. Davis withheld on the stump one illuminating comment which he made as president of the American Bar Association: "Much of the current discontent is caused perhaps by the publication of dissenting opinions which serve to fan the flame of public distrust." Evidently, the real culprits are men like Mr. Justice Hughes, Mr. Justice Holmes, Mr. Justice Brandeis, and occasionally even Chief Justice Taft (as in the minimum wage case), who, from time to time, expressed their objection to the slaughtering of social legislation on the altar of the dogma of "liberty of contract." Criticism of dissents is not to be wondered at in one who emphasizes, as did Mr. Davis in his Labor Day speech, "the right of free contract." It is this doctrine which the Supreme Court has used as a sword with which to slay most important social legislation and to deny the means of freedom to those least free. To invoke it is to indulge in sterile abstractions and cruelly to shut one's eyes to cases. . . . Mr. Davis is silent about such decisions, but he cannot be ignorant of them.

The contribution of Senator La Follette and the Progressive platform lies in the ventilation of this grave issue rather than in the specific remedies proposed. In this respect the Progressive campaign is not unlike that of 1912. No student of American constitutional law can have the slightest doubt that Mr. Roosevelt's vigorous challenge of judicial abuses was mainly responsible for a temporary period of liberalism which followed in the interpretation of the due process clauses, however abhorrent the remedy of judicial recall appeared to both bar and bench. The public opinion which the Progressive campaign aroused subtly penetrated the judicial atmosphere. In cases involving social-industrial issues, public opinion, if adequately informed and sufficiently sustained, seeps into Supreme Court decisions. Roosevelt shrewdly observed: "I may not know much about law, but I do know one can put the fear of God into judges." The "fear of God" was needed to make itself felt on the bench in 1912. The "fear of God" very much needs to make itself felt in 1924. Let any disinterested student of constitutional law read the decision of the Supreme Court last spring invalidating legislation fixing a standard weight for a loaf of bread and deny that we have never had a more irresponsible period in the history of that court.

But the "fear of God" is too capricious, too intermittent. We need most the wisdom of man. What is needed is a thorough understanding of our constitutional system in action, as a basis of determining what is the proper scope of judicial control, and what conditions are most likely to insure the exercise of this tremendous power by ordinary mortals, to avoid at once the abuses of tyranny and the timidities of dependence. Particularly does it behoove Progressives not to content themselves with mere abuse of abuses, nor to fall back upon mechanical contrivances when dealing with a process where mechanics can play but a very small part. An informed study of the work of the Supreme Court of the United States will probably lead to the conclusion that no nine men are wise enough and good enough to be entrusted with the power which the unlimited provisions of the due process clauses confer. We have had fifty years of experiment with the Fourteenth Amendment, and the centralizing authority lodged with the Supreme Court over the domestic affairs of forty-eight widely different states is an authority which it simply cannot discharge with safety either to itself or to the states. The due process clauses ought to go. It is highly significant that not a single constitution framed for English-speaking countries since the Fourteenth Amendment has embodied its provisions. And one would indeed be lacking in a sense of humor to suggest that life, liberty, or property is not amply protected in Canada, Australia, South Africa. By eliminating this class of cases the Supreme Court would really be relieved of a contentiously political burden. It would free itself to meet more adequately the jurisdiction which would remain and which ought to remain. The Court would still exercise the most delicate and powerful function in our dual system of government. To discharge it wisely, it needs a constant play of informed criticism by the professional as well as the lay press. This, in turn, implies an alertly progressive bar, the product of a lively spirit of legal education at our universities, and a public opinion trustful of the workings of our judiciary because the trust is justified by its exercise.

The American Leviathan

The following review of The American Leviathan: The Republic in the Machine Age, *by Charles A. Beard and William Beard,
appeared in the* Harvard Law Review *for February, 1931 (Vol.
44, p. 661).*

IT WILL not be the fault of the Beards if we fail to understand
how American society came to be what it is, and the part that
government now plays in that society. Three years ago hus-
band and wife gave us the most satisfactory single account of
American *Kulturgeschichte.* Now father and son do for our day
what Bryce did forty years ago—less magisterially than Bryce, but
with more regard for the teeming life beneath the decorous surface. If the reviewer had to place in the hands of a thoughtful foreigner one book on the history of the United States and another
on its contemporary government, *The Rise of American Civilization* and *The American Leviathan* would be the safest choices,
thereby proving that no single book, no matter how good, is
enough for any important field of inquiry. Whatever may be the
need of a foreigner, certainly to American lawyers the book of the
new Beards is as important as . . . the book of the old Beards.
For if law be, in essence, one of the systems of arrangements for
securing cohesion in society, no body of citizens needs more to be
reminded than lawyers of the forms and functions of government
within and through which the law of the lawyers must achieve the
social ends of law. The lawyer's contact with government begets
most immediately the doctrines and arrangements called public
law. The machine age, however, leads more and more to governmental permeation in matters which to some lawyers and judges
still seem peculiarly reserved for exclusively private arrangement,

17

immune against state interference. But the *laissez faire* of law is as doomed as the *laissez faire* of economics. Even to the most gallant survivor of economic individualism, the "economic man" is now seen in the context of society; the issues center upon the nature of the context and how the individual fits into it. Also law will more and more heed these realities and cease to concern itself with abstract individuals of an obsolete age.

The American Leviathan, in its quiet way, will further the continuous process of the law to shift without violence from past to future. The book is the more serviceable in that it is not a polemic, but the report of two naturalists. It conveys an analysis of our government in action, of the environment which determines it, and the influences by which it is shaped, drawn not from the fervors of Fourth of July orations and the jejune symmetries of textbooks on constitutional law and political science, but from the daily life of the myriad agencies, "official" and "unofficial," that make up government. Compared with the conventional conceptions of American constitutional law, the analysis in this book is as "heterodox" as was Charles A. Beard in 1913 in his *Economic Interpretation of the American Constitution.* But the times have caught up with him.

It is more accurate to say that Charles A. Beard has helped to make the times, thus achieving the ultimate success of every thinker in politics, namely, to rob his ideas of novelty. And so, without stirring bar associations to protest, the Beards now can write:

. . . the theory that the Constitution is a written document is a legal fiction. The idea that it can be understood by a study of its language and the history of its past development is equally mythical. It is what the government and the people who count in public affairs recognize and respect as such, what they think it is. More than this. It is not merely what it has been, or what it is today. It is always becoming something else, and those who criticize it and the acts done under it, as well as those who praise, help to make it what it will be tomorrow.

·   ·   ·   ·   ·   ·   ·

The entire Beard analysis of the processes of constitution-making through public opinion, formal amendments, and adjudication, lucidly expounded in thirty pages, is an admirable antidote to the stuffy unrealities that usually masquerade as descriptions of the Constitution of the United States. Being realistic, the Beards are keenly aware of the interplay between so-called fact and theory. They know that ultimately mankind is governed by ideas or by ideas about ideas. Thought-processes are implicit even in a machine age, and constitutional adjudications also involve logical coherences and are not a series of unrelated particulars.

All of which does not at all imply disregard of the enormous factor of the personalities who are the ultimate voices of our constitutional law. The Beards do well in pointing out the personal and party elements that enter into the selection of judges, through the personal and party values enforced by the appointing power. But the Beards are either ironic or too conventional in emphasizing the party choices made by party Presidents. The line of cleavage is far deeper than party, because within the parties are deep lines of cleavage regarding policy. Moreover, Presidents have suffered deep disappointment in the expectation that their appointees would vindicate public policies which Presidents have from time to time identified with the national well-being. For instruction of the laity, the Beards may well note hereafter that Chief Justice Chase declared unconstitutional the Legal Tender Act of the President who appointed him and of the administration of which he was a member. So also Mr. Justice Holmes decided against the government in the Northern Securities case, Roosevelt's pet litigation, although the latter thought it his duty to put on the Supreme Bench only men who would sustain "My Policies."

The chapters on the Constitution, on the Fundamental Principles of the Federal System and the Federal Judiciary minister most immediately to the professional interest of the lawyer. But the book as a whole analyzes contemporary governmental activities with shrewdness, clarity, and insight. If the Beards lack the pungency and sauciness with which Bagehot exposed the inner life of the English Constitution (would that Charles A. Beard smuggled into print the luminous gaiety of his talk!), they reveal penetratingly how government works and who works it in the United States of 1931.

The Supreme Court of the United States

This selection is from an article contributed by Mr. Frankfurter to the Encyclopedia of the Social Sciences *in 1934 (Vol. XIV, p. 424), reprinted by permission of the Macmillan Company, publishers.*

THE LEGISLATIVE history of the United States Senate began with a bill to implement Article III of the federal Constitution, providing for the establishment of "one Supreme Court" and "such inferior courts as the Congress may from time to time ordain and establish." The scheme for a federal judicial establishment, of which the chief architect was Oliver Ellsworth, himself a future Chief Justice, became law on September 24, 1789. There were many contenders for the Chief Justiceship and the five associates for which the first Judiciary Act provided, and not until February 1, 1790, was the day set for the organization of the Court. Even then a majority of the Court were not able to reach New York and the first formal session of the Court could not be held until the following day. From then on for a period fast approaching a century and a half the Supreme Court has maintained unbroken its very special relation to the constitutional scheme of American society, although during the first three years practically no business came before the Court. The Supreme Court mediates between citizen and government; it marks the boundaries between state and national authority. This tribunal is the ultimate organ—short of direct popular action—for adjusting the relationship of the individual to the separate states, of the individual to the United States, of the forty-eight states to one another, of the states to the union, and of the three departments of government to one another.

A tribunal having such stupendous powers inevitably stimulates romantic interpretation. Men of learning on both sides of the Atlantic have characterized the Supreme Court as the great political invention of the framers of the Constitution and have appraised it as their most successful contrivance. The most successful it is, but the claim of originality must be denied. Certainly neither the presidency nor the Congress has better withstood the fluctuating winds of popular opinion than the Supreme Court. Despite intermittent popular movements against it, the Court is more securely lodged in the confidence of the people than the other two branches of the government. But the establishment of the Court was not a fruit of the creative intelligence of the federal Constitutional Convention. It was a continuation of means for adjustment which the colonies first and then the thirteen sovereign states and finally the Confederation had evolved. The various controversies, most of them regarding boundaries between different colonies, had to be settled, and partly they were settled by the Privy Council. After independence these controversies did not cease. To them were later added difficulties between the states and the Confederation. At first the Continental Congress tried to adjust these conflicts, but eventually it became necessary to set up a technical judicial tribunal, the Court of Appeal. Not merely the recognition of the need for a body to compose the difference between the states *inter se* and between the states and a central government, but the practical response to that need evolved by the predecessor of the United States, dictated the necessity and furnished the materials for the Supreme Court which the Constitution outlined and the First Congress established. At least one litigation that began during the Confederation before its Court of Appeal had its final stage before the Supreme Court. In effect the Supreme Court constituted, not the invention of a new institution, but the perpetuation and perfection of an old one.

Indeed some mechanism for adjusting conflicts between the center and the constituent units is indispensable to a federalism. Such adjustments might be left to the federal legislature, as in part and ineffectively they were under the Confederation. But where the

powers in a federalism between the center and the circumference
are distributed by a legal document, certainly in any political society where the ideas of public law derive from the common law, it
is natural that conflict regarding this distribution of power should
become legal issues to be resolved by a judicial and not a political
tribunal. Canada, Australia, and the proposed dominion of India
represent three different forms of federalism. The distribution of
governmental authority as between center and circumference is
different in all three. In all three a court with functions similar
to our own Supreme Court is part of the scheme, not in imitation
of the American Supreme Court, but as an inevitable mechanism
of a federal state. To be sure the scope of authority of this adjusting mechanism may vary and is itself defined either explicitly or
by the implications imported into constitutions in the document
distributing governmental powers in a federalism. That the Supreme Court should have been given all the powers it has is of
course not a matter of natural law. But if any federalism is to
endure, it must provide for some checkrein on the constituent
units, and the history of the American colonies and states made it
inevitable that that checkrein should be a court and not Congress.
"I do not think," wrote Justice Holmes, "the United States would
come to an end if we lost our power to declare an Act of Congress
void. I do think the Union would be imperiled if we could not
make that declaration as to the laws of the several states. For one
in my place sees how often a local policy prevails with those who
are not trained to national views and how often action is taken
that embodies what the Commerce Clause was meant to end."

But judicial adjustments in the English-speaking world operate
within traditional limitations. By confining the power of the Supreme Court to the disposition of "cases" and "controversies" the
Constitution in effect imposed on a tribunal having ultimate power
over legislative and executive acts the historic restrictions governing adjudications in common law courts. Most of the problems of
modern society, whether of industry, agriculture or finance, of
racial interactions or the eternal conflict between liberty and authority, become in the United States sooner or later legal problems

for ultimate solution by the Supreme Court. They come before the Court, however, not directly as matters of politics or policy or in the form of principles and abstractions. The Court can only deal with concrete litigation. Its judgment upon a constitutional issue can be invoked only when inextricably entangled with a living and ripe lawsuit. In lawyers' language the Court merely enforces a legal right. . . .

In thus passing on issues only when presented in concrete cases the Supreme Court is true to the empiric process of Anglo-American law. But the attitude of pragmatism which evolved the scope and methods of English judicature, and subsequently its American versions, was powerfully reinforced by considerations of statecraft in defining the sphere of authority for a tribunal of ultimate constitutional adjustments. For in the case of the Supreme Court of the United States questions of jurisdiction are inevitably questions of power as between the several states and the nation or between the Court and the executive and Congress. Every decision of constitutionality is the assertion of some constitutional barrier. However much a judgment of the House of Lords may offend opinion, the Parliament can promptly change the law so declared. But a decision of constitutionality by the Supreme Court either blocks some attempted exercise of power or releases the cumbersome procedure of changes of fundamental law. Therefore the Supreme Court, and very early, evolved canons of judicial self-restraint. Thus it would avoid decisions on constitutionality not merely by observing common law conventions. The Court very early in its history refused to give merely advisory opinions. . . . Partly this was an assertion of its independence, a refusal of the rôle of subordination either to legislature or executive. The Court withholds utterance unless a controversy is so molded as to give the Court the last word. Partly also this is a manifestation of the psychology underlying the development of English law, which has special pertinence to the unfolding of American constitutional law. To refuse to give advisory opinions, to refuse to speak at large or indeed until litigation compels, is to rely more on the impact of reality than on abstract unfolding. In the workings of a constitution designed for a dynamic society this means a preference for "a judgment from experience as against a judgment from speculation." . . . To pass on legislation *in abstracto* or, still worse, in advance of enactment, would too often be an exercise in sterile dialectic and as a practical matter would close the door to new experience. But the Court has improved upon the common law tradition and evolved rules of judicial administration especially designed to postpone constitutional adjudications and therefore constitutional conflicts until they are judicially unavoidable. The Court will avoid decision on grounds of constitutionality if a case may go off on some other ground, as, for instance, statutory construction. So far has this doctrine been carried that at times the Court will give an interpretation to a statute much more restrictive than its text or the intention of Congress apparently indicated. Again, in order to avoid the projection of a conflict between state and national authority the Court, in reviewing state court decisions, is alert to find that the state court merely enforced some state law which the Supreme Court is bound to respect and thereby to deny the existence of a federal controversy.

The Court has thus evolved elaborate and often technical doctrines for postponing if not avoiding constitutional adjudication. In one famous controversy, involving a conflict between Congress and the President, the Supreme Court was able until recently to avoid decision of a question that arose in the First Congress. Such a system inevitably introduces accidental factors in decision-making. So much depends on how a question is raised and when it is raised. For the composition of the Court decisively affects its decisions in the application of constitutional provisions and doctrines which by their vagueness not only permit but invite conflicting constitutional views on the part of the Justices. But time is the decisive element in all phases of government, as in war. The cost of uncertainty in result due to changes in the personnel of the Court, through postponing constitutional adjudication until such a decision is unavoidable, is more easily absorbed than would be the mischief of premature judicial intervention in the multitudinous political conflicts arising in a vast federal society like the United

States. Political harmony would not be furthered and the Court's prestige within its proper sphere would be inevitably impaired. And so it is as important for the Court not to decide when a constitutional issue is not appropriately and unavoidably before it as it is to decide when its duty leaves no choice.

Some claims of unconstitutionality, however much they may be wrapped in the form of a conventional litigation, the Court will never adjudicate. Such issues are deemed beyond the province of a court and are compendiously characterized as political questions. Thus although according to the Constitution "The United States shall guarantee to every state in this union a republican form of government," the Supreme Court cannot be called upon to decide whether a particular state government is "republican." This and like questions are not suited for settlement by the training and technique and the body of judicial experience which guide a court. What such questions are and what they are not do not lend themselves to enumeration. In these, as in other matters, the wisdom of the Court defines its boundaries.

To be sure judicial doctrine is one thing, practice another. The pressure of so-called great cases is sometimes too much for judicial self-restraint, and the Supreme Court from time to time in its history has forgotten its own doctrines when they should have been most remembered. On the whole the Court has had to weather few popular storms. Even these few could have been avoided by a more careful regard for its own canons of judicial administration. The avoidable political conflicts which the Supreme Court has aroused by transgressing its own technical doctrines of jurisdiction demonstrate the large considerations of policy in which those doctrines are founded.

In the same soil of policy is rooted the canon of constitutional construction to which the Supreme Court throughout its history had avowed scrupulous adherence. The Court will avoid if possible passing on constitutionality; but if the issues cannot be burked, if it must face its responsibility as the arbiter between contending political forces, it will indulge every presumption of validity on behalf of challenged powers. This is not merely the wisdom of caution, but the insight of statesmanship. For the cases involving conflicts between the states and the nation or between Congress and the executive that touch the sensitive public nerves usually turn on such ambiguous language or such vague restrictions of the Constitution as to afford a spacious area of choice on the part of the primary political agencies of government. And the Supreme Court, being a court even in these matters affecting closely the nation's political life, has enunciated again and again the doctrine that the Court cannot enforce its notions of expediency or wisdom but may interpose its veto only when there is no reasonable doubt about constitutional transgressions. Here too the Supreme Court has sinned against its own rules. Especially in construing such vague generalities as "due process" and "equal protection of the laws" it has overlooked their significance and failed to observe that they express "moods and not commands." Cases like *Lochner* v. *New York* . . . and *Adkins* v. *Children's Hospital* . . . illustrate what Chief Justice Hughes has characterized as "self-inflicted wounds," because the deep resentment they aroused was due essentially to the Court's departure from its own postulates for deciding constitutional issues.

A rhythm, even though not reducible to law, is manifest in the history of Supreme Court adjudication. Manifold and largely undiscerned factors determine general tendencies of the Court, much too simplified by phrases like "the centralization" of Marshall or "the states' rights" of Taney. Thus there are periods when the Court seems to forget its doctrine against declarations of unconstitutionality so long as there is room for reasonable doubt. Thus the liberality of the Waite period was followed by the dominance of the strict views of Justice Field, in turn yielding to the reaction which made the Holmes outlook prevail. After the World War, during the decade when William H. Taft was Chief Justice, the Court again veered toward a narrow conception of the Constitution, although Taft himself, especially in a classic dissent, admonished against this tendency. Between 1920 and 1930 the Supreme Court invalidated more state legislation than during the fifty years preceding. Merely as a matter of statistics this is an impressive mortality rate, and it is no answer to point to the far larger number of laws which went through the Court unscathed. All laws are not of the same importance, and a single decision may decide the fate of a great body of legislation. Moreover the discouragement of legislative effort through an adverse decision and a general weakening of the sense of legislative responsibility are influences not measurable by statistics. The trend has been reversed since Charles E. Hughes became Chief Justice, and the Court is apparently in one of its alternating swings.

. . . With a too frequent misconception as to the nature of the judicial business and the conditions for its wise disposition, it was assumed that more business calls for more judges. The first Judiciary Act provided for a Supreme Court of six members, which was increased to seven in 1807 and to nine in 1837. Subject to short fluctuations from a tribunal of ten to one of seven between the years 1863 to 1869, this has remained the size of the court. There is no magic in the number nine, but there are limits to effective judicial action. Deliberation by the Court is the very foundation of sound adjudication, as is also a lively sense of responsibility by every member of the Court for its collective judgment. Experience is conclusive that to enlarge the size of the Supreme Court would be self-defeating. When this recurring proposal for increasing the number of Justices was once more made by the American Bar Association in 1922, Chief Justice Taft authoritatively rejected it.

Variants of the proposal to increase the membership of the Court for dealing with the increase of its business after the Civil War were recurrently urged. Thus a larger membership of the Court was proposed, ranging from fifteen to twenty-four, so as to permit shifts in the sittings of the Court or work by standing divisions. England and France were cited as examples of such schemes of judicial organization, and their experience has been drawn upon by some of the states of the United States. But either of these devices would be fatal for the special functions of the Supreme Court. A contemporaneously shifting personnel would disastrously accentuate the personal factor in constitutional adjudications, and divisional courts within the Supreme Court would require a mechanism for adjusting conflicts among the divisions. Happily these devices never attained enactment. But their persistent advocacy delayed the only efficacious remedy. Not till 1891 did Congress pass the requisite legislation. Instead of increasing the size of the Court, it decreased its business.

This was accomplished by establishing intermediate courts of appeal for each of the nine circuits (in 1929 increased to ten). These were given final authority over a large field of appeals which theretofore had gone to the Supreme Court, leaving the latter Court discretionary power to resolve conflicts among the intermediate courts or, when an important national interest otherwise required finality of determination, by the· Supreme Court itself. By thus giving to the Supreme Court obligatory appellate jurisdiction over a restricted type of litigation and for the rest letting the Supreme Court decide whether to review, the Congress enabled the Court to keep abreast of its docket. It did more. It introduced a principle of procedure capable of progressive application, which saved the Court for the discharge of duties peculiarly its own in maintaining the constitutional system. When after the Spanish-American War and the World War the vast expansion in economic enterprise and the resulting governmental regulation of business again produced a volume of judicial business beyond the Court's powers, Congress in 1925 came to the Court's rescue at its own request, by still further withdrawing the types of cases which can be taken to the Supreme Court as a matter of right and extending the area of litigation in which an appeal can be had in the Supreme Court only by its leave. At present in about nine hundred cases a year leave is asked of the Court for review, and in only about one case in six is the leave granted.

The Supreme Court has thus ceased to be a common law court. The stuff of its business is what on the continent is formally known as public law and not the ordinary legal questions involved in the multitudinous lawsuits of *Doe* v. *Roe* of other courts. The con-

struction of important federal legislation and of the Constitution is
now the staple business of the Supreme Court.

    .   .   .   .

These are tremendous and delicate problems. But the words of
the Constitution on which their solution is based are so unrestricted
by their intrinsic meaning or by their history or by tradition or by
prior decisions that they leave the individual Justice free, if indeed
they do not compel him, to gather meaning, not from reading the
Constitution, but from reading life. It is most revealing that members of the Court are frequently admonished by their associates not
to read their economic and social views into the neutral language
of the Constitution. But the process of constitutional interpretation
compels the translation of policy into judgment, and the controlling conceptions of the Justices are their "idealized political picture" of the existing social order. Only the conscious recognition of
the nature of this exercise of the judicial process will protect policy
from being narrowly construed as the reflex of discredited assumptions or the abstract formulation of unconscious bias.

Thus the most important manifestations of our political and economic life may ultimately come for judgment before the Supreme
Court, and the influence of the Court permeates even beyond its
technical jurisdiction. That a tribunal exercising such power and
beyond the reach of popular control should from time to time
arouse popular resentment is far less surprising than the infre-
quency of such hostility and the perdurance of the institution. No
political party has been consistent in its support or its hostility to
the Court. Every American political party at some time has sheltered itself behind the Supreme Court and at others has found in
the Court's decisions obstructions to its purposes. This is a reflection of the fact that the Court throughout its history has not been
the organ of any party or registered merely party differences.
Clashes of views, and very serious ones, there have been on the
Court almost from the beginning, but these judicial differences
have cut deeper than any differences as to old party allegiances;
they involve differences of fundamental outlook regarding the
Constitution and the judge's rôle in construing it.

Whenever Supreme Court decisions have especially offended some deep popular sentiment, movements have become rife to curb the Court's power. In Marshall's days such efforts were invoked by decisions promoting centralization and subordinating the states. In recent times invalidation of social legislation, both state and national, has aroused popular disfavor. In the earlier period we find proposals for repealing the famous Section 25 of the Judiciary Act of 1789, whereby the Supreme Court had power to review decisions of state courts denying some federal right. A brake upon a finding of unconstitutionality was also proposed by requiring the concurrence of seven Justices and not a mere majority. The latter safeguard was revived by Senator La Follette in 1924, while in an earlier stage of the Progressive movement, in 1912, Theodore Roosevelt proposed a recall by popular referendum of decisions nullifying state but not congressional legislation. But no proposal for curtailment of the Supreme Court's power over legislation has ever been adopted. The wise exercise of this power, it has shrewdly been discerned, cannot be assured by any mechanical device. The only reliance rests in the quality of the judges and the temper and training of the bar, for no graver responsibilities have ever confronted a judicial tribunal, no more searching equipment was ever required of judges. . . .

All told, seventy-five judges have thus far (1934) sat on the Supreme Court. A goodly number of them have been men of intellectual distinction. But hardly a half dozen are towering figures: Marshall, the creative statesman; Story, a scholar of vast learning; Taney, who adapted the Constitution to the emerging forces of modern economic society; Holmes, the philosopher become king; Brandeis, the master of fact as the basis of social insight. Confidence in the competence of the Court has not been won by the presence of a rare man of genius. The explanation lies rather in the capacity of the Court to dispose adequately of the tasks committed to it. The effective conditions for insuring the quality of judicial output of the Supreme Court have in the long run been maintained. Human limitations have been respected. While in response to the country's phenomenal increase in population and wealth and the resulting extension of governmental activities duties have been placed upon Congress, the executive departments, various federal administrative agencies and the lower federal courts which disregarded their strength and capacity, the duties of the Supreme Court have on the whole been kept within the capacities of nine judges who are not supermen.

The Supreme Court's internal procedure moreover has been an important factor in the achievement of its high standards of judicial administration. In its disposition of cases, in the rules and practices which determine argument, deliberation, and opinion-writing the Supreme Court operates under the following conditions, indispensable to a seasoned, collective, judicial judgment: (1) Encouragement of oral argument; discouragement of oratory. The Socratic method is applied; questioning, in which the whole Court freely engage, clarifies the minds of the Justices as to the issues and guides the course of argument through real difficulties. (2) Consideration of every matter, be it an important case or merely a minor motion, by every Justice before conference and action at fixed, frequent and long conferences of the Court. This assures responsible deliberation and decision by the whole Court. (3) Assignment by the Chief Justice of cases for opinion-writing to the different Justices after discussion and vote at conference. Flexible use is thus made of the talents and energies of the Justices, and the writer of the opinion enters upon the task, not only with knowledge of the conclusions of his associates, but with the benefit of their suggestions made at conference. (4) Distribution of draft opinions in print, for consideration by the individual Justices in advance of the conference, followed by their discussion at subsequent conferences. Ample time is thus furnished for care in formulation of the result, for recirculation of revised opinions if necessary, and for writing dissents. This practice makes for team play and encourages individual inquiry instead of subservient unanimity. (5) Discouragement of rehearings. Thoroughness in the process of adjudication excludes the debilitating habit of some state courts of being too prodigal with rehearing. (6) To these specific procedural habits must be added the traditions of the

Court, the public scrutiny which it enjoys and the long tenure of the Justices. The inspiration that comes from a great past is reinforced by sensitiveness to healthy criticism. Continuity and experience in adjudication are secured through length of service as distinguished from the method of selection of judges.

.   .   .   .

The Court and Statesmanship

The following selection is part of a book review of The Supreme Court of the United States: Its Foundation, Methods and Achievements, *by Charles Evans Hughes, which appeared in the* American Bar Association Journal *for April, 1930 (Vol. 16, p. 251).*

IN HIS analysis of the true nature of the most vital contests before the Court, and the general intellectual procedure which the wise discharge of the Court's duties requires, Chief Justice Hughes makes profoundly important observations. Upon a rigorous observance of them, I venture to believe, depends the Court's successful contribution to the statesmanship of the country.

First and foremost, these lectures leave no doubt that the new Chief Justice realizes that the effectiveness of the Court's work does not derive from any language of the Constitution or the compulsions of logic or the mechanical contrivances of its organization. It depends upon the self-denying ordinances of the Justices. He recognizes fully the subtle psychologic difficulties in drawing the line, at times the shadowy line, between questions of mere wisdom or policy and those of power by pointing out that "It is doubtless true that men holding strong convictions as to the unwisdom of legislation may easily pass to the position that it is wholly unreasonable. . . ."

In his book the new Chief Justice was alive to the fact that this danger is to be avoided only by the self-discipline of the Justices, by working "in an objective spirit." And so he found that

. . . the success of the work of the Supreme Court in maintaining the necessary balance between state and nation, and between individual rights as guaranteed by the Constitution and social interest as expressed

34

in legislation, has been due largely to the deliberate determination of the Court to confine itself to its judicial task, and, while careful to maintain its authority as the interpreter of the Constitution, the Court has not sought to aggrandize itself at the expense of either executive or legislature.

Thus he found that when damage has come to the reputation and usefulness of the Court, it came, not through criticism from without, but "from self-inflicted wounds."

The need for rigorous objectivity, for scrupulous alertness, against confounding personal convictions upon ephemeral policies with enduring principles of right and wrong, becomes all the more manifest when we consider the exact scope of issues that must frequently solicit the judgment of the Court. Again and again the future Chief Justice in these lectures took occasion to point out the narrow controversy regarding fact and experience upon which Supreme Court decisions turn:

> The division in the Court illustrates the vast importance of its function, as, after all, the protection both of the rights of the individual and of those of society rests not so often on formulas, as to which there may be agreement, but on a correct appreciation of social conditions and a true appraisal of the actual effect of conduct.

These are matters on which differences of opinion are common both within the Court and outside it. Because they turn so much on questions of fact and upon the meaning of experience, the utmost tolerance and detachment are demanded in the application of vague constitutional phrases, like that of the due process of law which represents "an American conception of extraordinary pervasiveness."

Such are the issues and such their demands upon rather uncommon gifts of intellectual objectivity. Since it is unavoidable that "judges will have their convictions," Chief Justice Hughes regarded it "of the essence of the appropriate exercise of judicial power that these should be independently expressed." Dissenting opinions have for him no terrors. Quite the contrary. He regards them as instruments of truth, as feeders to the stream of reason:

There are some who think it desirable that dissents should not be disclosed, as they detract from the force of the judgment. Undoubtedly, they do. When unanimity can be obtained without sacrifice of conviction, it strongly commends the decision to public confidence. But unanimity which is merely formal, which is recorded at the expense of strong, conflicting views, is not desirable in a court of last resort, whatever may be the effect upon public opinion at the time. This is so because what must ultimately sustain the court in public confidence is the character and independence of the judges.

A dissent in a court of last resort is an appeal to the brooding spirit of the law, to the intelligence of a future day, when a later decision may possibly correct the error into which the dissenting judge believes the court to have been betrayed.

Nor is this appeal always in vain. In a number of cases dissenting opinions have in time become the law.

Thus, the narrator of the Court's history. He now becomes the maker of its history to an extent that may be momentous in the life of the Court and of the country.

Taft and the Supreme Court

This selection appeared as an unsigned editorial in the New Republic *for October 27, 1920.*

Mr. Wilson is in favor of a latitudinarian construction of the Constitution of the United States, to weaken the protection it should afford against Socialist raids upon property rights. . . .

He has made three appointments to the Supreme Court. He is understood to be greatly disappointed in the attitude of the first of these [Mr. Justice McReynolds] upon such questions. The other two [Mr. Justice Brandeis and Mr. Justice Clarke] represent a new school of constitutional construction, which, if allowed to prevail, will greatly impair our fundamental law. Four of the incumbent Justices are beyond the retiring age of seventy, and the next President will probably be called upon to appoint their successors. There is no greater domestic issue in this election than the maintenance of the Supreme Court as the bulwark to enforce the guarantee that no man shall be deprived of his property without due process of law. . . .

THESE are the views of ex-President Taft, reputedly one of our greatest authorities in constitutional law. The lay reader of his article in the October *Yale Review* might naturally assume that Justices Brandeis and Clarke are a pair of firebrands who, as members of the Supreme Court, have enunciated novel and revolutionary doctrines. If Mr. Taft's words mean anything they mean that a study of the opinions of the Supreme Court will show that Brandeis and Clarke form a group apart from the other members of the Court, and, particularly, that in cases involving the due process clause these two Justices have gone off on frolics of their own—frolics strange and disruptive.

Suppose, however, some lay reader, with a curiosity exceeding his respect for Mr. Taft's weighty *ipse dixit*, retained some re-

sponsible lawyer to analyze the constitutional attitude of Brandeis
and Clarke as revealed by the recorded decisions. Such a lawyer
would at once put Mr. Justice Clarke on one side without a detailed examination. He would say that Clarke's sober and conventional attitude is sufficiently attested by the fact that on the gravest
issue which has recently divided the Supreme Court—the protection of freedom of speech when invoked by so-called radicals—he
was the Court's spokesman of views pleasing even to Attorney
General Palmer. But what of Brandeis? A careful lawyer would
report that at the bar Brandeis achieved distinction, not as the
propounder of new constitutional doctrines, but as the inventor of
a new technique in the application of settled constitutional law—
an innovation of *method* which received the unanimous approval
of a Supreme Court containing lawyers of such unquestionable
orthodoxy as Fuller, Brewer, and Peckham. And what is Brandeis's record as Justice? That means a study of his dissents, for
only in these can we discover "the new school" which, according
to Mr. Taft, he represents. For Mr. Taft can hardly mean that
Brandeis could have corrupted the constitutional views of appointees of Cleveland, McKinley, Roosevelt, and Taft.

Brandeis dissented alone in only four cases, he and Clarke alone
in six more—in all other cases Brandeis was associated with one or
more of the senior Justices. And what were the ten cases? Of the
four exclusive Brandeis dissents one involved a novel question of
equity jurisdiction, one a claim against the government in which
Brandeis held for a railroad against the government, two involved
a delimitation between federal and state power and Brandeis took
a rather conservative "states' rights" point of view; of the six
Brandeis-Clarke dissents two involved questions of procedure and
four concerned interpretation of franchises—issues as to which
courts everywhere and always show differences of opinion. Not
one of these ten cases involved the questions which particularly
trouble Mr. Taft—the due process clause—not one of them involved any novel constitutional construction, not one of them was
among the cases raising great public issues. Ten negligible dissents
—out of a total of over seventeen hundred decisions! The utter

disregard for accuracy in Mr. Taft's accusation shows that Professor Taft—teacher of Constitutional Law at Yale—does not control the irresponsibility of politician Taft.

But, after all, so much heat in Mr. Taft must have some provocation. Brandeis is the easy target, but what Mr. Taft really means is not that Brandeis brought new views to the Court, but that he brought new strength to an old conflict—the conflict between the liberals and the hidebound. The Supreme Court is hopelessly split, in constant throes of clash on vital issues. Social and economic questions divide the Justices according to the largeness of view with which they are able to dissociate the requirements of the Constitution from their personal bias. The last few years have shown many such divisions and the future is not likely to lessen them. What does Mr. Taft mean by his general language about "Socialist raids upon property rights"? Does he mean that he agrees with the nullification of the federal child labor law, that he agrees with the "school of constitutional construction" which invalidated the stock dividend tax and upheld the espionage convictions in the Abrams, Schaffer, and Pierce cases? Does Mr. Taft, who avows belief in the necessity of trade unions in the abstract, support the Hitchman case which throws all the weight of the injunction against unionization in the concrete? On these and kindred issues Mr. Taft will be called upon to act, and perhaps cast a deciding vote, should President Harding make him Mr. Justice Taft.

And we are entitled to know the answers to these specific questions *now*. For Mr. Taft justly says there is no greater domestic issue in this election than the personnel of the Supreme Court in the coming years. Mr. Taft deserves our gratitude for his candor in recognizing that the Supreme Court involves political issues to be discussed like other political issues. In 1912, Mr. Taft was shocked that Roosevelt should dare drag the Court into the political arena. But now Mr. Taft warns us that no issue is more important than the views of the candidates as to future Justices. Of course that means we must study past decisions, the line-up of the Justices, their attitude towards economic ("property") questions, the attitude of likely appointees towards such questions. Not only may specific decisions be popularly considered, but the justification of the whole function of final law making or unmaking exercised by the Supreme Court can hardly escape scrutiny. Mr. Taft has now made respectable what was heretofore tabooed. The door to the Holy of Holies has been opened. Others will follow where Mr. Taft's profanation leads.

The Same Mr. Taft

This selection appeared as an unsigned editorial in the New Republic *for January 18, 1922.*

The press greets Mr. Taft's appointment with almost universal acclaim. . . . The *New Republic* does not begrudge Mr. Taft this outpour of good-will. But the Chief Justiceship . . . is not a subject for mere good-nature. . . . Cases involving the social control allowed the states under the Fourteenth Amendment . . . will soon again call forth a clash of differing conceptions of policy and of the proper scope of the Court's ultimate veto power. Mr. Taft, even before he was one of its members, has been rather obsessed by the notion that the Supreme Court is a sacred priesthood immune from profane criticism. He is not likely to be more hospitable to criticism as the presiding Justice of the Court. But the *New Republic* cannot emphasize too often that the only safeguard against the terrible powers vested in the Supreme Court lies in continuous, informed and responsible criticism of the work of the Court. Only thus will it be able to function as a living organ of the national will and not as an obstructive force of scholastic legislation.

New Republic, July 27, 1921

ARIZONA became a state in 1912. Its first legislature was confronted with the task of formulating a civil code properly adapted to the needs of the people of Arizona. One of the most insistent and delicate problems was the just and effective settlement of industrial controversies. In case of a conflict between employer and employees what "legal rights" may be asserted and how should those rights be enforced? How much should be left to the pressure of public opinion, to enlightened self-interest, to the competition of economic forces, and how much should be dealt with by law, and what machinery should the law utilize within the field of its authority? These were and are very complicated questions, as to which differences of opinion are acute because experience has as yet not brought decisive answers. This, if anything can, affords peculiarly a field for the exercise of legislative discretion; if there can be any justification at all for having legislatures, a stronger case for determining the state's policy by the responsible judgment of its legislature can hardly be imagined. Nor was Arizona facing this problem in the abstract. Labor difficulties were not unknown in the past, and their recurrence was certainly a fact near the horizon of the lawmakers of the state.

Charged with the duty of devising rules for the future conduct of labor litigation the Arizona Legislature could hardly escape the necessity of some pronouncement upon the most contentious issue which presented itself in American labor law, to wit, the use of the injunction against picketing and the boycott, particularly where no violence was used and the claim of destruction of property was merely colorable. The highest courts of the country, acting solely upon their own lawmaking function, were hopelessly divided. Thus Massachusetts, California, Michigan, and New Jersey outlawed peaceful picketing while the courts of Ohio, Minnesota, Montana, New York, Oklahoma, and New Hampshire sanctioned it. The conviction of an impressive body of opinion, which had accumulated at the time the Arizona Legislature was considering this problem, has thus been summarized by Mr. Justice Brandeis:

> The equitable remedy, although applied in accordance with established practice, involved incidents which, it was asserted, endangered the personal liberty of wage-earners. The acts enjoined were frequently, perhaps usually, acts which were already crimes at common law or had been made so by statutes. . . . The effect of the proceeding upon the individual was substantially the same as if he had been successfully prosecuted for a crime; but he was denied, in the course of the equity proceedings, those rights which by the Constitution are commonly secured to persons charged with a crime.

>   •   •   •   •   •   •   •

> It was urged that the real motive in seeking the injunction was not ordinarily to prevent property from being injured nor to protect the

owner in its use, but to endow property with active, militant power which would make it dominant over men. In other words, that under the guise of protecting property rights, the employer was seeking sovereign power. And many disinterested men, solicitous only for the public welfare, believed that the law of property was not appropriate for dealing with the forces beneath social unrest; that in this vast struggle it was unwise to throw the power of the state on one side or the other according to principles deduced from that law; that the problem of the control and conduct of industry demanded a solution of its own; and that pending the ascertainment of new principles to govern industry, it was wiser for the state not to interfere in industrial struggles by the issuance of an injunction.

With this as a background, the Arizona Legislature yielded to the experience of England and several American states, by prohibiting interference, through extraordinary relief by injunction, between employer and employees in any case growing out of a dispute concerning terms of conditions of employment, unless injury through violence was at stake. In all other cases of industrial conflict it left the rights of the parties to be protected through the criminal law and ordinary suits for damages. This act was passed in 1913, has remained untouched since then, and has passed challenge in the Arizona courts.

But the Supreme Court of the United States now says otherwise. Eight years after the law has been in force the Supreme Court holds that Arizona has laid impious hands upon the Ark of the Covenant as enshrined in the Fourteenth Amendment. To a mere layman this result must appear as incredible as the process by which it is reached is mysterious—although the decision immediately affects some thirty million lay men and women, who earn their livelihood in industry, and it no less affects the whole hundred million lay population of this country, insofar as it involves the power of the Supreme Court of the United States to translate its views of social policy into the law of each of the forty-eight states. Nor will the layman's bewilderment be lessened by the fact that this appalling result is reached by the votes of five men as against the votes of four men. The Chief Justice helps neither

an understanding of the decision nor respect for the law in asserting that "It does not seem possible to escape the conclusion" that
the Arizona act is unconstitutional when in fact four of his associates—Justices Holmes, Pitney, Brandeis and Clarke—find not
the slightest difficulty in escaping that conclusion and in emphatically dissenting from it. Judged by its point of view and its significance for the future this decision of the Supreme Court is, in
our judgment, fraught with more evil than any which it has rendered in a generation. It challenges the whole scope of judicial
review under the Fifth and Fourteenth Amendments. We know
of no problem in the institutional life of this country which calls
for a more courageous searching and fundamental scrutiny than
the nature of the power which the majority of the Court exercises
in the Arizona case and the manner in which that power is wielded.

Let us recall the words of the Fourteenth Amendment to see
the exact terms of the limitations by which the states are circumscribed in determining for themselves, in the language of Mr. Justice Pitney, "their respective conditions of law and order, and what
kind of civilization they shall have as a result."

. . . nor shall any state deprive any person of life, liberty, or property
without due process of law; nor deny to any person within its jurisdiction the equal protection of the laws.

Chief Justice Taft finds that the denial in labor cases of extraordinary relief by injunction deprives the owner of a business of
"property" without "due process of law," and that in selecting the
class of employers and employees for special treatment, though
dealing with both sides alike, Arizona is guilty of a denial of "the
equal protection of the laws." Whence does the Court derive this
result? Surely not from the *words* of the Fourteenth Amendment.
That amendment, to be sure, imposes limitations upon state action,
but it does not define them. "Due process of law" and "the equal
protection of the laws" are not self-defining. Their content is derived from without. "The Constitution was intended," says the
Chief Justice, "to prevent experimentation with the fundamental
rights of the individual." Of course. But what "rights" are "funda-

mental" is *the* question to be answered. For Chief Justice Taft the beginning of the problem is the end. "When fundamental rights are thus attempted to be taken away," he says in speaking of the Arizona statute, and thus blithely indulges in a schoolboy's begging of the question. The very problem at issue is whether the use of the injunction in labor cases *is* a "fundamental right." It does not bring us one whit nearer solution to be told repeatedly that the Constitution safeguards "fundamental rights." The central problem is evaded by an effortless repetition of phrases.

.   .   .   .

Moreover, the Court has recognized that "while the cardinal principles of justice are immutable, the methods by which justice is administered are subject to constant fluctuations," and "the power of the people of the states to make and alter their laws at pleasure is the greatest security for liberty and justice." The Fourteenth Amendment, so the Supreme Court has told us again and again, is not the arbiter of policy. Only "immutable principles" are in its keeping.

Is it really possible for anyone living in the present day to insist that the restriction of the use of the injunction in labor cases is the denial of "a fundamental principle of liberty and justice which inheres in the very idea of free government and is the inalienable right of a citizen of such a government"? No wonder Mr. Justice Pitney, dealing with the issue in the concrete, writes, "I cannot believe that the use of the injunction in such cases—however important—is so essential to the right of acquiring, possessing and enjoying property that its restriction or elimination amounts to a deprivation of liberty or property without due process of law, within the meaning of the Fourteenth Amendment."

Equally incredible and ominous is an application of the requirement of the equal protection of the laws which excludes differentiating treatment of such a distinct problem as a labor controversy, compared with other types of litigation. Again let members of the Court speak. "I think further," writes Mr. Justice Holmes, "that the selection of the class of employers and employees for special treatment, dealing with both sides alike, is beyond criticism on principles often asserted by this Court. And especially I think that without legalizing the conduct complained of, the extraordinary relief by injunction may be denied to the class. Legislation may begin where an evil begins. If, as many intelligent people believe, there is more danger that injunction will be abused in labor cases than elsewhere, I can feel no doubt of the power of the legislature to deny it in such cases."

How is one to account for such a decision by the majority, and for this opinion by Chief Justice Taft? We venture the following analysis:

1. Chief Justice Taft deals with abstractions and not with the work-a-day world, its men and its struggles. To him, also, words are things and not the symbols of things. The jejune logomachy of his judicial process is thus exposed by Mr. Justice Holmes:

The dangers of a delusive exactness in the application of the Fourteenth Amendment have been adverted to before now. . . . By calling a business "property" you make it seem like land, and lead up to the conclusion that a statute cannot substantially cut down the advantages of ownership existing before the statute was passed. An established business no doubt may have pecuniary value and commonly is protected by law against various unjustified injuries. But you cannot give it definiteness of contour by calling it a thing. It is a course of conduct and like other conduct is subject to substantial modification according to time and circumstances both in itself and in regard to what shall justify doing it a harm. I cannot understand the notion that it would be unconstitutional to authorize boycotts and the like in aid of the employees' or the employers' interest by statute when the same result has been reached constitutionally without statute by courts with whom I agree.

For all the regard that the Chief Justice of the United States pays to the facts of industrial life, he might as well have written this opinion as Chief Justice of the Fiji Islands. Mr. Taft, as a member of the War Labor Board, came in contact with not a little that must have informed his mind as to the industrial struggle, and law's relation to it. But all those crude and sordid and unsymmetrical facts have no place in the mind of Chief Justice Taft. . . . From reading his opinion the historian of the future would have to assume that the Arizona Legislature withdrew injunctive relief in labor cases out of sheer malevolence or in a spirit of reckless oppression.

2. "What we call necessary institutions," says de Tocqueville, "are often no more than institutions to which we have grown accustomed." The Chief Justice, we venture to suggest, is a victim of this process of self-delusion. For him there never was a time when injunctive relief was not the law of nature. For him the world never was without it, and therefore the foundations of the world are involved in its withdrawal. And yet, 1888 marks the first recorded opinion of an injunction in labor litigation, and in 1896, the Chief Justice of Massachusetts still speaks of injunctions in such cases as "a practice of very recent origin." By 1921, the right to an injunction has become "an immutable principle of liberty and justice," world without end! The result is that while the due process clause does not guarantee trial by jury as at common law even in criminal cases, the due process clause *does* guarantee the right to trial *without jury*—for the nub of the matter is that the resort to equity for an injunction in labor disputes is due to a "greater probability of a conviction for contempt by a judge alone . . . than of conviction by a jury likely to sympathize in some degree with the offender."

3. As a result of both these tendencies—abstract reasoning and canonizing the familiar into the eternal—the judge's limitations are stereotyped into limitations of the Constitution. The danger has been voiced by one of the most discerning of recent judges, the late Mr. Justice Moody:

Under the guise of interpreting the Constitution, we must take care that we do not import into the discussion our own personal views of what would be wise, just and fitting rules of government to be adopted by a free people, and confound them with constitutional limitations.

This is precisely what Chief Justice Taft has done, and that too in the most sensitive field of social policy and legal control.

Social Issues before the Supreme Court

The following article appeared in the Yale Review *in the spring of 1933, copyright Yale University Press.*

IN OUR scheme of government, readjustment to great social changes means juristic readjustment. Our basic problems—whether of industry, agriculture, or finance—sooner or later appear in the guise of legal problems. Professor John R. Commons is therefore justified in characterizing the Supreme Court of the United States as the authoritative faculty of economics. The foundation for its economic encyclicals is the Constitution. Plainly, however, constitutional provisions are not economic dogmas and certainly not obsolete economic dogmas. . . .

By its very conception the Constitution has ample resources within itself to meet the changing needs of successive generations. For "it was made for an undefined and expanding future and for a people gathered and to be gathered from many nations and of many tongues." Through the generality of its language the Constitution provided for the future partly by not forecasting it. If the Court, aided by the bar, has access to the facts and heeds them, the Constitution is flexible enough to respond to the demands of modern society.

And so American constitutional law is not a fixed body of truth, but a mode of social adjustment. Indeed, the Constitution owes its continuity to an uninterrupted process of change. "The Constitution cannot make itself; somebody made it, not at once, but at several times. It is alterable; and by that draweth nearer to Perfection; and without suiting itself to differing Times and Circumstances, it could not live. Its Life is prolonged by changing seasonably the several Parts of it at several times." So wrote the shrewd

Lord Halifax, and his words are as true of our written Constitution as of that strange medley of imponderables, the British Constitution. A ready sense of the need for alteration is perhaps the most precious talent required of the Supreme Court. Upon it depends the vitality of our Constitution as a vehicle for life.

Public law is thus a most potent instrument of public policy. The significant cases before the Supreme Court are not just controversies between two litigants. They involve large public issues, and the general outlook of the Justices gives direction to their judicial views. In law also, where one ends, depends much on one's starting point.

The Supreme Court's right and wrong are drawn most frequently from broad and undefined clauses of the Constitution. A few simple-seeming terms like "liberty" and "property," indeterminate phrases like "regulate Commerce . . . among the several states" and "without due process of law," are invoked in judgment upon the shifting circumstances of a dynamic society. Phrases like "due process of law" are of "convenient vagueness." Necessarily their content is derived from without, not revealed within, the Constitution. The gloss that is put upon them controls the nation's efforts to meet its tasks. The capacity of states to control or mitigate unemployment, to assure a living wage for the workers, to clear slums and provide decent housing, to make city planning effective, to distribute fairly the burdens of taxation—these and like functions of modern government hinge on the Supreme Court's reading of the due process clause. The various attempts, in the past, to subject great economic instrumentalities to social responsibility—the Stockyards Act, the Grain Futures Act, the Transportation Act, the Child Labor Law—depended upon what the lawyers call interpretation of the Commerce Clause. But what is interpreted depends on who interprets. The fate of such laws turned on facts and assumptions which underlie the social valuations of the judges. Again, the thorny controversies affecting business combinations and trade unions are also described as interpretations of the Sherman Law and the Clayton Act. But the results were determined by the Court's view of our industrial scene. So also the opinions of the Justices regarding the activities of trade associations and co-operatives vary with the general context in which different Justices place the economic data deemed relevant to judgment. The sharp conflicts to which control of the railroads and other public utilities gives rise derive not from variant readings of the same English text. They are nurtured in different economic cultures; they are the concrete expressions of different social philosophies.

.　　　.　　　.　　　　　　.　　　.　　　.

In a period of rapid change like ours, the pace of social adjustments must be quickened. Poignant experience has made us realize the public implications of interests heretofore treated as private. Such interests must be stripped of many of their past immunities and subjected to appropriate responsibility. Courts will thus be called upon to make and to sustain extensive readjustments.

For example, the law must become more sophisticated in its conception of trustees' obligations. It must sharpen and extend the duties incident to the fiduciary relations of corporate directors and officers. The whole process of corporate salaries disproportionate to services rendered must be fearlessly faced, but especially the abuse of agreement for swollen contingent compensation. . . .

. . . The law cannot long continue to give such unbridled rein to the acquisitive motive. Our social health cannot afford it.

Disastrous defects have been exposed in our financial institutions; tighter controls must be devised. Secretary Mills calls for legislation that will "remedy the fundamental weakness of our banking structure." Schemes have been adumbrated for a unified national banking system which raise intricate questions of policy and administration as well as of constitutionality. All these will call for judicial understanding of banking and finance, their relation to government and industry and agriculture. . . .

Cutting across all our problems are the manifold aspects of taxation. The enormous increase in the cost of society and the subtle forms which modern wealth so largely takes are putting public finance to its severest test. To balance budgets, to pay for the cost of progressively civilized social standards, to safeguard the future and to divide these burdens with substantial fairness to the different interests in the community—these endeavors present problems more grueling than were ever faced by Colbert or Hamilton. Financial statesmanship must constantly explore new sources of revenue and find means to prevent the circumvention of their discovery. Such a task is bound to fail without wide latitude for experimentation, within the most promising areas of trial, in devising and executing fiscal measures. No finicky limitation upon the discretion of those charged with the duty of providing revenue, nor jejune conceptions about formal equality, should circumscribe the necessarily empirical process of tapping new revenue or stopping new devices for its evasion. The fiscal difficulties of government at best are hard and thorny. They ought not to be made insuperable by reading into the Constitution private notions of social policy. Too often, talk about scientific taxation is only a verbal screen for distributing the incidence of taxation according to traditional notions. Judgments of fairness in taxation, as in other activities of government, are functions of their time. Governing ideas of taxation of the eighteenth century, or even of the nineteenth century, were not permanently frozen into the Constitution.

Indeed, we must recognize the profound shift in the very purposes of taxation. Senator Root once reminded the American bar that "the vast increase of wealth resulting from the increased power of production is still in the first stages of the inevitable processes of distribution." Mr. Root was himself a member of an administration which employed the taxing power as one of the instruments for such distribution. Theodore Roosevelt was the first President avowedly to use the taxing power as a direct agency of social policy. More and more, it is bound to serve as a powerful means for directing the modern flow of wealth to social uses. The historical ambitions of American democracy and fiscal necessities alike demand it.

.   .   .   .

The law's concern with taxation covers a very wide front, and it must extensively modify its precedents and its predispositions.

Much new legislation is indispensable; effective investigation must precede legislation; sympathetic judicial insight will have to support the legislation. Leaks must be stopped; skillful avoidances and evasions must be circumvented. In part, this will involve a correction of detail, a reversal of rulings and decisions both of the taxing agencies and of the courts. More drastic changes will also be required. Professional skill and imagination, if directed to increase of revenue and not to protection of heavy taxpayers, will be able to overcome strained interpretations of the Supreme Court and to limit the baneful effects of some of its holdings of unconstitutionality. Thereby, without a doubt, vast sums will be reached which have been withdrawn from their fair share of taxation.

These are only a few of the new paths to be explored if we are to work ourselves out of the morass. Lawyers have a special responsibility in breaking these new paths and allowing free travel upon them. In this country, theirs is probably the greatest power for good or evil. High technical competence is, of course, demanded in formulating the complicated adjustments necessary for our complicated society. But technical power can thwart as well as promote necessary social invention. The times demand new methods adapted to new problems, the removal of what is obstructive and wasteful in old principles or old applications.

The Supreme Court is indispensable to the effective workings of our federal government. If it did not exist, we should have to create it. I know of no other peaceful method for making the adjustments necessary to a society like ours—for maintaining the equilibrium between state and federal power, for settling the eternal conflicts between liberty and authority—than through a court of great traditions free from the tensions and temptations of party strife, detached from the fleeting interests of the moment. But because, inextricably, the Supreme Court is also an organ of statesmanship and the most powerful organ, it must have a seasoned understanding of affairs, the imagination to see the organic relations of society, above all, the humility not to set

up its own judgment against the conscientious efforts of those
whose primary duty it is to govern. . . .

Unfortunately, the Supreme Court forgets at times to remember its own wisdom. In view of the tasks in hand, the price of
judicial obscurantism is too great. Let me give two or three instances reflecting controversies neither minor in character nor
resurrected from the dim past, but dealing with the liveliest issues
of our day.

The reorganization of the St. Paul has implications far beyond
the receivership even of an important railroad. In one form or
another, whether through administrative action or legislation or
voluntary arrangement, or a combination of these, we must contract the capital structures, certainly of some of the railroads. This
process will entail the interplay of financial and moral considerations and will demand the best thought of our regulatory agencies.
The recent decision of the Supreme Court in the St. Paul case
thus affects railroad credit, the financial burdens incident to railroad consolidation, the effective powers of the Interstate Commerce Commission to protect the public interest, and, not least,
the standards of fiduciary obligation of investment bankers.

.   .   .   .

Proposed railroad consolidations will involve issues similar to
those in the St. Paul case. For instance, among the men who will
guide the Eastern roads in these consolidations are lawyers and
bankers who successfully denied that the Interstate Commerce
Commission had jurisdiction over their St. Paul fees. Those fees
will probably appear petty in amount when compared with the
bankers' and lawyers' charges for consolidating the Eastern roads.
If these should prove to be excessive, the losers will be the railroads, and thus the investors and the public. If the Interstate
Commerce Commission attempts to determine whether the charges
are reasonable or not, its authority to do so may again be put
in question. These methods for avoiding control may also be employed in other phases of railroad affairs. In the past, the public
has relied on the Interstate Commerce Commission to regulate

the railroads in the public interest. That feeling of security is disturbed by the St. Paul decision.

Foreigners are fond of calling this the land of paradoxes. Our public finances certainly justify that characterization. The richest country in the world has been the most dilatory in balancing its budget, and appears the most distracted and embarrassed in its accomplishment. I venture to believe that a major explanation is the systematically inculcated hostility to the taxation of wealth. For a decade the press has sedulously repeated the Mellon doctrine that the immunity of the rich from taxation is a blessing for the poor. In times of prosperity taxes on bloated incomes will discharge enterprise; in days of adversity there are no bloated incomes—such was the governing philosophy.

It ought not to be too surprising that this deep-seated sentiment against the taxation of wealth should be shared by members of our Supreme Court. How easily private notions of economic or social policy are transmuted into constitutional dogma is amply proved by the United States Reports since the War. Enormous wealth has been withdrawn from the taxing power of the nation and the states on the gossamer claim that otherwise governmental instrumentalities would be defeated. The history of taxation is, to no small extent, a battle of wits between skill in devising taxes and astuteness in evading them. By creating constitutional obstructions to safeguards against evasion, the Supreme Court has put the Constitution at the disposal of the evaders. A few years ago the Supreme Court sheltered great wealth by interposing the benevolent "due process" clause on behalf of rich donors who made gifts in anticipation of tax measures especially designed for them. One might suppose the Supreme Court would at least be friendly to the effective enforcement of the inheritance tax. The social justification of that tax has become an accepted postulate even of our individualistic society. But the other day the Court, again under the blessed versatility of "due process," nullified the attempt of Congress, in response to the compelling experience of the Treasury Department, to prevent gross evasions of the inheritance tax.

From the original enactment of the estate tax law in 1916, it was realized that a single tax on estates could be too easily avoided by well-timed and astute disposition of property before death. To check such practices, the Act of 1916 contained two safeguards. Gifts made "in contemplation of death," and those in which the donor retained a joint interest during his lifetime, were taxed as part of his estate at death. But other means remained by which property might be withdrawn from the operation of the tax and yet remain within the effective control of the donor: he might, for example, place it in trust with a power of revocation or control reserved in himself. The possibility of escape by this device was materially reduced by legislation, which taxed gifts, by way of trust, taking effect "in possession or enjoyment" at the time of the donor's death. The courts threatened the effectiveness of much of this legislation by technical and sterile definitions of "possession or enjoyment," and in 1931 Congress was forced to close a broad avenue of escape from the estate tax by making specific provision for the inclusion of property which is transferred on trust for another but from which the income is reserved for the donor during his life.

Meanwhile, the tax authorities were beset by difficulties growing out of the vague phrase, "in contemplation of death." In what degree the donor must have apprehended his end, and how to prove that apprehension, were questions which made the collection of a tax precarious at best. The devil himself, the lawyers are fond of quoting, knoweth not the mind of man; and even if he did, the devil's advocate might experience considerable difficulty in proving it to a court of law. Realizing that the limited omniscience of the taxing authorities was finding it impossible to isolate successfully those gifts that were made "in contemplation of death," Congress in 1924 imposed a tax on all gifts, irrespective of date or motive, at rates equal to those under the estate tax. This general gift tax was upheld by the Supreme Court. In addition, the tax on gifts made in contemplation of death was retained, giving the government a second string to its bow, although, of course, credit was allowed where a gift tax had already been paid on the transfer.

The arm of the government was strengthened, moreover, by requiring the representatives of the estate to prove, where the gift was within two years of death, that it was not in contemplation thereof. But this shift of the burden of proof was of little value to the government in a contest against an elderly man of wealth contemplating death with one eye and the tax law with the other. The gift tax itself promised better results, but in 1926 it was repealed. (By the revenue Act of 1932 it has been restored.)

Congress was alive to the need of conserving the gain which the gift tax had made in the enforcement of the estate tax. Ten years' experience in administering the revenue acts had taught its lesson. Congress provided that gifts made within two years of death should be "deemed to have been made in contemplation of death," and so might be assessed under the estate tax. "The inclusion of this provision," reported the Ways and Means Committee of the House, "will prevent most of the evasion and is the only way in which it can be prevented." This is the provision which the Supreme Court declared unconstitutional. Again "due process" worked its charm on behalf of wealth.

In thus setting at naught the considered effort of Congress to obtain a really effective tax on decedents' estates, a majority of the Court found the provision arbitrary and unreasonable because it might apply to gifts made with no thought of death or taxes. "The young man in abounding health," writes Mr. Justice Sutherland, "bereft of life by a stroke of lightning within two years after making a gift, is conclusively presumed to have acted under the inducement of the thought of death, equally with the old man and ailing who already stands in the shadow of the inevitable." The pity aroused by this affecting apparition of the benevolent young plutocrat is somewhat mollified by the fact that if the property had not been given to kith and kin—gifts to charity being exempted—so shortly before the donor's end, it would in all likelihood have passed by will and been taxed accordingly.

The apparition fades completely before the picture drawn by

Mr. Justice Stone in a dissenting opinion, in which he was joined by Mr. Justice Brandeis. (Mr. Justice Cardozo did not sit in the case.) This opinion reveals graphically by whom these gifts are made, and with what effect on the operation of the taxing system. Mr. Justice Stone analyzes one hundred and two cases in which the government and the decedent's estate engaged in litigation over the question whether a gift had been made "in contemplation of death," under the law as it existed before the 1926 provision. . . .

This decision does not touch technical issues that are in the special province of learned judges. How taxes are evaded and how fine a net must be woven to keep big fish from escaping, what the experience of a decade of federal estates administration indicated, and what means are adapted to prevent wholesale evasion—these are matters which tax administrators, members of the Ways and Means Committee, students of public finance, are as competent to understand as Mr. Justice Sutherland and his brethren. Is it not the plain truth that Mr. Justice Stone's powerful opinion deals with actualities and demolishes the hollow fabric of unreality erected by the majority? And if it be the truth, the Supreme Court has its duty towards a balanced budget—it ought not to sanctify gross tax evasion or call the word-spinning by which it does so the Constitution.

Finally, what of the Supreme Court's attitude towards the most inclusive of all our problems, namely, how to subdue our anarchic competitive economy to reason, how to correct the disharmonies between production and consumption? This issue was raised last spring in the now famous Oklahoma Ice case. On the basis of watchful scrutiny of the actual operation of the ice industry in Oklahoma, the legislature of that state, acting upon the recommendation of its Corporation Commission, availed itself of a well-tested instrument of public control—the device of a certificate of public convenience and necessity—to subject the ice business to a regulated instead of a wildcat economy. By this means, Oklahoma, within the limited area of the ice industry, endeavored to avoid excessive equipment and the demoralization of deflation and unemployment, and thereby promote stability. But the majority of the Court struck down this very modest essay in regulated economy. It denied Oklahoma's right to act upon its own experience, and, for a time at least, unbridled competition was given the sanction of the United States Constitution.

Against such an attitude, Mr. Justice Brandeis raised his magistral voice. It is not hazardous prophecy to believe that Mr. Justice Brandeis's opinion (concurred in by Mr. Justice Stone, Mr. Justice Cardozo taking no part in the decision) merely anticipates history, even the history of future opinions of the Court. The closing observations of this memorable dissent deserve quotation:

> To stay experimentation in things social and economic is a grave responsibility. Denial of the right to experiment may be fraught with serious consequences to the nation. It is one of the happy incidents of the federal system that a single courageous state may, if its citizens choose, serve as a laboratory and try novel social and economic experiments without risk to the rest of the country. This Court has the power to prevent an experiment. We may strike down the statute which embodies it on the ground that, in our opinion, the measure is arbitrary, capricious or unreasonable. We have power to do this, because the due process clause has been held by the Court applicable to matters of substantive law as well as to matters of procedure. But in the exercise of this high power, we must be ever on our guard, lest we erect our prejudices into legal principles. If we would guide by the light of reason, we must let our minds be bold.

The faith and enterprise which built this nation are unimpaired. Our intrinsic resources are greater than ever. We have also the unparalleled advantage of a fluid society. Under the guidance of a Supreme Court responsive to the potentialities of the Constitution to meet the needs of our society, it would now lie within our power to have an enduring diffusion of the goods of civilization to an extent never before attainable.

The Elements of Judicial Greatness:
Three Great Justices

Justice Holmes Defines the Constitution

Shortly after the commencement of Mr. Frankfurter's service in Washington with the War Department, his long personal intimacy with Mr. Justice Holmes began. Mr. Justice Holmes became not only a friend, but an important intellectual interest. The nature and extent of this interest are indicated by three of Mr. Frankfurter's articles in the Harvard Law Review (*Vol. 29, p. 683; Vol. 36, p. 909; Vol. 41, p. 101*) *as well as his book,* Mr. Justice Holmes and the Supreme Court, *published in 1938. The following selection from the book appeared in the* Atlantic Monthly *for October, 1938, and is reprinted by permission of the President and Fellows of Harvard College.*

THE HISTORY of the Supreme Court would record fewer explosive periods if, from the beginning, there had been a more continuous awareness of the rôle of the Court in the dynamic process of American society. Lawyers, with rare exceptions, have failed to lay bare that the law of the Supreme Court is enmeshed in the country's history; historians no less have seemed to miss the fact that the country's history is enmeshed in the law of the Supreme Court. Normally historians, much more than lawyers, guide the general understanding of our institutions. But historians have, in the main, allowed only the most spectacular decisions—the Dred Scott controversy or the Legal Tender cases—to intrude upon the flow of national development through their voluminous pages. The vital share of the Court in the interplay of the country's political and economic forces has largely escaped their attention. Not unnaturally the Court has been outside the permanent focus of the historian's eye. For the momentum of the Court's influence has been achieved undra-

matically and imperceptibly, like the gradual growth of a coral
reef, as the cumulative product of hundreds of cases, individually
unexciting and seemingly even unimportant, but in their total
effect powerfully telling in the pulls and pressures of society.

From the very beginning the Court has had business which
in form was an ordinary lawsuit but which affected the nation as
much as action either by the Congress or by the President. The
raw material of modern government is business. Taxation, utility
regulation, agricultural control, labor relations, housing, banking
and finance, control of the security market—all our major domestic
issues—are phases of a single central problem: namely, the interplay of economic enterprise and government. These are the issues
which for more than a generation have dominated the calendar
of the Court.

> .   .   .   .

We speak of the Court as though it were an abstraction. To
be sure the Court is an institution, but individuals, with all their
diversities of endowment, experience, and outlook, determine its
actions. The history of the Supreme Court is not the history of
an abstraction, but the analysis of individuals acting as a Court
who make decisions and lay down doctrines, and of other individuals, their successors, who refine, modify, and sometimes even
overrule the decisions of their predecessors, reinterpreting and
transmuting their doctrines. In law also men make a difference.
It would deny all meaning to history to believe that the course
of events would have been the same if Thomas Jefferson had had
the naming of Spencer Roane to the place to which John Adams
called John Marshall, or if Roscoe Conkling rather than Morrison
R. Waite had headed the Court before which came the Granger
legislation. The evolution of finance capital in the United States,
and therefore of American history after the Reconstruction period,
would hardly have been the same if the views of men like Mr.
Justice Miller and Mr. Justice Harlan had dominated the decisions of the Court from the Civil War to Theodore Roosevelt's
administration. There is no inevitability in history except as men
make it.

II

The United States got under way one hundred and fifty years ago, and only seventy-seven men have shaped its destiny, in so far as law has shaped it. To understand what manner of men they were who have sat on the Supreme Bench is vital for an understanding of the Court and its work. Yet how meager is our insight into all but a very few! A lawyer's life before he becomes a judge, like that of an actor, is largely writ in water unless he has had a rich political career. And legal opinions are not conducive to biographical revelation. On the whole, we have a pitifully inadequate basis for understanding the psychological and cultural influences which may be the roots of judicial opinions. The obvious map to the minds of the Justices—the opinions of the Court—is deceptive precisely because they are the opinions of the Court. They are symphonies, not solos. Inferences from opinions to the distinctive characteristics of individual Justices are treacherous, except in so far as a man's genius breaks through a collective judgment, or his vivid life before he went on the bench serves as commentary, or as he expresses individual views in dissent or through personal writings. Not to speak of the present Court, Mr. Justice Holmes possessed these qualities of personal genius perhaps in richer measure than any member in the Court's history.

The Chief Justice of Massachusetts became Mr. Justice Holmes of the Supreme Court on December 4, 1902, and resigned on January 12, 1932. He was thus a member of the Court for a fifth of its entire active history, and participated in more than a third of its adjudications. More important than these items of duration or volume is the historic significance of the period. Long-maturing social forces which the Civil War released or intensified found powerful political expression just about the time that Mr. Justice Holmes went to Washington. Time did not abate these conflicts. And so it came about that the Court, during his whole thirty years, was sucked into political controversies more continuous and of more immediate popular concern than at any other time in its history.

To the discerning, the burst of capitalistic activity following the victory of the North early revealed that reconciliation of unfettered individual enterprise with social well-being would be the chief issue of politics. A letter by Mr. Justice Miller, written in 1878, which has recently come to light, is a straw showing the way the wind was blowing. Miller, an appointee of Lincoln, and probably the most powerful member of his Court, kept a close watch on events in Washington as well as from the vantage point of the agricultural Middle West, where he traveled much on circuit:

I have met with but few things of a character affecting the public good of the whole country that have shaken my faith in human nature as much as the united, vigorous, and selfish effort of the capitalists—the class of men who as a distinct class are but recently known in this country—I mean those who live solely by interest and dividends. Prior to the late war they were not numerous. They had no interest separate from the balance of the community, because they could lend their money safely and at high rates of interest. But one of the effects of the war was greatly to reduce the rate of interest by reason of the great increase in the quantity of the circulating medium. Another was by the creation of a national funded debt, exempt from taxation, to provide a means for the investment of surplus capital. This resource for investment was quadrupled by the bonds issued by the states, by municipal corporations, and by railroad companies. The result has been the gradual formation of a new kind of wealth in this country, the income of which is the coupons of interest and stock dividends, and of a class whose only interest or stake in the country is the ownership of these bonds and stocks. They engage in no commerce, no trade, no manufacture, no agriculture. They produce nothing.

Mr. Justice Miller was here describing early manifestations of the impact of technological science upon society. Finance capital was in its early stages. Its evolution since Mr. Justice Miller wrote has been analyzed in Veblen's writings and in Brandeis's *Other People's Money;* the pungent details are recorded in the massive volumes of the Pujo and the Pecora investigating committees. In brief, technological advances led to large-scale industry, large-scale industries flowered into mergers and monopolies, thereby producing in considerable measure a subordination of industry to finance. On the social side came the shift from a dominantly agricultural to an urbanized society. Big business vigorously stimulated trade-unionism. Since modern politics is largely economics, these conflicting forces soon found political expression. After several abortive attempts, the various agrarian and progressive movements, in combination with organized labor and other less defined groups, three times won the Presidency. For the "square deal" of Theodore Roosevelt, the "new freedom" of Woodrow Wilson, and the "new deal" of Franklin D. Roosevelt have a common genealogy. Disregarding for the moment detailed or minor differences, the three eras which these slogans summarize derived from efforts to reconcile modern economic forces with the demands of a popular democracy.

. . . .

Short of the immediate issues of today, Mr. Justice Holmes's period of service on the Court covered the years of most intense interaction between government and business. Barring the tariff and the National Bank Act, there were only two important measures of economic legislation on the federal statute books when Mr. Justice Holmes came to the Court, and these two, the Interstate Commerce Act of 1887 and the Sherman Law of 1890, had only somnolent vitality. Nor had state legislation, after the flurry of the Granger days, proved itself an effective device for social control over economic circumstance. Theodore Roosevelt's presidency marked the change. Under him the federal government for the first time embarked upon a positive program of social welfare. Through use of the taxing power and by regulatory legislation, not only were abuses to be remedied, but benefits to be achieved for the common man. A vast field of hitherto free enterprise was brought under governmental supervision. Regardless of the political complexion of successive administrations, the area of national oversight of business was extended. From 1903 to 1932, an invigorated Interstate Commerce Commission, the Federal Trade Commission, the Federal Reserve Board, the Farm Loan Board, the Tariff Commission, the Federal Power Commission, the Railroad Labor Board, followed each other in quick succession.

This vigorous legislative movement was partly a reflex of energetic state action and partly stimulated states to action. Wisconsin, under the elder La Follette, and New York, under Charles E. Hughes, took the lead in effective state regulation of utilities. In the decade between 1910 and 1920 all but half a dozen states enacted workmen's compensation laws. Local anti-trust laws, shorter-hours acts, minimum-wage laws, blue-sky laws, banking laws, conservation enactments, illustrate only some of the topics on which laws came from the forty-eight states. Such were the problems that were presented to Mr. Justice Holmes for adjudication.

III

What equipment did Mr. Justice Holmes bring to the Court for dealing with these problems? What qualities did Theodore Roosevelt look for in appointing a Supreme Court Justice at this time? Thanks to Senator Lodge, the elder, to whom President Roosevelt unburdened his mind, we know both the hopes and the doubts that he felt about Mr. Justice Holmes's qualifications for the Supreme Bench at that particular time:

First of all, I wish to go over the reasons why I am in his favor. . . . The labor decisions which have been criticized by some of the big railroad men and other members of large corporations constitute to my mind a strong point in Judge Holmes's favor. The ablest lawyers and the greatest judges are men whose past has naturally brought them into close relationship with the wealthiest and most powerful clients, and I am glad when I can find a judge who has been able to preserve his aloofness of mind so as to keep his broad humanity of feeling and his sympathy for the class from which he has not drawn his clients. I think it eminently desirable that our Supreme Court should show in unmistakable fashion their entire sympathy with all proper effort to secure the most favorable possible consideration for the men who most need that consideration.

Now a word as to the other side. . . . In the ordinary and low sense which we attach to the words "partisan" and "politician," a judge of the Supreme Court should be neither. But in the higher sense, in the proper sense, he is not in my judgment fitted for the position unless he is a party man, a constructive statesman, constantly keeping in mind his adherence to the principles and policies under which this nation has been built up and in accordance with which it must go on; and keeping in mind also his relations with his fellow statesmen who in other branches of the government are striving in co-operation with him to advance the ends of government.

. . . The majority of the present Court who have, although without satisfactory unanimity, upheld the policies of President McKinley and the Republican party in Congress, have rendered a great service to mankind and to this nation. The minority—a minority so large as to lack but one vote of being a majority—have stood for such reactionary folly as would have hampered well-nigh hopelessly this people in doing efficient and honorable work for the national welfare. . . .

Now I should like to know that Judge Holmes was in entire sympathy with our views, that is, with your views and mine . . . before I would feel justified in appointing him. Judge Gray has been one of the most valuable members of the Court. I should hold myself as guilty of an irreparable wrong to the nation if I should put in his place any man who was not absolutely sane and sound on the great national policies for which we stand in public life.

In taking account of the general philosophy of a prospective member of the Supreme Court towards major public issues likely to come before it, Theodore Roosevelt was merely following the example of other Presidents, notably Lincoln in appointing Chase as Chief Justice. The psychological assumptions made by Theodore Roosevelt and Lincoln that the past in which a man is inured may have a powerful effect upon his future decisions are supported by weighty judicial experience.

When judges decide issues that touch the nerve center of economic and social conflict, the danger, in de Tocqueville's phrase, of confounding the familiar with the necessary is especially hazardous. The matter was put with candor by Lord Justice Scrutton, a great English judge:

> The habits you are trained in, the people with whom you mix, lead to your having a certain class of ideas of such a nature that, when you have to deal with other ideas, you do not give as sound and accurate judgment as you would wish. This is one of the great difficulties at present with Labor. Labor says: "Where are your impartial Judges? They all move in the same circle as the employers, and they are all educated and nursed in the same ideas as the employers. How can a labor man or a trade-unionist get impartial justice?" It is very difficult sometimes to be sure that you have put yourself into a thoroughly impartial position between two disputants—one of your own class and one not of your class.

Unlike the great men on the Court before him, Mr. Justice Holmes had been singularly outside the current of public affairs or of interest in them. He was essentially the philosopher who turned to law. Ultimate issues of the destiny of man, not the evanescent events of the day, preoccupied his mind. That he did not read newspapers revealed neither affectation nor a sense of superiority; it mirrored his worldly innocence. When Senator Lodge tried to induce him to run for Governor, with the bait that it would inevitably lead to a seat in the United States Senate, Mr. Justice Holmes blandly replied: "But I don't give a damn about being a Senator." And yet, though he did not bring to the Court the experience of great affairs, not even Marshall exceeded him in judicial statesmanship. Other great judges have been guided by the wisdom distilled from an active life; Mr. Justice Holmes was led by the divination of the philosopher and the imagination of the poet.

Because he had an organic philosophy, he was not distracted by the infinite diversity of detail in the appearance of the same central issues. No one realized better than he that, while principles gain significance through application, concrete instances are inert except when galvanized into life by a general principle. And so it is perhaps more true of him than of any other judge in the history of the Court that the host of public controversies in which he participated was subdued to reason by relatively few guiding considerations. This was true whether he was called upon to strike a balance between the claims of property and its obligations, or between the rights of individuals and their duties, or between the limits of state action and the authority of the federal government.

What is the rôle of a judge in making these adjustments between society and the individual, between the states and the nation? The conception which a judge has of his own function, and the fastidiousness with which he follows it, will in large measure determine the most delicate controversies before him. Justices of the Court are not architects of policy. They can nullify the policy of others; they are incapable of fashioning their own solutions for social problems. The use which a judge makes of this power of negation is largely determined by two psychological considerations. It depends first on the judge's philosophy, conscious or implicit, regarding the nature of society; that is, on his theory of the clash of interests. This, in turn, will influence his conception of the place of the judge in the American constitutional system.

Mr. Justice Holmes's view of the play of forces in society hardly differed from that of Madison in his classic statement in the *Federalist:*

Those who hold and those who are without property, have ever formed distinct interests in society. Those who are creditors, and those who are debtors, fall under a like discrimination. A landed interest, a moneyed interest, with many lesser interests, grow up of necessity in civilized nations and divide them into different classes, actuated by different sentiments and views. The regulation of these various and interfering interests forms the principal task of modern legislation, and involves the spirit of party and faction in the necessary and ordinary operations of the government.

Thirty years before he went on the Supreme Court, Mr. Justice Holmes expressed this view in his own way:

This tacit assumption of the solidarity of the interests of society is very common, but seems to us to be false. . . . In the last resort a man rightly prefers his own interest to that of his neighbors. And this is as true in legislation as in any other form of corporate action. All that can be expected from modern improvements is that legislation should easily and quickly, yet not too quickly, modify itself according to the will of the *de facto* supreme power in the community, and that the spread of an educated sympathy should reduce the sacrifice of minorities to a minimum. . . . The objection to class legislation is not that it favors a class, but either that it fails to benefit the legislators, or that it is dangerous to them because a competing class has gained in power, or that it transcends the limits of self-preference which are imposed by sympathy. . . . But it is no sufficient condemnation of legislation that it favors one class at the expense of another; for much or all legislation does that; and none less when the bona fide object is the greatest good of the greatest number. . . . If the welfare of all future ages is to be considered, legislation may as well be abandoned for the present. . . .

The fact is that legislation in this country, as well as elsewhere, is empirical. It is necessarily made a means by which a body, having the power, puts burdens which are disagreeable to them on the shoulders of somebody else.

Mr. Justice Holmes never forgot that the activities of government are continual attempts by peaceful means to adjust these clashes of interest, and he was equally mindful of the fact that the body to whom this task of adjustment is primarily delegated is the legislature. . . . He scrupulously treated the Constitution as a broad charter of powers for the internal clashes of society, and did not construe it as though it were a code which prescribed in detail answers for the social problems of all time.

Thus the enduring contribution of Mr. Justice Holmes to American history is his constitutional philosophy. He gave it momentum by the magic with which he expressed it. Great judges are apt to be identified with what lawyers call great cases. Mr. Justice Holmes's specialty was great utterance. "Great cases," he himself has said, "are called great, not by reason of their real importance in shaping the law of the future, but because of some accident of immediate, overwhelming interest which appeals to the feelings and distorts the judgment." He saw the vital in the undramatic; to him, inconspicuous controversies revealed the clash of great social forces. And so the significance of his genius would evaporate in any analysis of his specific decisions. In his case, form and substance were beautifully fused. His conception of the Constitution must become part of the political habits of the country if our constitutional system is to endure; and if we care for our literary treasures the expression of his views must become part of our national culture.

IV

The Constitution is, of course, a legal document, but a legal document of a fundamentally different order from an insurance policy or a lease of timberland. For the Justice, the Constitution was not primarily a text for dialectic, but a means of ordering the life of a progressive people. While its roots were in the past, it was projected for the unknown future.

. . . The provisions of the Constitution are not mathematical formulas having their essence in their form; they are organic living institutions transplanted from English soil. Their significance is vital, not formal; it is to be gathered not simply by taking the words and a dictionary, but by considering their origin and the line of their growth.

. . . When we are dealing with words that also are a constituent act, like the Constitution of the United States, we must realize that they have called into life a being the development of which could not have been foreseen completely by the most gifted of its begetters. It was enough for them to realize or to hope that they had created an organism; it has taken a century and has cost their successors much sweat and blood to prove that they created a nation. The case before us must be considered in the light of our whole experience and not merely in that of what was said a hundred years ago.

While the Supreme Court is thus in the exacting realm of government, it is itself freed from the terrible burdens of governing. The Court is the brake on other men's actions, the judge of other men's decisions. Responsibility for action rests with legislators. The range of the Court's authority is thus very limited, but its exercise may vitally affect the nation. No wonder John Marshall spoke of this power of the Court as "delicate."

No one man who ever sat on the Court has been more keenly or more consistently sensitive than Mr. Justice Holmes to the dangers and difficulties inherent in the power of judges to review legislation. For it is subtle business to decide, not whether legislation is wise, but whether legislators were reasonable in believing it to be wise. In view of the complexities of modern society and the restricted scope of any man's experience, tolerance and humility in passing judgment on the worth of the experience and beliefs of others become crucial faculties in the disposition of cases. The successful exercise of such judicial power calls for rare intellectual disinterestedness and penetration, lest limitations in personal experience and imagination operate as limitations of the Constitution. These insights Mr. Justice Holmes applied in hundreds of cases, and expressed in memorable language:

> It is a misfortune if a judge reads his conscious or unconscious sympathy with one side or the other prematurely into the law, and forgets that what seem to him to be first principles are believed by half his fellow men to be wrong. . . . When twenty years ago a vague terror went over the earth and the word "socialism" began to be heard, I thought and still think that fear was translated into doctrines that had no proper place in the Constitution or the common law.
>
> While the courts must exercise a judgment of their own, it by no means is true that every law is void which may seem to the judges who pass upon it excessive, unsuited to its ostensible end, or based upon conceptions of morality with which they disagree.
>
> Considerable latitude must be allowed for differences of view as well as for possible peculiar conditions which this court can know but imperfectly, if at all. Otherwise a constitution, instead of embodying only relatively fundamental rules of right, as generally understood by all English-speaking communities, would become the partisan of a particular set of ethical or economical opinions, which by no means are held *semper ubique et ab omnibus.*

While in the '80s and '90s our economy was in process of drastic transformation, members of the Supreme Court continued to reflect the economic order in which they grew up. Between the presidencies of Grant and the first Roosevelt, *laissez faire* was the dominant economic social philosophy, and it was imported into the Constitution. Ephemeral facts were translated into legal absolutes; abstract conceptions concerning "liberty of contract" were erected into constitutional dogmas. Malleable and undefined provisions of the Constitution were applied as barriers against piecemeal efforts of adjustment through legislation to a society permeated by the influence of technology, large-scale industry, progressive urbanization, and the general dependence of the individual on economic forces beyond his control. The due-process clauses were especially the destructive rocks on which this legislation foundered. Judge Learned Hand, one of the most eminent of our judges, has said that the requirement of due process is merely an embodiment of the English sporting idea of fair play. . . .

Yet, as late as 1905, the Supreme Court held it unconstitutional to limit the working hours of bakers to ten, and as recently as 1936 the Court adhered to its ruling that it was beyond the power both of the states and of the nation to assure minimum-wage rates for women workers obviously incapable of economic self-protection. Every variety of legislative manifestation to subject economic power to social responsibility encountered the judicial veto.

The doctrinal process by which the majority reached such results was thus explained by Mr. Justice Holmes in dissenting from his brethren in the minimum-wage case:

. . . The only objection that can be urged [against a minimum-wage law for women for the District of Columbia] is found within the vague contours of the Fifth Amendment, prohibiting the depriving any person of liberty or property without due process of law. To that I turn.

The earlier decisions upon the same words in the Fourteenth Amendment began within our memory and went no farther than an unpretentious assertion of the liberty to follow the ordinary callings. Later that innocuous generality was expanded into the dogma, Liberty of Contract. Contract is not specially mentioned in the text that we have to construe. It is merely an example of doing what you want to do, embodied in the word "liberty." But pretty much all law consists in forbidding men to do some things that they want to do, and contract is no more exempt from law than other acts.

For a short time after the bakeshop case the views of Mr. Justice Holmes were in the ascendant. Chief Justice White was heard to attribute to the influence exerted by President Theodore Roosevelt's messages and speeches no inconsiderable share in the shift of the Court's emphasis. The fact is that for less than a decade, between 1908 and the World War, the Court did allow legislation to prevail which, in various aspects, regulated enterprise with reference to its social consequences and withdrew phases of industrial relations from the area of illusory individual bargaining.

But those who had assumed a permanent change in the Court's outlook were soon disappointed. Changes in the Court's personnel and in the general economic and social climate of the Harding-Coolidge era soon reflected themselves in decisions. Until after the 1936 election, the Court was back to the high tide of judicial negation reached in the Lochner case in 1905. Mr. Justice Holmes's classic dissent in that case will never lose its relevance:

This case is decided upon an economic theory which a large part of the country does not entertain. If it were a question whether I agreed with that theory, I should desire to study it further and long before making up my mind. But I do not conceive that to be my duty, because I strongly believe that my agreement or disagreement has nothing to do with the right of a majority to embody their opinions in law. It is settled by various decisions of this court that state constitutions and state laws may regulate life in many ways which we as legislators might think as injudicious or, if you like, as tyrannical as this, and which equally with this interfere with the liberty of contract. Sunday laws and usury laws are ancient examples. A more modern one is the prohibition of lotteries. The liberty of the citizen to do as he likes so long as he does not interfere with the liberty of others to do the same, which has been a shibboleth for some well-known writers, is interfered with by school laws, by the Post Office, by every state or municipal institution which takes his money for purposes thought desirable, whether he likes it or not. The Fourteenth Amendment does not enact Mr. Herbert Spencer's Social

Statics. . . . Some of these laws embody convictions or prejudices which judges are likely to share. Some may not. But a constitution is not intended to embody a particular economic theory, whether of paternalism and the organic relation of the citizen to the state or of *laissez faire*. It is made for people of fundamentally differing views, and the accident of our finding certain opinions natural and familiar or novel and even shocking ought not to conclude our judgment upon the question whether statutes embodying them conflict with the Constitution of the United States.

This was the great theme of his judicial life—the amplitude of the Constitution as against the narrowness of some of its interpreters. And so, having analyzed with brave clarity the governing elements in the modern economic struggle, he did not shrink from giving his analysis judicial recognition. "One of the eternal conflicts out of which life is made up," he wrote, more than forty years ago, "is that between the effort of every man to get the most he can for his services, and that of society, disguised under the name of capital, to get his services for the least possible return. Combination on the one side is patent and powerful. Combination on the other is the necessary and desirable counterpart, if the battle is to be carried on in a fair and equal way." Mr. Justice Holmes therefore found nothing in the Constitution to prevent legislation which sought to remove some of the more obvious inequalities in the distribution of economic power.

Economists and historians are now largely agreed that the resistance to a natural and responsible trade-unionism has been one of the most disturbing factors in our economy. Had the views of Mr. Justice Holmes prevailed, the Constitution would not have been used as an obstruction to the healthy development of trade-unionism. More than thirty years ago he protested when a majority of the Court invalidated an act of Congress against the "yellow dog" contract which was drawn by Richard Olney, as Attorney General, and sponsored by President Cleveland. The need for legislation to remove disabilities against the effective right of association by workers became more manifest with time.

State after state, therefore, passed laws to assure trade-unions the opportunity which they already had in the rest of the English-speaking world. But a majority of the Court remained obdurate and imposed a doctrinaire view of the Constitution against such legislation. One can only surmise what would have been the gain to social peace and economic security had the dissenting views expressed more than twenty years ago by Mr. Justice Holmes been the Court's views. . . .

v

Mr. Justice Holmes denied that the Constitution stereotyped any particular distribution of economic power for all time. With the clean precision of a surgeon he uncovered the process by which, under the guise of deductive reasoning, partial claims were given the shelter of the Constitution as comprehensive interests of property:

> Delusive exactness is a source of fallacy throughout the law. By calling a business "property" you make it seem like land, and lead up to the conclusion that a statute cannot substantially cut down the advantages of ownership existing before the statute was passed. An established business no doubt may have pecuniary value and commonly is protected by law against various unjustified injuries. But you cannot give it definiteness of contour by calling it a thing. It is a course of conduct, and like other conduct is subject to substantial modification according to time and circumstances both in itself and in regard to what shall justify doing it a harm.

By a steady extension of doctrines which, to Mr. Justice Holmes, had no justification in the Constitution, a majority of the Court persistently denied exertions of the legislature toward reconciling individual enterprise and social welfare. Abstract conceptions regarding property and "liberty of contract" were the swords with which these measures were struck down. Mr. Justice Holmes was finally roused to an unusual judicial protest. His dissent from the decision of the majority in declaring unconstitutional a New York statute regulating theatre-ticket scalping fully reveals his mind. It also gives a glimpse of the importance he attached to art throughout life:

We fear to grant power and are unwilling to recognize it when it exists . . . when legislatures are held to be authorized to do anything considerably affecting public welfare it is covered by apologetic phrases like the police power, or the statement that the business concerned has been dedicated to a public use. The former expression is convenient, to be sure, to conciliate the mind to something that needs explanation: the fact that the constitutional requirement of compensation when property is taken cannot be pressed to its grammatical extreme; that property rights may be taken for public purposes without pay if you do not take too much; that some play must be allowed to the joints if the machine is to work. But police power often is used in a wide sense to cover, as I said, to apologize for the general power of the legislature to make a part of the community uncomfortable by a change.

I do not believe in such apologies. I think the proper course is to recognize that a state legislature can do whatever it sees fit to do unless it is restrained by some express prohibition in the Constitution of the United States or of the state, and that courts should be careful not to extend such prohibitions beyond their obvious meaning by reading into them conceptions of public policy that the particular court may happen to entertain. Coming down to the case before us, I think . . . that the notion that a business is clothed with a public interest and has been devoted to a public use is little more than a fiction intended to beautify what is disagreeable to the sufferers. The truth seems to me to be that, subject to compensation when compensation is due, the legislature may forbid or restrict any business when it has a sufficient force of public opinion behind it. Lotteries were thought useful adjuncts of the state a century or so ago; now they are believed to be immoral, and they have been stopped. Wine has been thought good for man from the time of the Apostle until recent years. But when public opinion changed it did not need the Eighteenth Amendment, notwithstanding the Fourteenth, to enable a state to say that the business should end. . . . What has happened to lotteries and wine might happen to theatres in some moral storm of the future, not because theatres were devoted to a public use, but because people had come to think that way.

But if we are to yield to fashionable conventions, it seems to me that theatres are as much devoted to public use as anything well can be. We have not that respect for art that is one of the glories of France. But to many people the superfluous is the necessary, and it seems to me that government does not go beyond its sphere in attempting to make life livable for them. I am far from saying that I think that this particular law is a wise and rational provision. That is not my affair. But if the people of the state of New York, speaking by their authorized voice, say that they want it, I see nothing in the Constitution of the United States to prevent their having their will.

Taxation is perhaps the severest testing ground for the objectivity and wisdom of a social thinker. The enormous increase in the cost of society and the extent to which wealth is now represented by intangibles, the profound change in the relation of the individual to government and the resulting widespread insistence on security, are subjecting public finance to the most exacting demands. To balance budgets, to pay for the costs of progressively civilized social standards, to safeguard the future, and to divide these burdens fairly among different interests in the community, put the utmost strain on the ingenuity of statesmen. They must constantly explore new sources of revenue and find means of preventing the circumvention of their discoveries. Subject as they are, in English-speaking countries, to popular control, they should not be denied adequate latitude of power for their extraordinarily difficult tasks.

Mr. Justice Holmes never yielded to finicky limitations or doctrinaire formulas, drawn from the general language of the Constitution, as a means of circumscribing the discretion of legislatures in the necessarily empirical process of tapping new revenue or stopping new devices for evasion. He did not have a curmudgeon's feelings about his own taxes. A secretary who exclaimed, "Don't you hate to pay taxes!" was rebuked with the hot response, "No, young feller. I like to pay taxes. With them I buy civilization." And as a judge he consistently refused to accentuate fiscal difficulties of government by injecting into the Constitution his own notions of fiscal policy. Nor did he believe that there was anything in the Constitution to bar even a conscious use of the taxing power for readjusting the social equilibrium. . . .

I have indicated the general direction of Mr. Justice Holmes's judicial mind on the great issues of the constitutional position of property in our society. During most of his thirty years on the Supreme Bench, and especially during the second half of his tenure, his were not the views of a majority of the Court. But the good that men do lives after them. In the spring of 1937 the old views of Mr. Justice Holmes began to be the new constitutional direction of the Court.

His own constitutional outlook was, throughout a long life, free from fluctuations. This was so because it was born of a deeply rooted and coherent philosophy concerning the dynamic character of the American Constitution and of a judge's function in construing it. If he threw the weight of his authority on the side of social readjustments through legislation it was not because of any faith in panaceas in general or in measures of social amelioration in particular. He personally "disbelieved all the popular conceptions of socialism" and came dangerously close to believing in the simplicities of the wage-fund theory. But his skepticism and even hostility, as a matter of private judgment, toward legislation which he was ready to sustain as a judge only serve to add cubits to his judicial stature, for he thereby transcended personal predilections and private notions of social policy and became truly the impersonal voice of the Constitution.

The Early Writings of O. W. Holmes, Jr.

This selection appeared in the Harvard Law Review *for March, 1931 (Vol. 44, p. 717), as one of the essays celebrating the nine-tieth anniversary of Mr. Justice Holmes's birth.*

OUR TIMES may well come to be named, by future dealers in half-truths, the Tired Age. Disillusionment is a mood of fashion as much as a form of ennui after the war's great effort. Whatever the cause, our politics are devoid of ardor, and social reform has lost its romance. Such being the mental climate, one would expect jurisprudence to be in the doldrums and to earn its title as the dreary science. Alas for these generalizations about the main currents of thought! The waters of law are unwontedly alive. New winds are blowing on old doctrines, the critical spirit infiltrates traditional formulas, philosophic inquiry is pursued without apology as it becomes clearer that decisions are functions of some juristic philosophy.

New situations, the offspring of technology and changing social conceptions, make new demands upon law. The absorption of new facts and the reconcilement of new conflicts entail a re-examination of the *fundamenta* of the legal order. What are the sources of law, and what its sanctions? What do judges do when they "decide"? What are the wise bounds of *stare decisis* and when is the judicial process free from its own past? What is appropriate to the fluid empiricism of case-law, and when is codification desirable? What is the proper area of law-making by courts and what should be left to legislation? These are issues of moment to society. Happily, they are the dominant concern of contemporary legal scholarship on the bench, at the bar, in law schools. And these problems are now seen, not in isolation, but as aspects of the function of reason and the art of thinking. Science and philosophy illumine the interplay of form and substance in legal history, and the logic of law draws sustenance from the laws of logic.

In grappling with these issues, the youngest and most daring thinkers salute as leader him who was born when William Henry Harrison was President. It is a favorite *aperçu* of Mr. Justice Holmes's that the ideas of an earlier generation are absorbed but its writings die. The Justice, however, escapes his own verdict. *The Common Law* and half a dozen essays have given the most powerful direction to modern legal science. But they are classic not merely in their influence. They belong to our day.

The Common Law is already fifty years old. Its philosophic underpinning is even older. Ten years before he gave the famous Lowell Lectures, O. W. Holmes, Jr., became editor of the *American Law Review*. Beginning with Volume V (October, 1870) and through Volume VII (July, 1873), the *American Law Review* printed six essays and at least sixty reviews and comments which, though unsigned, bear the unmistakable *imprimatur* of its editor's thought and style. These earliest of his legal writings canvass all the juristic issues with which the air is now rife. To be sure, the current jargon had not been invented, and so his muscular and luminous English is not outmoded. In his analysis of judicial psychology, Holmes was conscious of the rôle of the unconscious a generation before Freud began to reorient modern psychology. Though another half-century was to elapse before the appearance of Ogden and Richards's *The Meaning of Meaning*, exploration of the meaning of the meaning of law was Holmes's pioneer enterprise.

Later, after he ceased to be editor, he published over his own signature five more essays in the *American Law Review:* "Primitive Notions in Modern Law" (Pts. I and II), "Possession," "Common Carriers and the Common Law," "Trespass and Negligence." All these papers were drawn upon for his *Common Law,* but simply as raw material for the finished product. "I have made," he tells us in its Preface, "such use as I thought fit of my articles in the [*American*] *Law Review,* but much of what has been taken from that source has been rearranged, rewritten, and enlarged, and the greater part of the work is new." Only one as rich as he could so lavishly discard what he had previously written. Thus, in his "Common Carriers and the Common Law," he reveals the imaginative gift which in a great scientist reconstructs an extinct species from a single vertebra. In Holmes, it takes the form of drawing a profound lesson for the whole story of law from the particular instance of the development of the carriers' liability. His analysis deserves wider currency than the seared pages of the *American Law Review* now give it. For it epitomizes much of what is most significant in recent jurisprudence:

The little piece of history above very well illustrates the paradox of form and substance in the development of law. In form its growth is logical. The official theory is that each new decision follows syllogistically from existing precedents. But as precedents survive like the clavicle in the cat, long after the use they once served is at an end and the reason for them has been forgotten, the result of following them must often be failure and confusion from the merely logical point of view. It is easy for the scholar to show that reasons have been misapprehended and precedents misapplied.

On the other hand, in substance the growth of the law is legislative. And this in a deeper sense than that which the courts declare to have always been the law is in fact new. It is legislative in its grounds. The very considerations which the courts most rarely mention, and always with an apology, are the secret root from which the law draws all the juices of life. We mean, of course, considerations of what is expedient for the community concerned. Every important principle which is developed by litigation is in fact and at bottom the result of more or less definitely understood views of public policy; most generally, to be sure, under our practice and traditions, the unconscious result of instinctive preferences and inarticulate convictions, but none the less traceable to public policy in the last analysis. And as the law is administered by able and experienced men, who know too much to sacrifice good sense to a syllogism, it will be found that when ancient rules maintain themselves in this way, new reasons more fitted to the time have been found for them, and that they gradually receive a new content and at last a new form from the grounds to which they have been transplanted. The importance of tracing the process lies in the fact that it is unconscious, and involves the attempt to follow precedents, as well as to give a good reason for them, and that hence, if it can be shown that one half of the effort has failed, we are at liberty to consider the question of policy with a freedom that was not possible before.

What has been said will explain the failure of all theories which consider the law only from its formal side, whether they attempt to deduce the *corpus* from *a priori* postulates or fall into the humbler error of supposing the science of the law to reside in the *elegantia juris,* or logical cohesion of part with part. The truth is, that law hitherto has been, and it would seem by the necessity of its being is always, approaching and never reaching consistency. It is forever adopting new principles from life at one end, and it always retains old ones from history at the other which have not yet been absorbed or sloughed off. It will become entirely consistent only when it ceases to grow.[1]

Of the unsigned essays, four dealt explicitly with major problems of jurisprudence: "Codes, and the Arrangement of the Law" (two papers), "The Theory of Torts," "Misunderstandings of the Civil Law," and two are penetrating inquiries into what were then new perplexities of the substantive law: "How Far Are Corporations Liable for Acts Not Authorized by Their Charters," and "On the Title to Grain in Public Warehouses." In his reviews and comments, Holmes ranged the gamut of the legal literature of his day; he made his own the entire kingdom of law. Reports, digests, casebooks, fresh editions of old texts, new treatises, inaugural lectures, essays—all were judged by his learning and in turn enriched it.

These early pieces should be collected into a volume—even those that are no longer as intrinsically relevant as they were when written. For all of us, truth is born when we discover it. But intellectual genealogy is important. The history of ideas is essential to culture; thereby we are saved from being intellectually *nouveaux riches.* For the present, however, it must suffice

---

1 "Common Carriers and the Common Law" (1879), 13 *Am. L. Rev.* 608, 630-31; *cf. The Common Law* (1881), 35-36.

to make more available only a portion of Holmes's anonymous writings. The four essays now reprinted pose juristic issues still, or, more accurately, again in controversy. The shorter commentaries furnish samples of his reviewing, whetted, appropriately enough, on the writings of Dicey, Pollock, and Fitzjames Stephen. They give, as well, compact formulations of Holmes's theory of legislation—beside which most talk about legislation sounds hollow and partisan—and foreshadow an outlook which, thirty years later, he was to apply on the Supreme Bench by his forbearance in exercising the power of judicial review.

The masters of art and science are their own best commentators. I shall attempt no gloss upon these Holmesiana. But they insistently raise one question: How is one to account for them? In the basic problems which preoccupied them, in the way they conceived law and its judicial unfolding, they are so out of the legal current of their time. "The study of English law," Mr. Justice Holmes told us, in welcoming Holdsworth's *History*, "has been slow to feel the impulse of science." And later, when he gave his blessing to the Continental Legal Historical Series, he indicated the legal environment in which, strangely enough, his own work flowered:

> I can but envy the felicity of the generation to whom it is made so easy to see their subject as a whole. When I began, the law presented itself as a ragbag of details. The best approach that I found to general views on the historical side was the first volume of Spence's *Equitable Jurisdiction*, and, on the practical, Walker's *American Law*. The only philosophy within reach was Austin's *Jurisprudence*. It was not without anguish that one asked oneself whether the subject was worthy of the interest of an intelligent man. One saw people whom one respected and admired leaving the study because they thought it narrowed the mind; for which they had the authority of Burke. It required blind faith— faith that could not yet find the formula of justification for itself.

Happily, he was thrown back upon the deep impulses of his own nature. He was born invincibly to ask the meaning of things and to cut beneath the skin of formulas, however respectable. His mind had commerce, not with ragbag-minded lawyers, but with impractical philosophers like William James and Charles S. Peirce; his pastime was not courtroom gossip, but "twisting the tail of the cosmos." Native predilection was reinforced by the experience of the Civil War. "Polite conversation" did not satisfy Captain Holmes; he was driven to deeper questioning.

There were other personal attributes not at all peculiar to unique creative powers. Holmes mastered the materials of his profession, such as they were. "I should think Wendell worked too hard," wrote William James in 1869. He has never made a fetish of long hours, but he worked—and works—with intensity. He soaked himself in the details of the law, and his imagination saw organic connection between discrete instances. The magistral summaries of his later opinions were the concentrations of his vast and accurate reading in the apprentice years. Not the least characteristic note in his book reviews is Holmes's insistence on accuracy —accuracy to the utmost nicety.

But the Zeitgeist moved also through O. W. Holmes, Jr. He came to maturity when Darwin had upset men's most ancient beliefs. The evolutionary doctrines worked as ferment beyond their immediate scope. If Genesis had to be "reinterpreted," the texts of the law could hardly claim sanctity. To their contemporaries, great men inevitably appear as sports, for they mark revolutions in ideas. We now see the kinship of Whitman and Melville and Holmes. All three express man's passionate effort in the face of the illimitable mystery of the universe—Whitman and Melville as artists, Holmes as thinker.

Forty years ago, an enviable group of young men were vouchsafed glimpses into the inner life of the thinker—his tortures and triumph: "I say to you in all sadness of conviction, that to think great thoughts you must be heroes as well as idealists. Only when you have worked alone—when you have felt around you a black gulf of solitude more isolating than that which surrounds the dying man, and in hope and in despair have trusted to your own unshaken will—then only will you have achieved. Thus only can you gain the secret isolated joy of the thinker, who knows that, a hundred years after he is dead and forgotten, men who never heard of him will be moving to the measure of his thought. . . ." [2] To Mr. Justice Holmes, who thus spoke to youth for all time, has been granted the crowning gift of witnessing himself, the sway of his mind over men's thought and action. And this response has come as the victories of the mind always come— by its inner force and worth. For Mr. Justice Holmes has lived his chosen life unflinchingly and without worldly compromise— the life of the thinker under fire, applying the philosopher's temper to the passions of men and the conflicts of society.

His insights have become part of the common stock of our culture. Wherever law is known, he is known. Whatever name classifiers may give to the variants of the legal order in different parts of the world, the contribution of Mr. Justice Holmes is universally acknowledged—in China and Japan, in South Africa and Australia, by the civilians on the Continent, in the home of the Common Law. He, above all others, has given the directions of contemporary jurisprudence. He wields such a powerful influence upon today because his deep knowledge of yesterday enables him to extricate the present from meaningless entanglements with the past and yet to see events in the perspective of history.

Since his mind is scrupulously skeptical, he has escaped sterile dogma and romantic impressionism. Only the methods of reason, unsubordinated by ephemeral episodes, can unite coherence with vitality. To this life of reason he has passionately adhered in responding to the most exacting demand that is made upon judges— to compose clashing interests of an empire by appeal to law. The philosopher's stone which Mr. Justice Holmes has constantly employed for arbitrament is the conviction that our constitutional system rests upon tolerance and that its greatest enemy is the Absolute.

In a thousand instances, he has been loyal to his philosophy. Thereby he has resolved into comprehending larger truths the conflicting claims of state and nation, of liberty and authority, of

---

[2] *Collected Legal Papers* (1920), 32.

individual and society. The composer of strife, Mr. Justice Holmes has wrought with serene detachment. His deepest allegiance is to civilization—a civilization neither parochial nor utopian, but groping for realization on the stage of the new world as part of the whole world.

Mr. Justice Cardozo and Public Law

Mr. Frankfurter's interest in Mr. Justice Cardozo was also the accompaniment of a long friendship. The following selection appeared in January, 1939, as one of the Essays Dedicated to the Memory of Mr. Justice Cardozo, published jointly by the Harvard Law Review, *the* Columbia Law Review, *and the* Yale Law Journal. *It was the last piece Mr. Frankfurter wrote before he was nominated for membership on the Supreme Court in January, 1939.*

THE FAIRIES that presided over Benjamin N. Cardozo's birth were not wholly benign. But they endowed him with one gift of grace far more significant than his rare talents of mind. He was given a contagious goodness which brought to life the goodness in others. In no invidious sense was the New York Court of Appeals, especially during his presidency, Cardozo's court. And the compulsions of Cardozo's spirit upon those with whom he labored were revealed even through the austerity which insulates the Supreme Court from public knowledge of its intimate life. It is not surprising that the persuasiveness of his personality subdued his immediate environment by its sheer unconscious radiations. It is astonishing that so cloistered a spirit should have attained such a hold on popular feeling.

Other judges have had much more influence upon the governing forces of American society than fell to Cardozo's lot. Perhaps a few, but at best a very few, judges had as keen an insight into the peculiar rôle of the judge in the American scheme. Finally, there was one judge of greater originality and deeper penetration into the intellectual presuppositions of the judicial process. For it was not merely the language of playful deference which made

Cardozo always speak of Holmes as "the Master." But the history of the Supreme Court affords no analogue to the unanimity of lay as well as professional opinion that Chief Judge Cardozo was the one man adequate to fill the historic place vacated by Holmes; nor is there a parallel to the deep feeling of the country as a whole that the death of Cardozo was not merely the premature termination of a distinguished judicial career, but the end of the living energy of one of the most powerful moral resources of the nation.

Ordinarily observations like these are properly uncongenial to pages concerned with the discussion of juristic problems. But in the case of Cardozo the main path to his views on public law leads from his character. His conception of the Constitution cannot be severed from his conception of a judge's function in applying it. His views of the judge's function derive from his convictions on philosophic issues which implicate the workings of the judicial mind. Such issues in turn involve a man's notions of his relation to the universe. These are abstractions. They seem far removed, let us say, from No. 180 of the October Term, 1936. But the clarity with which a specific controversy is seen in the context of the larger intellectual issues beneath the formal surface of litigation, and the courage with which such analysis infuses decision and opinion, are the ultimate determinants of American public law.

I

That the task of constitutional construction is a function, not of mechanics, but of imponderables is now known even by Macaulay's omniscient schoolboy. There is, however, no authorized catalogue of the imponderables; still less is there an accepted organon for striking the balance among competing and conflicting values. Partly because of the wise common law tradition of *ad hoc* adjudication, partly because of the distinctive temperament and experience of judges, an avowed juristic philosophy of which individual decisions are particular expressions seldom emerges from the opinions of a judge. The formulation of such a philosophy before a judge ascends the Supreme Bench is a still rarer phenomenon. Barring only Holmes, no man had so completely revealed the map of his mind before he went on the Court as had Cardozo. If surprise there was in anything that he wrote as a Justice, it was not for want of disclosure by him as to the way he looked at questions that would come before him.

Ultimately, a particular decision in a realm not obviously foreclosed by authority—the decisive field for the play of a judge's creative powers—is the exercise of a high art, what in the happier phraseology of the seventeenth century was called a "mystery." But it is a most subtle and complicated art, at its best the end of a long ratiocinative process. Scientific discoveries, we are told, come to the prepared mind. So the art of adjudication is most imaginatively exercised by those judges who know that the ultimate determination of values is not within the power of formula or measurement. Therefore they explore to the uttermost the rational foundations of what they affirm and what they reject, in order to avoid confusion between their private universe and the universe. All of Cardozo's writings, but more particularly *The Nature of the Judicial Process* and *The Paradoxes of Legal Science* are suffused with intimations of what later came from his pen as a Justice, as well as glosses upon what is so shyly expressed in opinions. . . .

Whereas Holmes all his life was much more occupied with his first love, philosophy, than was Cardozo, he never formulated his philosophy as systematically as did Cardozo except in a short essay or two. Indeed, while Holmes was a conscientious student of all the great systems of philosophy and reread such disparate thinkers as Spinoza and John Dewey again and again, he distrusted system, and inclined to the view that systems are apt to be merely the elegant elaborations of a few profound insights. On the other hand, Holmes often made his opinions the vehicles of his philosophic beliefs. He summarized his own views as to ultimates in the amber of his apothegms. While he was alert to the dangers of what the shrewd Lincoln called "pernicious abstractions," particularly in the business of judging, the flair of his mind was for abstractions.

Thus it is that from his opinions may be culled sentences which convey his vision of the Constitution in its relation to the organic process of human society and his conception of the judge as a custodian of that vision.

With Cardozo it was otherwise. Perhaps because he had spelled out his philosophic beliefs and directions in his trilogy, his opinions stuck close to the circumstance of the particular record and indulged sparingly in detachable epigrammatic utterance. But the specific inevitably implicates the general, and in a few instances Cardozo expressed the underlying principles that guided his constitutional function in language and accent not confined to the immediacies of the case.

Indeed the only scope for originality in elucidating the process of constitutional adjudication is the power of putting old truths with freshness. In the abstract, the appropriate ways of looking at the Constitution, when brought within the focus of the judiciary, have been stated in essentially similar terms since Marshall first intoned them in the solemn rhetoric of his day. The sanctions of statesmanship which vindicate this viewpoint were stated with the finality of exquisite scholarship by James Bradley Thayer nearly fifty years ago. Nor have the intermittent deviations in the applications of Marshall's canons and Thayer's philosophy ever explicitly challenged either canons or philosophy. That the Constitution contains within itself the formulated past, but was also designed for the unfolding future; that it is a source of governmental energy no less than of governmental restriction; that in the most difficult areas of adjudication the issues which come before the Court do not primarily present questions as to the meaning of words, but invite judgment upon ultimate issues of society which in the now classic language of Mr. Justice Holmes "must be considered in the light of our whole experience and not merely in that of what was said a hundred years ago"—these are generalities to which fealty is never denied.

But the recognition of their relevance to a specific controversy and the fidelity with which they are applied are the turning points of decisions. Difference among judges is not in knowledge of constitutional precepts but in the persistence and insight with which they respect them. Normally, the raw materials of public law controversies are contemporary affairs, and understanding of their significance is seldom achieved on the bench without considerable prior immersion in affairs. Cardozo is a striking exception. The market place was not his milieu. Sociological problems were not the preoccupation of his leisure moments, his spontaneous writings, or his talk. Like Holmes, he was sensitive to social tensions and the conflicts of interest not by the bent of his mind, but because the scholar in him made him realize that to be a good judge he had to become conversant with the processes of government and industry.

·   ·   ·   ·   ·   ·   ·

II

The main stuff of contemporary Supreme Court litigation is fairly indicated by the fact that both the first and the last opinions written by Mr. Justice Cardozo arose out of the interaction of government and business. Nor does it urge significance unduly to note that in his first opinion Cardozo spoke only for himself, Mr. Justice Brandeis and Mr. Justice Stone, while his last opinion, announced in his absence by the Chief Justice, was on behalf of a majority of the Court. The economic and social context of Cardozo's period of service, the spate of legislation which came from Congress and the states, and the resistance to which it gave rise, are too familiar to call even for summary.

. . . Supreme Court decisions have on occasion furnished materials for popular discussion. But never in our history was interest in the Court so continuous nor were its opinions so extensively canvassed in the lay press as during the incumbency of Cardozo. To a very considerable degree, therefore, his opinions have become common property. This is not the place for their detailed review. A conspectus of his attitude toward the subjection of economic legislation to judicial review must suffice.

The radiations of taxation have steadily extended the intrusion of government into economic affairs. The tasks of statesmanship in tapping new sources of revenue without killing the goose that lays the golden eggs have correspondingly multiplied. The enormous diversity in types of business activity, the nice calculations involved in making classifications at once fair and effective, the repercussions of different taxes upon diverse enterprises are among the most exigent but elusive riddles for those charged with governing. Clichés like "scientific taxation" cover up a thousand perplexities not susceptible of solution by procedures and criteria familiar to the natural sciences. It is in this perspective of pervasive fiscal needs and the intractable problems they present to legislators that tax measures must be seen when brought under the scrutiny of such large phrases as "due process" and "the equal protection of the laws." . . .

Taxation primarily for revenue can hardly exclude social consequences. The complexities of tax legislation are intensified whenever social policy is its predominant aim. From the day of Hamilton's Report on Manufactures, American statesmen have employed taxation for purposes other than revenues. Beginning with Theodore Roosevelt's administration, taxation has assumed a mounting share in the process of social adjustment. "A motive to build up through legislation the quality of men," Cardozo was allowed to say for a narrow majority of the Court, "may be as creditable in the thought of some as a motive to magnify the quantity of trade. Courts do not choose between such values in adjudging legislative powers. They put the choice aside as beyond their lawful competence. . . . The tax now assailed may have its roots in an erroneous conception of the ills of the body politic or of the efficacy of such a measure to bring about a cure. We have no thought in anything we have written to declare it expedient or even just, or for that matter to declare the contrary. We deal with power only." [1]

Thus, various forms of exaction have been devised as one response to the problems presented by economic concentration. Whether to differentiate between big and smaller business, and how to do so— these are questions which divide expert as well as lay opinion. It

[1] *Fox* v. *Standard Oil Co.*, 294 U.S. 87, 100-01 (1935).

is not disrespectful for a lawyer to suggest that this is a realm
of public finance in which the fog of doubt and confusion has not
yet been wholly lifted by economists. That nevertheless this is a
field into which the state may enter no one will deny. And yet
there is no legal litmus to give ready answers when state action
is challenged. Again the ultimate canons for constitutional construction must do service. The Constitution does not have preferences between competing theories, and the wide range of discretion which this leaves to the legislative judgment must not be cur-
tailed by judicial intrusion, under the guise of abstract absolutes,
into the domain of policy. By Cardozo these generalities were
translated into living practice. For he viewed measures of social
taxation with a shrewd eye for actuality undiverted by hypothe-
sized unrealities. . . .

A healthy society is as much dependent upon wise price policies
as upon sound systems of taxation. But the puzzles of a proper
price mechanism are perhaps even less amenable to unequivocal
solutions than are ways for achieving appropriate fiscal measures.
The operation of pricing schemes in the market is very different
from what it appears to be in economic treatises. Not the least of
these perplexities is the influence of governmental intervention in
pricing. It is more than sixty years since the Supreme Court gave
sanction to price regulation within the limited field of "public callings." Yet even within this circumscribed field confusion and friction, with resulting waste, have been more prominent than agreement on procedure and criteria for fixing values and rates. But in
this area of government no less than in that of taxation, legislation
cannot wait for accord among economists or general acceptance of
their theories. Powerful economic forces produce problems which
must be dealt with by legislators with whatever fallible and tentative wisdom they can utilize. The competing claims of consumers
and producers, of large producers and small, of large consumers
and small, of producers and distributors, of distributors and consumers, press for adjustment. Fallible wisdom produces fallible

legislation. To deny government the right to act except with omniscience and prescience is to deny it the right to act at all.

The right to act is evolving empirically and waveringly. In dealing with these new exertions of governmental power, as where he concerned himself with novel methods of taxation, Cardozo found his bearings in loyal adherence to the classic doctrines for constitutional adjudication. He sharply differentiated the austere responsibility of a judge from the ample discretion of the legislator. He found no barriers to legislative recognition of differences among different industries or among different groups within the same industry; he found no warrant for any doctrine that afforded greater immunity to the price mechanisms of industry than to its other aspects.

· · · · · · ·

III

The ample scope which Cardozo thus gave to legislative discretion in devising policy did not make him indifferent to those procedural safeguards in the exercise of governmental powers which give historic basis to "due process." Prices may be fixed and profits limited, certainly for the "public callings," but not without fair inquiry and an adequate canvass of the factors relevant to adjustment between private and public interests. . . .

The accomplishments of half a century have won for the Interstate Commerce Commission a place in the Supreme Court's esteem not second to that accorded the lower federal courts. Mr. Justice Cardozo gave voice to that esteem. . . .

But the very complexity of the technical tasks entrusted to such a commission led to the requirement that it formulate the basis of its determinations. This is the justification for findings, that they serve to illumine and thereby to safeguard the Commission's own procedures. It was not in the spirit of Baron Parke that Cardozo spoke for the Court in vindicating the rationale of findings. . . .

But insistence on procedural regularity was not, for Cardozo, an expression of inhospitality to the process behind the development of administrative law. Nor did he see administrative law as a collection of explicit rules uniformly applicable throughout the domain of what the British call "delegated legislation." Cardozo recognized that the broad concepts of hearing, findings, and judicial review summarized a variety of diversified situations in which the large aims expressed by these concepts were variously achieved. . . .

Cardozo had, if not Maitland's genius, the latter's perception of the social forces that mold law. He had, to be sure, an enormous fund of technical learning. But he escaped that dangerous narrowness of the mere legal pedant which has been the subject of classic animadversions by Burke and Bagehot. He did so by seeing law as part of our whole cultural history. Cardozo was not imprisoned by the tags and rags of learning, for he was guided by understanding of the circumstances summarized in historic clichés and by philosophic insight into their significance. Thus he never forgot that forms are related to function; that court procedures not expressive of ultimate liberties are not necessarily norms of universal applicability; that practices of administration may have a momentum of rationality; and that activities of government which are not the immediate province of courts ought not to be circumscribed by formalities historically appropriate to courts. He used his learning in technical law, not as the standard for judgment of allowable development in new branches of the law, but as a fertile source for proving that old principles have creative energies for new situations.

Thus viewing administrative law, Cardozo eschewed unreal abstractions and stuck close to the practicalities of government as revealed by history, by legislative ends and administrative responsibilities. . . .

IV

In the domain of economic affairs, the penumbral region where law and policy blend, Cardozo walked humbly. But when those ethical precepts which are embodied in the Bill of Rights were invoked, he responded with all the certitude of one whose most constant companion was reason and whose life was rooted in the moral law. Unfortunately, the brevity of his tenure and the contingencies upon which the assignment of opinions depends gave him only limited opportunity in Washington to express with new vitality the claims of civilization expressed by constitutional protection to civil liberties. Doubtless his presence on the Court, particularly in these matters, made itself felt otherwise than through his own opinions. For, while the conferences in Washington could hardly have had for Cardozo the intimate camaraderie which so gladdened his days at Albany, the contagion of his ethical qualities must have affected the currents of his newer associations. To trace such influences upon the actions and opinions of others is, however, too elusive a pursuit for one outside the inner mysteries of the Court.

We do not therefore have in his Supreme Court opinions such full-bodied expression of his philosophy of spiritual freedom as that which opportunities enabled Holmes to add to our permanent literature.[2] Happily, however, he wrote on the great theme of

[2] Friendly critics have suggested that Cardozo viewed encroachments upon civil liberties with less deference to the legislative judgment than that which he accorded to economic measures. The same seeming inconsistency has been suggested against Holmes, and the answer made in Holmes's case applies to Cardozo as well:

"The Justice deferred so abundantly to legislative judgment on economic policy because he was profoundly aware of the extent to which social arrangements are conditioned by time and circumstances, and of how fragile, in scientific proof, is the ultimate validity of a particular economic adjustment. He knew that there was no authoritative fund of social wisdom to be drawn upon for answers to the perplexities which vast new material resources had brought. And so he was hesitant to oppose his own opinion to the economic views of the legislature. But history had also taught him that, since social development is a process of trial and error, the fullest possible opportunity for the free play of the human mind was an indispensable prerequisite. Since the history of civilization is in considerable measure the displacement of error which once held sway as official truth by beliefs which in turn have yielded to other truths, the liberty of man to search for truth was of a different order than some economic dogma defined as a sacred right because the temporal nature of its origin had been forgotten. And without freedom of expression, liberty of thought is a mockery. Nor can truth be pursued in an atmosphere hostile to the endeavor or under dangers which only heroes hazard.

"Naturally, therefore, Mr. Justice Holmes attributed very different legal sig-

the freedom of the human mind in perduring language to which
not even an opinion could have added intrinsic authority:

> Many an appeal to freedom is the masquerade of privilege or inequal-
> ity seeking to intrench itself behind the catchword of a principle. There
> must be give and take at many points, allowance must be made for the
> play of the machine, or in the clash of jarring rivalries the pretending
> absolutes will destroy themselves and ordered freedom too. Only in one
> field is compromise to be excluded, or kept within the narrowest limits.
> There shall be no compromise of the freedom to think one's thoughts
> and speak them, except at those extreme borders where thought merges
> into action. There is to be no compromise here, for thought freely com-
> municated, if I may borrow my own words, is the indispensable condi-
> tion of intelligent experimentation, the one test of its validity. There is
> no freedom without choice, and there is no choice without knowledge—
> or none that is not illusory. Here are goods to be conserved, however
> great the seeming sacrifice. We may not squander the thought that will
> be the inheritance of the ages.[3]

.   .   .   .

Civil liberties were for Cardozo not empty slogans but cher-
ished protections of the human spirit. They derived meaning from
history and were given pertinence by contemporary society. He
was, however, too steeped in the history of the law not to detect
quickly meretricious uses of history. . . . And so he never rested
on a formula, even one that embodied the most precious victory of
reason. Had Cardozo ever been called upon to vindicate the security which the Constitution guarantees to "the free exercise" of religion, he doubtless would have done so in majestic utterance. But
when immunity from compulsory instruction in military science in

nificance to those liberties of the individual which history has attested as the
indispensable conditions of a free society from that which he attached to liberties
which derived merely from shifting economic arrangements. . . . Because these
civil liberties were explicitly safeguarded in the Constitution or conceived to be
basic to any notion of the liberty guaranteed by the Fourteenth Amendment,
Mr. Justice Holmes was far more ready to find legislative invasion in this field
than in the area of debatable economic reform."—Frankfurter, *Mr. Justice
Holmes and the Supreme Court* (1938), 50-51.
   [3] Cardozo, "Mr. Justice Holmes" (1931), 44 *Harv. L. Rev.* 682, 687-88.

a state university sought the shelter of religious liberty, he rejected the claim sympathetically but robustly. . . .

V

The constitutional history of our federal system as disclosed in Supreme Court decisions is in no small measure the still unwritten story of the rhythm of emphasis now upon national power, now upon state power. But no period of the Court's life contained such extreme fluctuations of rhythm within so short a span as the less than six terms during which Cardozo sat.

Certainly constitutional dialectic has never been employed to more self-defeating ends than when a narrow majority of the Court invoked state sovereignty against the Municipal Bankruptcy Act as a means of destroying the state's freedom of action. Such a doctrine of impotence, Cardozo protested, was consonant neither with reason nor with the whole "evolutionary process" of our constitutional law. . . . But Cardozo's conception of the federal system became the law of the land within two years. . . .

. . . Mr. Justice Cardozo was permitted to speak for a majority of the Court in sustaining one of the most ramifying exertions of federal power. For a hundred years the implications of the general welfare clause were debated by publicists and statesmen. The Supreme Court, with wise abstention, avoided this thorny conflict. Excepting only the creative interpretations of Marshall, whereby great national powers were breathed into the inert words of the Constitution, probably no other adjudications of the Court initiated such far-reaching recognition of federal authority as that which was given in the Social Security cases.[4] From such powerful and luminous opinions as those which Cardozo rendered there, the choice of short excerpts becomes an invidious necessity:

Congress may spend money in aid of the "general welfare." . . . The conception of the spending power advocated by Hamilton and strongly reinforced by Story has prevailed over that of Madison, which

[4] *Steward Machine Co. v. Davis*, 301 U.S. 548 (1937); *Helvering v. Davis*, 301 U.S. 619 (1937).

has not been lacking in adherents. Yet difficulties are left when the power is conceded. The line must still be drawn between one welfare and another, between particular and general. Where this shall be placed cannot be known through a formula in advance of the event. There is a middle ground, or certainly a penumbra, in which discretion is at large. The discretion, however, is not confided to the courts. The discretion belongs to Congress, unless the choice is clearly wrong, a display of arbitrary power, not an exercise of judgment. . . . Nor is the concept of the general welfare static. Needs that were narrow or parochial a century ago may be interwoven in our day with the well-being of the nation. What is critical or urgent changes with the times.

The purge of nation-wide calamity that began in 1929 has taught us many lessons. Not the least is the solidarity of interests that may once have seemed to be divided. Unemployment spreads from state to state, the hinterland now settled that in pioneer days gave an avenue of escape. . . .

The problem is plainly national in area and dimensions. Moreover, laws of the separate states cannot deal with it effectively. Congress, at least, had a basis for that belief. . . . Only a power that is national can serve the interests of all.

Whether wisdom or unwisdom resides in the scheme of benefits set forth in Title II, it is not for us to say. The answer to such inquiries must come from Congress, not the courts. Our concern here, as often, is with power, not with wisdom. Counsel for respondent has recalled to us the virtues of self-reliance and frugality. There is a possibility, he says, that aid from a paternal government may sap those sturdy virtues and breed a race of weaklings. If Massachusetts so believes and shapes her laws in that conviction, must her breed of sons be changed, he asks, because some other philosophy of government finds favor in the halls of Congress? But the answer is not doubtful. One might ask with equal reason whether the system of protective tariffs is to be set aside at will in one state or another whenever local policy prefers the rule of *laissez faire*. The issue is a closed one. It was fought out long ago. When money is spent to promote the general welfare, the concept of welfare or the opposite is shaped by Congress, not the states. So the concept be not arbitrary, the locality must yield.[5]

[5] *Helvering* v. *Davis*, 301 U.S. 619, 640-41, 644-45 (1937).

Cardozo did not deem it necessary to reconcile these cases with the Butler case,[6] decided fourteen months earlier, and this is not the place to make the attempt.

In these phases of our federal system Cardozo dealt with relatively novel issues which gave full play to his learning, imagination, and serene devotion to the ultimate but narrowly confined function of the Court in assessing the validity of legislation. He left his special mark in every case he wrote, but when dealing with the commerce clause he wrote upon a heavily encrusted palimpsest. In view of the illumination which the Chief Justice has shed upon the organic relation of modern industry in his opinions in the Labor Board cases,[7] the earlier exposition by Cardozo of the ramifications of modern industry has become part of the established corpus of the law of the commerce clause. . . .

If he seemed to throw his weight to the side of national power it was not because of any strong doctrinaire beliefs or political preferences. Thus he decided against New York in one aspect of its milk control legislation, doubtless with special sympathy for the difficulties which confronted the state, because he could not escape the conviction that New York was in effect erecting a barrier where the commerce clause enjoined free trade. . . . These were not matters that closely touched his private intellectual interests. He decided as he decided and wrote what he wrote because the judicial function as he conceived it and so candidly set it forth in his philosophic writings compelled his votes and indicated the direction of his opinions.

To adapt a favorite quotation of his, these extracts are but little fragments of the golden fleece that Cardozo has left upon the hedges of his judicial life. But even the fullest reading of his

---

[6] *United States* v. *Butler*, 297 U.S. 1 (1936) (invalidating the AAA— Ed. Note).

[7] *NLRB* v. *Jones & Laughlin Steel Corp.*, 301 U.S. 1 (1937); *NLRB* v. *Fruehauf Trailer Co.*, id. at 49; *NLRB* v. *Friedman-Harry Marks Clothing Co.*, id. at 58; *Associated Press* v. *NLRB*, id. at 103; and *Washington, Va. & Md. Coach Co.* v. *NLRB*, id. at 142.

opinions merely gives intimations of his depth of thought and beauty of character. The permanent influence of this great judge was achieved only partially by his own writings, for the current of his culture permeated in ways more subtle than even his opinions can express. Perhaps his qualities are best defined by saying that Cardozo completely satisfied the requirements of a judge wholly adequate for the Supreme Bench.

I venture to believe that it is as important to a judge called upon to pass on a question of constitutional law, to have at least a bowing acquaintance with Acton and Maitland, with Thucydides, Gibbon, and Carlyle, with Homer, Dante, Shakespeare, and Milton, with Machiavelli, Montaigne, and Rabelais, with Plato, Bacon, Hume, and Kant, as with the books which have been specifically written on the subject. For in such matters everything turns upon the spirit in which he approaches the questions before him. The words he must construe are empty vessels into which he can pour nearly anything he will. Men do not gather figs of thistles, nor supple institutions from judges whose outlook is limited by parish or class. They must be aware that there are before them more than verbal problems; more than final solutions cast in generalizations of universal applicability. They must be aware of the changing social tensions in every society which make it an organism; which demand new schemata of adaptation; which will disrupt it, if rigidly confined.[8]

[8] Learned Hand, "Sources of Tolerance" (1930), 79 *U. of Pa. L. Rev.* 1, 12.

When Judge Cardozo Writes

The following book review of Law and Literature, and Other Essays and Addresses, *by Benjamin N. Cardozo, appeared in the* New Republic *for April 8, 1931.*

To LAYMEN, the dichotomy between law and literature is merely one aspect of the conflict between law and life. A feeling so widely and deeply held by even the most cultivated outside the law cannot be nurtured wholly upon untruth. And yet it conceals a fine covey of paradoxes which would have been fair game for a Hazlitt, though for all I know he himself shared the feeling or put to flight at least some of its paradoxes. That nothing which is human is alien to him, is truer of the lawyer than even of doctor or priest. For the lawyer's office is frequently a confessional, and long before psychiatry had its name wise lawyers had to practice its arts. The work of courts is in essence the composition of human rivalries, the arbitrament of conflicting human desires. Something of its human origin ought therefore to be secreted in the records of the law; at least an occasional heartbeat ought to be found within law-sheep binding. And the adventurous-minded, the sophisticated who do not like to slumber too easily on the dogma that law is outside of life or that life is without law, would be rewarded more richly than they suspect by those records of the variegated human scene we call the law reports. Thus, in a single pamphlet of recent opinions may be found an exciting analysis of the originality, if any, of the dramatic qualities of "Abie's Irish Rose" and disclosures regarding the practice of birth control in the United States, the more revealing because set forth with calculated sobriety. If it be true, as Robert Louis Stevenson said, that the writer who knew what to omit could turn a daily paper into an Odyssey, then, as the lawyers would say, it is *a fortiori* true of the law reports.

But I am afraid that even with these few remarks I have added further proof that of the many mansions in the house of literature, law is not one. Incurably subdued by the materials of my profession, I seemingly cannot write a paragraph without "if anys" and *a fortioris*. Here is the inevitable lawyer's writing—the dull qualifications and circumlocutions that sink any literary barque or even freighter, the lifeless tags and rags that preclude grace and stifle spontaneity. In good measure one may admit the charge, without implying that the limits of one of her votaries are the law's limits. It will not do to press the claims of law upon literature by denying that the law has its own great preoccupation distinct from that of literature. Once and for all, Mr. Justice Holmes has put our case, with colors flying and without arrogance: "Of course the law is not the place for the artist or the poet. The law is the calling of thinkers." Literature is not the goal of lawyers, though they occasionally attain it. With more explicitness to the matter in hand, though wholly free from didacticism, Chief Judge Cardozo in this volume of essays makes clear why the artist's search for beauty cannot be the lawyer's prime concern. For the judge, with us the ultimate spokesman of the law, must be "historian and prophet all in one." The law must be declared "not only as the past has shaped it in judgments already rendered, but as the future ought to shape it in cases yet to come. Those of us whose lives have been spent on the bench and at the bar have learned caution and reticence, perhaps even to excess. We know the value of the veiled phrase, the blurred edge, the uncertain line." Here we have the source of the antinomy between law and literature. "Caution and reticence" are not the wellsprings of literature, but they are indispensable to wisdom in law, certainly to wisdom in adjudication. Since judges must be prophets, in other words since judges not merely register the past but direct the future, they had best not presume too much upon a wisdom that was denied the Delphic oracles. By a strange inconsistency, those who chafe most against the governance of the present by the edicts of the past too frequently want the present to pronounce against the future, forgetting that for the future the present will be the past.

Law, then, is not part of belles-lettres. But within the limits of its responsibility and its themes, law has not come empty-handed to the altars of literature. A comprehensive account of English literature, as the expression of English thought, could hardly omit Mansfield, Stowell and Bowen, to mention only modern judges, and Maitland's genius shows with what imagination and charm the story of the law can be invested.

When I think thus of the law, I see a princess mightier than she who once wrought at Bayeux, eternally weaving into her web dim figures of the ever-lengthening past—figures too dim to be noticed by the idle, too symbolic to be interpreted except by her pupils, but to the discerning eye disclosing every painful step and every world-shaking contest by which mankind has worked and fought its way from savage isolation to organic social life.

So wrote an American judge, Mr. Justice Holmes, who among judges has the supreme place in any adequate anthology of English prose. But there are other judges who wrote with the memorable uniqueness of expression that is style. There is of course John Marshall, whom Judge Cardozo, in the exhilarating essay which gives its name to this volume, selects for the "type magisterial or imperative" in his critical and playful analysis of the varieties of judicial opinions. "We hear the voice of the law speaking by its consecrated ministers with the calmness and assurance that are born of a sense of mastery and power. Thus Marshall seemed to judge, and a hush falls upon us even now as we listen to his words. Those organ tones of his were meant to fill cathedrals. . . ." There is not space to follow Judge Cardozo in his serio-humorous categories of opinions and their exemplars. I have, besides, my own favorites. Who among non-lawyers writes as Judge Charles M. Hough wrote, and as Judge Learned Hand now writes? One might also be tempted to intrude on Judge Cardozo's gentle silences about the versatile forms of judicial stuffiness. Unlike the new Earl Russell, judges are prone to "regard solemnity as a means of attaining truth."

Deference for the well-known shyness of the author has held this review much too long in check. If Judge Cardozo will publish, he must suffer the pains of public appreciation. Who better than he has demonstrated that law is stunted and undernourished by life, if it falls below the dignity of literature? The bar reads his opinions for pleasure, and even a disappointed litigant must feel, when Judge Cardozo writes, that a cause greater than his private interest prevailed. And so it has come to pass that the court over which Judge Cardozo presides enjoys an eminence second only to that of the Supreme Court of the United States. Its Chief must be included in the first half-dozen judges of the English-speaking world.

This volume gives the lay reader a taste of Judge Cardozo's qualities—grace in the service of solidity, sensitiveness directing judgment, awareness of the limits of reason and of the subtle guises of self-deception. Judge Cardozo elsewhere has quoted Chesterton's remark that the most important thing about a man is his philosophy. And this distillate of Judge Cardozo's reflections is inevitably judicial self-revelation. These seven papers were born of distinct occasion; formally they have no common theme. And yet they have the unity of their common source, drawn as they are from the same deep brooding over law's meanings and methods.

The enduring contributions of thinkers, maintains one of the acutest, are not systems but insights. Indeed, systems are apt to be overrefined elaborations of penetrating glimpses into truth. At all events, the two judges who in our day have given powerful direction to juristic thinking have done so not by heavy treatises on jurisprudence. Mr. Justice Holmes has gradually refashioned the whole outlook and methods of American legal thought through his essays no less than his opinions. The work of philosophic permeation begun by his master sixty years ago (and happily still continued in his opinions) is being carried on by New York's Chief Judge, and again by essays. . . .

"It is the first step in sociological wisdom," according to Whitehead, "to recognize that the major advances in civilization are processes which all but wreck the societies in which they occur—like unto an arrow in the hand of a child. The art of free society consists first in the maintenance of the symbolic code; and secondly in fearlessness of revision, to secure that the code serves those purposes which satisfy an enlightened reason." In the service of this "sociological wisdom" no one is more deeply enlisted than the author of these essays.

Brandeis

When Mr. Frankfurter was a student in the Harvard Law School, Louis D. Brandeis was becoming the "people's lawyer" of Boston. When Mr. Frankfurter returned to the faculty of the school in 1914, Mr. Brandeis had become a controversial figure in the community. His activities enlisted the enthusiastic interest of Mr. Frankfurter, and the friendship which the two men formed in Boston has continued to the present time. For Mr. Justice Brandeis, as for Mr. Justice Holmes, Mr. Frankfurter annually selected a secretary from among the young graduates of the Harvard Law School. The following selection was written shortly after President Wilson nominated Mr. Brandeis to the Supreme Court, and appeared as an unsigned editorial in the New Republic *for February 5, 1916.*

ONE PUBLIC benefit has already accrued from the nomination of Mr. Brandeis. It has started discussion of what the Supreme Court means in American life. From much of the comment since Mr. Brandeis's nomination it would seem that multitudes of Americans seriously believe that the nine Justices embody pure reason, that they are set apart from the concerns of the community, regardless of time, place, and circumstances, to become the interpreter of sacred words with meaning fixed forever and ascertainable by a process of ineluctable reasoning. Yet the notion not only runs counter to all we know of human nature, it betrays either ignorance or false knowledge of the actual work of the Supreme Court as disclosed by two hundred and thirty-nine volumes of United States Reports. It assumes what is not now and never was the function of the Supreme Court.

· · · · · · · ·

To generalize about periods and tendencies in the history of the Supreme Court is to omit many details and qualifications, but that the great problems of statesmanship have determined the character of the Court at different periods in our history there can be no doubt. In the first period, barring a negligible opening decade, the Court under Marshall's great leadership dealt with the structure of government. It gave legal expression to the forces of nationality. Marshall also laid down what may be called the great canon of constitutional criticism by insisting that it is a "Constitution that we are construing, a great charter of government with all the implications that dynamic government means." After Marshall the ever-present conflict of state and national power absorbed attention until the Civil War. Then followed a third period in which national power was ascendant, a period of railroad and industrial development, of free lands and apparently unlimited resources, a period in which the prevailing philosophy was naturally enough *laissez faire*. It was a period of luxuriant individualism. The Fourteenth Amendment was made the vehicle of its expression, the quality of the Court was exemplified in the sturdy personalities of Justices like Brewer and Peckham. "Liberty of contract" flourished, social legislation was feared, except during the sound but brief leadership in the opposite direction by Chief Justice Waite.

The period of individualism and fear is over. Occasionally there is a relapse, but on the whole we have entered definitely upon an epoch in which Justice Holmes has been the most consistent and dominating force, and to which Justices Day and Hughes have been great contributing factors. It is the period of self-consciousness as to the true nature of the issues before the Court. It is the period of realization that basically the questions are not abstractions to be determined by empty formula, that contemporary convictions of expediency as to property and contract must not be passed off as basic principles of right. It is this new spirit which led Justice Holmes to say that it was the Court's duty "to learn to transcend our own convictions, and to leave room for much that we hold dear to be done away with, short of revolution, by the orderly change of law."

    .   .   .   .

To the consideration of these very questions Mr. Brandeis has given his whole life. To their understanding he brings a mind of extraordinary power and insight. He has amassed experience enjoyed by hardly another lawyer to the same depth and richness and detail, for it is the very condition of his mind to know all there is to be known of a subject with which he grapples. Thus he is a firsthanded authority in the field of insurance, of industrial efficiency, of public franchises, of conservation, of the transportation problem, of the interrelations of modern business and modern life.

But his approach is that of the true lawyer, because he seeks to tame isolated instances to as large a general rule as possible, and thereby to make the great reconciliation between order and justice. Mr. Brandeis would extend the domain of law, as he only very recently put it before the Chicago Bar Association, by absorbing the facts of life, just as Mansfield in his day absorbed the law merchant into the common law. This craving for authentic facts on which law alone can be founded leads him always to insist on establishing the machinery by which they can be ascertained. It is this which has led him to create practically a new technique in the presentation of constitutional questions. Until his famous argument on the Oregon ten-hour law for women, social legislation was argued before our courts practically *in vacuo,* as an abstract question unrelated to a world of factories and child labor and trade unions and steel trusts. In the Oregon case for the first time there were marshaled before the Supreme Court the facts of modern industry which reasonably called for legislation limiting hours of labor. This marked an epoch in the argument and decision of constitutional cases and resulted not only in reversal of prior decisions, but in giving to the courts a wholly new approach to this most important class of present-day constitutional issues. As advocate Mr. Brandeis has secured the approval of every constitutional case which he has argued—argued always for the public—not only from the Supreme Court of the United States but from the courts of New York, Illinois, and Oregon.

We may be perfectly certain, then, that Mr. Brandeis is no doctrinaire. He does not allow formulae to do service for facts. He has remained scrupulously flexible. While, for example, he has made us realize that there may be a limit to the efficiency of combination, yet he has insisted that the issue must be settled by authoritative data, that such data must be gathered by a permanent non-partisan commission. So Mr. Brandeis helped to give us the Federal Trade Commission. He sees equally clearly that there are limits to the uses of competition, and no man has spoken more effectively against the competition that kills or more vigorously for the morality of price maintenance.

The very processes of his mind are deliberate and judicial—if we mean by deliberation and judicial-mindedness a full survey of all relevant factors of a problem and courageous action upon it. He has an almost unerring genius for accuracy, because his conclusion is the result of a slow mastery of the problem. Events have rarely failed to support his judgments. In the New Haven situation, for instance, the conclusions which Mr. Brandeis had reached and for which he sought quiet acceptance a decade ago were finally vindicated. So of all his public activities—the adoption of a sliding scale in franchise returns, the adoption of a savings-bank insurance, the settlement of industrial disputes, the regulation of conditions of labor, the conservation of our natural resources—in each problem there have been three stages: thorough investigation by and with experts; education of the public to the results of such investigation; and then political action with informed public opinion behind it, either by legislation for the government or by changes in the structure of one of the great groups of the state, such as the trade union or employers' organizations.

Mr. Brandeis says of himself: "I have no rigid social philosophy; I have been too intense on concrete problems of practical justice." A study of his work verifies this analysis. It is true he has a passion for justice and a passion for democracy, but justice and democracy enlist a common fealty. It is by his insistence on translating these beliefs into life, by his fruitful intellectual inventiveness in devising the means for such translation, that Mr. Brandeis is distinguished. One who has brought the agency of a vitalizing peace to the most anarchistic of all industries, the garment trades, and has done it, not by magic, but by turning contending forces into co-operative forces, has that balance of head and heart and will which constitutes real judicial-mindedness.

It is said of him that he is often not amiable in a fight. There is truth in the statement. The law has not been a game to him; the issues he has dealt with have been great moral questions. He has often fought with great severity. He has rarely lost. His great fights have been undertaken in the public interest. In the course of his career he has made enemies, some of whom were malicious, others honestly convinced that he had wronged them. A number of charges have been made against him, no one of which has been proved, though no one can question that Mr. Brandeis's enemies have spared no pains to prove them. His friends who are in a position to know the details of his career believe in him passionately. They are delighted that so able a committee of the Senate should have undertaken the work of running down every insinuation. They believe that no man's career can stand as much scrutiny as his. They want the insinuations crystallized, examined, and disposed of, so that the nation may begin to employ this man who has at once the passion of public service and the genius for it.

Mr. Justice Brandeis and the Constitution

This selection appeared in the Harvard Law Review *for November, 1931* (*Vol. 44, p. 33*), *in a series of essays celebrating Mr. Justice Brandeis's seventy-fifth birthday. It later appeared in a book of essays,* Mr. Justice Brandeis (*1932*), *which Mr. Frankfurter edited.*

A DEFINITIVE history of great political events may challenge the fecundity of historians, but of necessity escapes them. Even an adequate history of the Supreme Court awaits writing, to say which is no failure of gratitude to Mr. Charles Warren, who did not purport to paint a full canvas. He attempted only an essay on *The Supreme Court in United States History*. To write the history of the Court presupposes an adequate social history of the United States, which, as yet, we lack. Much brave scholarship is now enlisted to give a critical understanding of our past. And the illuminating chapters of the Beards and of Parrington, together with the *History of American Life*, edited by Professors Schlesinger and Fox, bring nearer the day of a comprehensive history of our civilization.

Moreover, the work of the Supreme Court is the history of relatively few personalities. However much they may have represented or resisted their Zeitgeist, symbolized forces outside their own individualities, they were also individuals. The fact that they were *there* and that others were not, surely made decisive differences. To understand what manner of men they were is crucial to an understanding of the Court. Yet how much real insight have we about the seventy-four men who constitute the Supreme Court's roll of judges? How much is known about the inner forces that directed their action and stamped the impress of their unique influence upon the Court? Only of Marshall have we an adequate biography; Story's revealing correspondence takes us behind his scholarly exterior; very recently not a little light has been shed on the circumstances and associations that helped to mold Field's outlook. About most of the Justices we have only mortuary estimates.

However little we may know about the personal and social influences in which the Court's history is enmeshed, we know enough to know that the essential history of the United States is mirrored in the controversies before the Court. The thrust of the American empire against the hostility to extension, the eternal conflict between creditor and debtor classes and between rich and poor, the push toward economic concentration and the resistance of individual enterprise, the struggles between *étatisme* and libertarianism, between racial homogeneity and diversity of strains, the conflict between the attachments of localism and the march of centralization—all the contending forces in our society, throughout our national life, lie buried within the interstices of the two hundred and eighty-three volumes of the United States Reports, ready to be quickened into life by the magic touch of the artist.

Of spontaneous generation there is little in history. Epochal changes germinate slowly, and dates in history are deluding. They mark fruition rather than beginning. Yet "every schoolboy knows," though without the omniscience which Macaulay attributed to that imaginary lad, that the Great War ushered in a new era. While the forces which burst upon the world in a cataclysmic war had long been burrowing underground, the débâcle of three mighty empires, the Russian Revolution and its violent break with the past, the intensification of technological processes induced by the War, loosed economic and social forces far more upsetting to the pre-existing equilibrium than the changes wrought by the French Revolution and the Napoleonic Wars. All these conflicts and confusions of recent history also are registered in the current annals of the Supreme Court. Mr. Justice Brandeis came to the Supreme Court at the threshold of this new epoch.[1]

II

Time is an almost indispensable condition for weaving the impress of distinction upon the work of the Court. Mr. Justice Brandeis has now entered upon his sixteenth term and written four hundred and fifteen opinions. These reveal an organic constitutional philosophy, which in turn expresses his response to the deepest issues of society. Other Justices have brought to the Court the matured philosophy of a lifetime's brooding. But probably no other man has come to the Court with his mind dyed, as it were, in the very issues which became his chief judicial concern. Indeed, his work as Justice may accurately be described as a continuation of devotion to the solution of those social and economic problems of American society with which he was preoccupied for nearly a generation before his judicial career. Some years before going on the Court he had practically withdrawn from private practice and given unique meaning to what Senator Root has called the "public profession" of the law. Whenever some particularly pressing or difficult issue absorbed his interest and his energy, his passion for law and his mastery of its processes were engaged on behalf of the community; the community which he served was increasingly as wide as the nation. And he gave himself to public affairs as a private citizen. He is one of the very few men who became a Justice without having held prior judicial or political office, except for his service as special counsel for the Interstate Commerce Commission

[1] "On January 28, 1916, President Wilson nominated Louis D. Brandeis of Massachusetts to succeed Mr. Justice Lamar deceased: he was confirmed by the Senate on June 1, 1916; his commission was dated June 1, 1916, and he took his seat upon the bench June 5, 1916."—241 U.S. iii. The reporter thus veils one of the most stirring occurrences in the Court's history. This is not the occasion to explore the meaning of the contest that resulted in the confirmation of the nomination of Mr. Brandeis. See "Hearings and Report on Nomination of Louis D. Brandeis," Sen. No. 409, 64th Cong., 1st Sess.

in the proceedings for general rate increases in 1913-14. Even this inquiry he conducted not as a partisan but in a judicial spirit, to see "that all sides and angles of the case are presented of record without advocating any particular theory for its disposition."

Thus for years Mr. Justice Brandeis had been immersed in the problems which modern industry and finance have created for society and in the conflicts engendered by them. Hardly another lawyer had amassed experience over so wide a range and with so firm a grip on the details that matter. The intricacies of large affairs, railroading, finance, insurance, the public utilities and the conservation of our natural resources, had yielded to him their meaning. In all these fields the impact of the concrete instance started his inquiries, but it is of the very nature of his mind to explore a subject with which he is grappling until he sees it in all its social bearing.

At a time when our constitutional law was becoming dangerously unresponsive to drastic social changes, when sterile clichés instead of facts were deciding cases, he insisted, as the great men of law have always insisted, that law must be sensitive to life. And he preached the doctrine by works more than by faith. By a series of arguments and briefs he created practically a new technique in the presentation of constitutional questions. Until his famous brief in *Muller* v. *Oregon*,[2] social legislation was supported before the courts largely *in vacuo*—as an abstract dialectic between "liberty" and "police power," unrelated to a world of trusts and unions, of large-scale industry and all its implications. In the Oregon case, the facts of modern industry which provoke regulatory legislation were, for the first time, adequately marshaled before the Court. It marks an epoch in the disposition of cases presenting the most important present-day constitutional issues.

III

Never was there an easier transition from forum to bench than when Mr. Brandeis became Mr. Justice Brandeis. Since the signifi-

[2] 208 U.S. 412 (1908).

cant cases before the Supreme Court always involve large public issues and are not just cases between two litigants, the general outlook of the Justices largely determines their views and votes in doubtful cases. Thus the divisions on the Court run not at all along party lines. They reflect not past political attachments, but the philosophy of the judges about government and our government, their conception of the Constitution and of their own function as its interpreter.

Rich experience at the bar confirmed the teachings which Mr. Brandeis had received from James Bradley Thayer, the great master of constitutional law, that the Constitution had ample resources within itself to meet the changing needs of successive generations. The Constitution provided for the future partly by not forecasting it and partly by the generality of its language. The ambiguities and lacunae of the document left ample scope for the unfolding of life. If only the Court, aided by the bar, has access to the facts and heeds them, the Constitution, as he had shown, is flexible enough to respond to the demands of modern society. The work of Mr. Justice Brandeis is in the tradition of Marshall, for, underlying his opinions, is the realization "that it is a *constitution* we are expounding." In essence, the Constitution is not a literary composition but a way of ordering society, adequate for imaginative statesmanship, if judges have imagination for statesmanship.

.   .   .   .

This general point of view has led Mr. Justice Brandeis to give free play to the states and the nation within their respective spheres.

.   .   .   .

Taxation has always been the most sensitive nerve of government. The enormous increase in the cost of society and the extent to which wealth is represented by intangibles are putting public finance to its severest tests. To balance budgets, to pay for the cost of progressively civilized social standards, to safeguard the future and to divide these burdens with substantial fairness to the different interests in the community, strains to the utmost the ingenuity of statesmen. They must constantly explore new sources of revenue and find means to prevent the circumvention of their discovery. Subject as they are, in English-speaking countries, to popular control, they must be allowed the widest latitude of power. No finicky limitation upon their discretion nor jejune formula of equality should circumscribe the necessarily empirical process of tapping new revenue or stopping new devices for its evasion. To these needs Mr. Justice Brandeis has been especially alive. He has consistently refused to accentuate the fiscal difficulties of government by injecting into the Constitution his own notions of fiscal policy. In the "vague contours of the Fifth Amendment" he reads no restriction upon historic methods of taxation. Nor has he found in the Constitution compulsion to grant additional immunity or benefit to taxpayers merely because they already hold tax-exempt securities.

.   .   .   .

I V

For the states, within their ambit, Mr. Justice Brandeis also finds ample scope in the Constitution. He feels profoundly the complexities of their problems. The widest opportunity for experimentation should not, he believes, be denied to them by a static conception of the Constitution. Here, again, the general intimations of fairness and reason in the due process clause were not intended to shut off remedies, however tentative, for the moral and economic waste, the friction of classes, urban congestion, the relaxation of individual responsibility, the subtler forms of corruption, and the abuses of power which have followed in the wake of a highly developed *laissez faire* industrialism.

.   .   .   .

Particularly, the states should not be hampered in dealing with evils at their points of pressure. Legislation is essentially *ad hoc*. To expect uniformity in law where there is diversity in fact is to bar effective legislation. An extremely complicated society inevitably entails special treatment for distinctive social phenomena. If legislation is to deal with realities, it must address itself to important variations in the needs, opportunities and coercive power of the different elements in the state. The states must be left wide latitude in devising ways and means for paying the bills of society and in using taxation as an instrument of social policy. Taxation is never palatable. Its essential fairness must not be tested by pedantic arguments derived from hollow abstractions. Even more dangers than have been revealed by the due process clause may lurk in the requirement of "the equal protection of the laws," if that provision of the Fourteenth Amendment is to be applied with "delusive exactness." That tendency, often revealed during the post-war period, Mr. Justice Brandeis has steadily resisted.

·   ·   ·   ·   ·   ·   ·

The veto power of the Supreme Court over the social-economic legislation of the states, when exercised by a narrow conception of the due process and equal protection of the law clauses, presents undue centralization in its most destructive and least responsible form. The most destructive, because it stops experiment at its source, preventing an increase of social knowledge by the only scientific method available: namely, the tests of trial and error. The least responsible, because it so often turns on the fortuitous circumstances which determine a majority decision, and shelters the fallible judgment of individual Justices, in matters of fact and opinion not peculiarly within the special competence of judges, behind the impersonal authority of the Constitution. The inclination of a single Justice, the buoyancy of his hopes or the intensity of his fears, may determine the opportunity of a much-needed social experiment to survive, or may frustrate for a long time intelligent attempts to deal with a social evil. Against these dangers the only safeguards are judges thoroughly awake to the problems of their day and open-minded to the facts which may justify legislation. His wide experience, his appetite for fact, his instinct for the concrete and his distrust of generalities, equip Mr. Justice Brandeis with unique gifts for the discharge of the Court's most difficult and delicate tasks.

·   ·   ·   ·   ·   ·   ·

VII

Marshall could draw with large and bold strokes the boundaries of state and national power; today most crucial issues involve the concrete application of settled, general doctrines. The fate of vast interests and hopeful reforms, the traditional contest between centralization and local rule, now turn on questions of more or less, on matters of degree, on drawing lines, sometimes very fine lines. Decisions therefore depend more and more on precise formulation of the issues embedded in litigation, and on alertness regarding the exact scope of past decisions in the light of their present significance. The Court's conception of its own function and awareness of its processes in constitutional adjudication determine the Constitution in action.

In his whole temperament, Mr. Justice Brandeis is poles apart from the attitude of the technically minded lawyer. Yet no member of the Court invokes more rigorously the traditional limits of its jurisdiction. In view of our federalism and the Court's peculiar function, questions of jurisdiction in constitutional adjudications imply questions of political power. The history of the Court and the nature of its business admonish against needless or premature decisions. It has no greater duty than the duty not to decide or not to decide beyond its circumscribed authority. And so Mr. Justice Brandeis will decide only if the record presents a *case*—a live, concrete, present controversy between litigants.

. . . .

When the record does present a case and judgment must be rendered, constitutional determination must be avoided if a non-constitutional ground disposes of the immediate litigation.

. . . .

Moreover, the duty to abstain from adjudicating, particularly in the field of public law, may arise from the restricted nature of the judicial process. The specific claim before the Court may be enmeshed in larger public issues beyond the Court's reach of investigation, or a suitable remedy may exceed judicial resources.

Such a situation, even though formally disguised as a case, eludes adjudication. To forgo judgment under such circumstances is not abdication of judicial power, but recognition of rational limits to its competence. Law is only partly in the keeping of courts; much must be left to legislation and administration. Nor does the absence of legislation create a vacuum to be occupied by judicial action.

. . . .

Even though the abstract conditions for judicial competence exist, the Supreme Court may not be the fittest tribunal for its exercise. When cases depend on subtle appreciation of complicated local arrangements or the interpretation of state enactments not yet interpreted by state courts nor yielding their meaning merely to a reading of English, original interpretations by the Supreme Court are likely to be *in vacuo*. The local court, whether state or federal, has judicial antennae for local situations seldom vouchsafed to the tribunal at Washington. The Supreme Court should draw on the experience and judgment of the local courts before giving ultimate judgment upon local law.

. . . .

And when, finally, a constitutional decision is rendered, not the language in explanation of it, but the terms of the controversy which called it forth, alone determine the extent of its sway. This is merely the common law lawyer's general disrespect for dicta; but in constitutional adjudications dicta are peculiarly pernicious usurpers. To let even accumulated dicta govern is to give the future no hearing. And immortality does not inhere even in constitutional decisions. The Constitution owes its continuity to a continuous process of revivifying changes. "The Constitution cannot make itself; some body made it, not at once, but at several times. It is alterable; and by that draweth nearer Perfection; and without suiting itself to differing Times and Circumstances, it could not live. Its Life is prolonged by changing seasonably the several Parts of it at several times." So wrote the shrewd Lord Halifax, and it is as true of our written Constitution as of that strange medley of imponderables which is the British Constitution. A ready and delicate sense of the need for alteration is perhaps the most precious talent required of the Supreme Court. Upon it depends the vitality of the Constitution as a vehicle for life.

.   .   .   .

VIII

A philosophy of intellectual humility determines Mr. Justice Brandeis's conception of the Supreme Court's function: an instinct against the tyranny of dogma and skepticism regarding the perdurance of any man's wisdom, though he be judge. No one knows better than he how slender a reed is reason—how recent its emergence in man, how powerful the countervailing instincts and passions, how treacherous the whole rational process. But just because the efforts of reason are tenuous, a constant process of critical scrutiny of the tentative claims of reason is essential to the very progress of reason. Truth and knowledge can function and flourish only if error may freely be exposed. And error will go unchallenged if dogma, no matter how widely accepted or dearly held, may not be questioned. Man must be allowed to challenge it by speech or by pen, not merely by silent thought. Thought, like other instincts, will atrophy unless formally exercised. If men cannot speak or write freely, they will soon cease to think freely. Limits there are, of course, even to this essential condition of a free society. But they do not go beyond the minimum requirements of an imminent and substantial threat to the very society which makes individual freedom significant. Together with his colleagues, Mr. Justice Brandeis has refused to make freedom of speech an absolute. But the test of freedom of speech is readiness "to allow it to men whose opinions seem to you wrong and even dangerous."

.   .   .   .

Freedom of speech and freedom of assembly are empty phrases if their exercise must yield to unreasonable fear. Great social convulsions like the Russian Revolution are bound to have their repercussions of panic among the timid and humorless, particularly panic stimulated by all the modern incitements to mass feeling. Such times present the decisive occasions for a stern enforcement of the right to air grievances, however baseless, and to propose remedies even more cruel than the grievances.

This Court has not yet fixed the standard by which to determine when a danger shall be deemed clear; how remote the danger may be and yet be deemed present; and what degree of evil shall be deemed sufficiently substantial to justify resort to abridgment of free speech and assembly as the means of protection. To reach sound conclusions on these matters, we must bear in mind why a state is, ordinarily, denied the power to prohibit dissemination of social, economic, and political doctrine which a vast majority of its citizens believes to be false and fraught with evil consequences.

Those who won our independence believed that the final end of the state was to make men free to develop their faculties; and that in its government the deliberative forces should prevail over the arbitrary. They valued liberty both as an end and as a means. They believed liberty to be the secret of happiness, and courage to be the secret of liberty. They believed that freedom to think as you will and to speak as you think are means indispensable to the discovery and spread of political truth; that without free speech and assembly discussion would be futile; that with them, discussion affords ordinarily adequate protection against the dissemination of noxious doctrine; that the greatest menace to freedom is an inert people; that public discussion is a political duty; and that this should be a fundamental principle of the American government. They recognized the risks to which all human institutions are subject. But they knew that order cannot be secured merely through fear of punishment for its infraction; that it is hazardous to discourage thought, hope, and imagination; that fear breeds repression; that repression breeds hate; that hate menaces stable government; that the path of safety lies in the opportunity to discuss freely supposed grievances and proposed remedies; and that the fitting remedy for evil counsels is good ones. Believing in the power of reason as applied through public discussion, they eschewed silence coerced by law—the argument of force in its worst form. Recognizing the occasional tyrannies of governing majorities, they amended the Constitution so that free speech and assembly should be guaranteed.

Fear of serious injury cannot alone justify suppression of free speech and assembly. Men feared witches and burnt women. It is the function of speech to free men from the bondage of irrational fears. To justify suppression of free speech there must be reasonable ground to fear that serious evil will result if free speech is practiced. There must be reasonable ground to believe that the danger apprehended is imminent. There must be reasonable ground to believe that the evil to be prevented is a serious one. Every denunciation of existing law tends in some measure to increase the probability that there will be violation of it. Condonation of a breach enhances the probability. Expressions of approval add to the probability. Propagation of the criminal state of mind by teaching syndicalism increases it. Advocacy of law-breaking heightens it still further. But even advocacy of violation, however reprehensible morally, is not a justification for denying free speech where the advocacy falls short of incitement and there is nothing to indicate that the advocacy would be immediately acted on. The wide difference between advocacy and incitement, between preparation and attempt, between assembling and conspiracy, must be borne in mind. In order to support a finding of clear and present danger it must be shown either that immediate serious violence was to be expected or was advocated, or that the past conduct furnished reason to believe that such advocacy was then contemplated.

Those who won our independence by revolution were not cowards. They did not fear political change. They did not exalt order at the cost of liberty. To courageous, self-reliant men, with confidence in the power of free and fearless reasoning applied through the processes of popular government, no danger flowing from speech can be deemed clear and present, unless the incidence of the evil apprehended is so imminent that it may befall before there is opportunity for full discussion. If there be time to expose through discussion the falsehood and fallacies, to avert the evil by the processes of education, the remedy to be applied is more speech, not enforced silence. Only an emergency can justify repression. Such must be the rule if authority is to be reconciled with freedom. Such, in my opinion, is the command of the Constitution. It is therefore always open to Americans to challenge a law abridging free speech and assembly by showing that there was no emergency justifying it.[3]

Utterance also has responsibility. To misrepresent fact is to corrupt the source of opinion. No compensating social gain de-

[3] *Whitney* v. *California*, 274 U.S. 357, 374-77 (1927) (concurring).

mands the right to such misrepresentation. But the free exchange
of opinion upon complicated issues must not be turned into crime
by treating the prevailing view as a fact and proscribing unpopular
dissent.

·   ·   ·   ·   ·   ·   ·

The press is the most important vehicle for the dissemination
of opinion. The Constitution precludes its censorship. Equally
inadmissible should be all oblique methods to censor the press.
Particularly offensive is the coercive power of unregulated administrative control.

·   ·   ·   ·   ·   ·   ·

XI

To quote from Mr. Justice Brandeis's opinions is not to pick
plums from a pudding, but to pull threads from a pattern. He
achieves not by epigrammatic thrust but through powerful exposition. His aim is not merely to articulate the grounds of his judgment, but to reach the mind even of the disappointed suitor,
deeming it essential for defeated interests to know that their
claims have adequately entered the judicial process. His opinions
march step by step towards demonstration, with all the auxiliary
reinforcement of detailed proof. The documentation of his opinions is one aspect of his reliance on reason. To sever text from
accompanying footnotes is therefore to dismember an organic
whole.

The style of his opinions befits their aim. The dominant note
is Doric simplicity. Occasionally, as in the terrible case of Ziang
Sung Wan,[4] his restraint attains austerity. And sometimes the
majesty of his theme stirs him to eloquence. When the issue is
freedom of speech, he gives noble utterance to his faith and to
the meaning of our institutions as the embodiment of that faith.

In truth, Mr. Justice Brandeis is a moral teacher, who follows
Socrates in the belief that virtue is the pursuit of enlightened
purpose. His long years of intimate connection with the history

[4] *Wan* v. *United States*, 266 U.S. 1 (1924).

of the Harvard Law School symbolize his dominant impulse. Problems, for him, are never solved. Civilization is a sequence of new tasks. Hence his insistence on the extreme difficulty of government and its dependence on sustained interest and effort, on the need for constant alertness to the fact that the introduction of new forces is accompanied by new difficulties. This, in turn, makes him mindful of the limited range of human foresight, and leads him to practice humility in attempting to preclude the freedom of action of those who are to follow.

The Justice himself, while at the bar, disavowed allegiance to any general system of thought or hope. "I have no rigid social philosophy; I have been too intent on concrete problems of practical justice." Devotion to justice is widely professed. By Mr. Justice Brandeis it has been given concrete expression in a long effort towards making the life of the commonplace individual more significant. His zest for giving significance to life is not sentimentality; it arises from a keen sensitiveness to quality. He not only evokes the best qualities in others; he exacts the best in himself. Stern self-discipline of a mind preternaturally rich and deep has fashioned a judge who, by common consent, is a great and abiding figure of the world's most powerful court.

The Liberties of a Free People:
Their Protection in the Courts

Press Censorship by Judicial Construction

This selection appeared as an unsigned editorial in the New Republic *for March 30, 1921.*

IF PEOPLE truly acted according to self-interest, it has been observed, this would be a very different world. The dictum finds striking confirmation in the attitude of the press towards the recent decision of the Supreme Court in the Milwaukee *Leader* case. With few exceptions, newspapers have either approved or have been indifferent to a decision which immediately affects only a despised Socialist sheet, but which involves nothing less than the control of the press.

As the Milwaukee *Leader* had for weeks systematically carried matter which the Postmaster General deemed non-mailable, in September, 1917, he denied second-class postal rates to all future issues of the *Leader*. To deny mail service to a newspaper except at six times the usual cost of the service furnished to papers is normally, of course, to make its circulation impossible. The Supreme Court has now sustained this power of suppression in the Postmaster General. Our government, we are constantly told, is "a government of laws and not of men"; whence, then, is this power derived? Since the offending matter in the *Leader* was obstructive to the conduct of the war, was the power to deny second-class rates found in the Espionage Act? No; Congress did not confer such power upon the Postmaster General even in that drastic war legislation. Was the Supreme Court, then, able to point to any general statute giving the Postmaster General discretionary authority over the life and death of a paper by denying it second-class rates in the future because of infractions of the postal laws in the past? No; there is no such statute. How then does the Supreme Court give the action of the Postmaster General the color of law? It does so by making two parallel lines of law meet. Let us trace this freak of legal geometry.

Congress from time to time by specific statutes has forbidden the deposit in the mails of certain printed matter. It seeks by this means to keep the mails free from publications offensive to decency or otherwise counter to the policy of the law, as for instance matter violative of the copyright law or information concerning abortion. This legislation makes the use of the mails for transmission of papers carrying non-mailable matter criminal and also authorizes the Postmaster General to refuse to carry papers containing the non-mailable matter. But there is no law which, either by way of punishment or prevention, authorizes the Postmaster General to order that future issues of a past offender shall be refused transmission. The Espionage Act enlarged the class of non-mailable matter; it did not enlarge the power of the Postmaster General in dealing with it. Violations of the Espionage Act through the newspapers could be dealt with only as violations of Section 211 of the Federal Criminal Code, prohibiting obscenities, can be dealt with, namely, by criminal prosecution and by refusal to transmit the issues containing the non-mailable matter. In other words—and it cannot be emphasized too often—Congress trusted to criminal prosecution with all its constitutional safeguards, and to a denial of the mails to the offending *thing,* but not to the offender.

Alongside of this exercise by Congress of its power to police the mails is legislation dealing with the cost of the mail service. Since 1879 a tariff of postal rates has been in force, graduated according to the nature of the mail matter. The second-class mail rate is confined to newspapers and other periodicals which possess the qualifications and comply with the conditions prescribed by Congress. The rate is very low and non-compensatory. "Justification for this non-compensatory service lies in the belief that education in its broad sense—intellectual activity fostered through the dissemination of information and of ideas—is essential to the life of a free, self-governing and striving people." Undoubtedly the Postmaster General, subject to a limited review by the courts, must determine whether or not a publication satisfies the conditions for second-class prescribed by Congress. Does, for instance, the *Tip Top Weekly*, each issue carrying a story complete in itself, or the *Riverside Literary Series* meet the definitions of a newspaper laid down by the law? He must answer such questions; but there is not a scintilla of a suggestion in the Mail Classification Act which makes the rating as second-class matter by the Postmaster General contingent upon the Postmaster General's verdict as to the legality either of the past or of the future issues of a newspaper. In other words, the low newspaper rate was not used as a means of policing the mails. "The question of the rate has nothing to do with the question of whether the matter is mailable." A newspaper is a newspaper even though a Victor Berger edit it.

The Mail Classification Act provides that a newspaper to be mailable at the second-class rate "must be regularly issued at stated intervals as frequently as four times a year," and that it must be "originated and published for the dissemination of information of a public character." Mr. Burleson held that if any issue of the paper contained matter violative of the Espionage Act, the paper is "no longer regularly issued," and that it has likewise ceased to be a paper "published for the dissemination of information of a public character." Mr. Burleson certainly deserves high rank as a sophist. No wonder Mr. Justice Holmes makes short shrift of this contention by calling it "a quibble." The Classification Act empowers the Postmaster General to determine whether a publication is a newspaper; it does not make him a censor of the press nor qualify him to distinguish good newspapers from bad.

The majority of the Court sustains Mr. Burleson's order on a somewhat less specious claim. Inasmuch as the *Leader* was found by the Postmaster General to have violated the Espionage Act in the past, "it is a reasonable presumption" that the character of the publication will continue and, therefore, will continue to violate the act in the future. Nor would it be "practicable to examine each issue of a newspaper" to determine whether the issue is offending. "Government is a practical institution adapted to the practical conduct of public affairs." The menacing implications of the "practical" powers thus conferred by the Supreme Court need not be labored. Without warrant of express grant of authority to the Postmaster General the Supreme Court derives this terrific power solely through administrative necessity. . . .

It will not do to say that this issue concerns only the Milwaukee *Leader*, or the New York *Call*. Newspapers of high respectability not only may, but have, run afoul of the postal laws. The decision reveals a lethal remedy against their misbehavior—or rather the Postmaster General's finding of their misbehavior, for *there* is the rub. The Postmaster General, without court or jury, may find that newspapers are non-mailable. The old New York *Herald*, for instance, was convicted by a jury for sending systematically obscene matter through the mail in its "personal" columns. The Burleson decision would have justified "a reasonable presumption" by the Postmaster General that the character of the publication will continue and second-class rates might have been denied to the New York *Herald*. The New York *World* was prosecuted for libel by Mr. Roosevelt's administration. To be sure, this prosecution failed. But if Mr. Roosevelt's Attorney General had not denied the very power which the Supreme Court has now sanctioned, there is little doubt that President Roosevelt would have ordered the withdrawal of second-class rates to the *World*. It is a fact worth noting that the *World* is one of the few papers which has pointed out the sinister significance of this decision.

For the present, the Espionage Act of 1918 has been repealed. But there is no guarantee that it may not be revived in peacetime and again forbid the publication of "any language intended to bring the form of the government of the United States or the Constitution of the United States . . . into contempt, scorn, contumely, or disrepute." An attack of Mr. Gompers's *Federationist*, or of Mr. Bryan's *Commoner*, upon the power of the Supreme Court to nullify legislation may easily be the basis of a finding by the Postmaster General that they are publications bringing the form of the government of the Constitution of the United States "into disrepute," resulting in denial of second-class rates and consequent guillotining of those papers. Or Colonel Harvey, upon his return from the Court of St. James's, may resume his bizarre editing, and find a Democratic Postmaster General denying him second-class rates for publishing another offending cartoon. Little evidence is necessary to justify the administrative finding, particularly where the finding involves offenses depending on opinion. Administrative partisanship and bigotry are poisons too subtle for detection by the process of appeal. It is for this reason that Mr. Justice Brandeis interprets the power which the Supreme Court has now conferred upon the Postmaster General as one making him "the universal censor of publications."

But there is an even deeper significance, if possible, to this decision than the control which it sanctions over the sources of public opinion. More perhaps than any of the decisions which the war has engendered, it shakes confidence in the judicial process. Again and again behind so-called questions of "statutory construction"—what has Congress said, and what does its language mean, in terms of power?—lurk great issues of policy. Instead of exercising a detached and disinterested calm, the Supreme Court seems to have been torn from its judicial moorings by the passions of the time. For the real basis of the decision apparently is that "a government competent to wage war against its foreign enemies" is not "powerless against its insidious foes at home." "Government" is a large abstraction for a little Burleson.

Against these fallibilities of the Court there is no simple panacea. We must look to a broader and more conscious legal education. "I cannot but believe," Mr. Justice Holmes has told us, "that if the training of lawyers led them habitually to consider more definitely and explicitly social advantages on which the rule they lay down must be justified, they sometimes would hesitate where they now are confident, and see that really they were taking sides upon debatable and often burning questions." Above all, a sustained and informed public opinion must exercise a continuous critique of the decisions of the courts. Roosevelt's "recall of judicial decisions" was an inadequate mechanical recognition of the truth that the Supreme Court is not apart from, but a part of, our national life. The extent of the public understanding of what the Supreme Court does, and how the Court does it, will largely determine the Supreme Court's responsiveness to the best traditions and the deepest needs of the country.

Károlyi, Kellogg, and Coolidge

This selection appeared as an unsigned editorial in the New Republic *for December 2, 1925.*

IRRESPONSIBILITY is perhaps the chief characteristic of the Coolidge administration. The public accountability of the President which was implied in Roosevelt's outspokenness was respected even by Taft, Wilson, and Harding. These Presidents partly relied on publicity for their policies and partly responded to an active public curiosity about public affairs. Mr. Coolidge has systematically muffled the public mind and denied official responsibility in action. By calculated taciturnity and the irresponsible anonymity of the official White House spokesman, public apathy has been cultivated and questionable conduct screened. These basic vices for a democratic society have spread from the White House and infected the whole administration. A complacent press completes the mischief.

A striking illustration of the whole color of the Coolidge régime is furnished by the Károlyi incident. The granddaughter of Count Andrassy, one of the great European statesmen of the nineteenth century, herself a woman of distinction, is denied a visa on her passport for the United States, whither she seeks to come to visit friends. The American Consul at Paris refused in fact both a visa and any reason for withholding it. This arbitrary conduct is accentuated by the fact that the only surface cause appears to be the fact that the lady is the wife of Count Michael Károlyi, the first President of the Hungarian Republic, but now under the ban by the Horthy régime. Inquiry at the State department secures at first a vague claim that "the law" compelled refusal. "The White House spokesman," now known by every schoolboy to be Mr. Coolidge, but not speaking with his authority, echoes that "the law" hath said Countess Károlyi must be kept out. Fortunately, the American host of the Countess is a wealthy influential Republican politician whose friendship for the Countess is outraged. He is allowed to appear in the very presence of the Secretary of State to seek a reason for the exclusion. Face to face with simple questions Mr. Kellogg fumbles and falters and finally slips into the honest answer that the department is irritated by the performances of Count Károlyi after his recent visit to America. "The Countess is not the Count," Mr. Strassburger remonstrates, only to be advised by Mr. Kellogg's expert on European affairs that the Countess is really the more influential of the two. Surely feminists should rejoice.

American opinion has been only feeble and flickering against this crass outrage upon one of the most vital doctrines of political liberty. But the Kossuth tradition is strong with the Károlyis. And so the Countess has pressed her case through counsel who are pertinaciously asking questions. Insistent inquiry is the true remedy, for the practice of arbitrariness can only survive if sheltered by secrecy and silence. Mr. James F. Curtis, who was one of Mr. Taft's assistant secretaries of the Treasury, has at last elicited a statement of "the law" under which Mr. Kellogg is acting. . . .

The two Acts now relied on by the department are accurately described by their titles. The Act of May 22, 1918, was "an act to prevent in time of war departure from or entry into the United States contrary to the public safety." This Act was extended on March 2, 1921, at which time we were at least technically still at war with Germany in the sense that a treaty of peace had not formally terminated war. Will Mr. Coolidge step out of the anonymity of the White House spokesman and say in his own person that the denial of the visa to the Countess Károlyi was required or justified, "to prevent in time of war" entry by Countess Károlyi into the United States because it would be "contrary to the public safety"?

The Act of October 16, 1918, was "an act to exclude and expel from the United States aliens who are members of the anarchistic and similar classes." Again we invite President Coolidge to abandon his irresponsible anonymity and say on the responsibility of his office that the Countess Károlyi is a member of "the anarchistic" or "similar classes." The Act of June 5, 1920, greatly extended the prohibited classes of dangerous aliens. It is the most extreme legislation against opinion ever enacted by Congress. It makes the Alien and Sedition Laws of 1797 seem like poor instruments of repression. "This statute," wrote John Lord O'Brian in 1920, "carries the doctrine of constructive knowledge and imputed guilt far beyond any view hitherto entertained by an American court or legislative body and presents a distinct anomaly in our jurisprudence." But, broad as the statute is, no candid mind acting on facts instead of on undisclosed prejudice can possibly bring the Countess Károlyi within its tentacles. Who are excluded?

(a) "Anarchists." Let President Coolidge or Secretary Kellogg say in downright English that Countess Károlyi is an anarchist.

(b) "Aliens . . . who are affiliated with any organization . . . that advises opposition to all organized government." Let President Coolidge or Secretary Kellogg charge Countess Károlyi with any such membership.

(c) "Aliens . . . who are members affiliated with any organization . . . that believes in . . . (1) the overthrow by force of the government of the United States or of all forms of law, or (2) the unlawful killing of any officer of the United States or of any other organized government, or (3) the unlawful damage of property, or (4) sabotage." Let President Coolidge or Secretary Kellogg charge Countess Károlyi explicitly with membership in any organization devoted to these purposes.

(d) "Aliens who write or knowingly have in their possession any printed matter advocating (1), (2), (3), or (4) just enumerated." Let President Coolidge or Mr. Kellogg charge Countess Károlyi with conduct violative of this provision if the facts warrant.

(e) "Aliens who are affiliated with any organization that prints or has in its possession any printed matter of the character described under subdivision (d)." Will President Coolidge or Mr. Kellogg name the offensive organization to which the Countess belongs?

No evidence implicating the Countess has been forthcoming, although her life has been raked fore and aft by the minions of espionage. Nothing has been vouchsafed by the President or the Secretary of State except their *ipse dixits* and their pious references to "law." But with us the law is still particular and defined and not merely the unregulated will of a Mussolini. Broad as is the Act of June 5, 1920, it looks in its ordinary course to enforcement through the immigration authorities. That gives assurances of an orderly procedure, before administrative authorities, summary though it be, with recourse to the courts to curb at least gross abuse of discretion and to assure some evidence for the ruling of the Immigration Officers. No such safeguards whatever restrict the arbitrary whim of the Secretary of State in granting or withholding visas. There is no way of haling him before the court. An alien at our gates can invoke habeas corpus. The Countess Károlyi in Paris is dependent exclusively upon the sensitiveness of American opinion to traditional standards of liberty.

President Coolidge in his recent Omaha address reaffirmed our professed allegiance to those historic safeguards which are enshrined in the bills of rights and those practices of tolerance which are deemed synonymous with American freedom. His utterance to the Legionnaires is worse than hollow so long as he continues to tolerate arbitrary conduct by his Secretary of State and so long as he sanctions it by his own anonymous approval. While Mr. Coolidge merely voiced the views expressed in his series of articles on the Reds in our women's colleges a Károlyi incident was consistent with his philosophy. But in the light of his Omaha speech, his failure to correct the Károlyi exclusion borders close on hypocrisy. The President's consistency is a matter for his own conscience. But tolerance of arbitrary conduct, such as that of Secretary Kellogg, sheltered behind a false claim of law, touches vitally the whole foundation of our political structure. We commend to his party associates the words of a distinguished Republican, Mr. John Lord O'Brian, in commenting on the Act of 1920, although Mr. O'Brian was not dealing with so outrageous a misuse of the Act as exemplified by the Károlyi case.

"Nothing so quickly undermined public confidence in government as the exercise of arbitrary power. Arrogance in a nation is as serious a moral defect as it is in an individual."

The Case of Sacco and Vanzetti

This article, which is reprinted verbatim *from the* Atlantic Monthly *for March, 1927, brought the* cause célèbre *of* Sacco and Vanzetti *into national prominence. Shortly afterwards Mr. Frankfurter expanded the article into a book of the same name,* The Case of Sacco and Vanzetti (*1927*).

FOR MORE than six years the Sacco-Vanzetti case has been before the courts of Massachusetts. In a state where ordinary murder trials are promptly dispatched such extraordinary delay in itself challenges attention. The fact is that a long succession of disclosures has aroused interest far beyond the boundaries of Massachusetts and even of the United States, until the case has become one of those rare *causes célèbres* which are of international concern. The aim of this paper is to give in the briefest compass an accurate résumé of the facts of the case from its earliest stages to its present posture.

I

At about three o'clock in the afternoon of April 15, 1920, Parmenter, a paymaster, and Berardelli, his guard, were fired upon and killed by two men armed with pistols as they were carrying two boxes containing the pay roll of the shoe factory of Slater and Morrill, amounting to $15,776.51, from the company's office building to the factory through the main street of South Braintree, Massachusetts. As the murder was being committed, a car containing several other men drew up to the spot. The murderers threw the two boxes into the car, jumped in themselves, and were driven away at high speed across some near-by railroad tracks. Two days later this car was found abandoned in woods at a distance from the scene of the crime.

At the time of the Braintree holdup the police were investigating a similar crime in the neighboring town of Bridgewater. In both cases a gang was involved. In both they made off in a car. In both eyewitnesses believed the criminals to be Italians. In the Bridgewater holdup the car had left the scene in the direction of Cochesett. Chief Stewart of Bridgewater was therefore, at the time of the Braintree murder, on the trail of an Italian owning or driving a car in Cochesett. He found his man in one Boda, whose car was in a garage awaiting repairs. Stewart instructed the garage proprietor to telephone to the police when anyone came to fetch it. Pursuing his theory, Stewart found that Boda had been living in Cochesett with a radical named Coacci. Now on April 16, 1920, which was the day after the Braintree murders, Stewart, at the instance of the Department of Justice, then engaged in the wholesale rounding up of Reds, had been to the house of Coacci to see why he had failed to appear at a hearing regarding his deportation. He found Coacci packing a trunk and apparently very anxious to leave. At the time, Coacci's trunk and his haste to depart for Italy were not connected in Chief Stewart's mind with the Braintree affair. But when, subsequently, the tracks of a smaller car were found near the murder car, he surmised that this car was Boda's; and in the light of his later discoveries he jumped to the conclusion that Coacci, Boda's pal, had "skipped with the swag." As a matter of fact, the contents of the trunk were found eventually to be wholly innocent. In the meantime, however, Chief Stewart continued to work on his theory that whosoever called for Boda's car at Johnson's garage would be suspect of the Braintree crime. On the night of May 5, Boda and three other Italians did in fact call. To explain how they came to do so we must go back a few days.

During the proceedings for the wholesale deportation of Reds under Attorney-General Palmer in the spring of 1920, one Salsedo was held incommunicado in a room in the New York offices of the Department of Justice, on the fourteenth floor of a

Park Row building. This Salsedo was a radical friend of Boda and his companions. On May 4 these friends learned that Salsedo had been found dead on the sidewalk outside the Park Row building. Already frightened by the Red raids, they bestirred themselves to "hide the literature and notify the friends against the federal police." For this purpose an automobile was needed, and they turned to Boda.

Such were the circumstances under which the four Italians appeared on the evening of May 5 at the Johnson garage. Two of them were Sacco and Vanzetti. The car was not available and the Italians left, but the police were notified. Sacco and Vanzetti were arrested on a street car, Boda escaped, and the fourth, Orciani, was arrested the next day.

Chief Stewart at once sought to apply his theory of the commission of the two "jobs" by one gang. The theory, however, broke down. Orciani had been at work on the days of both crimes, so he was let go. Sacco, a shoe operative, in steady employment at 'a shoe factory in Stoughton, had taken a day off, and this was April 15. Hence, while he could not be charged with the Bridgewater crime, he was charged with the Braintree murder. Vanzetti, as a fish peddler at Plymouth and his own employer, could not give the same kind of alibi for either day and so he was held for both crimes. Stewart's theory that the crime was committed by these Italian radicals was not shared by the head of the State Police, who always maintained that it was the work of professionals.[1]

Charged with the crime of murder on May 5, Sacco and Vanzetti were indicted on September 14, 1920, and put on trial May 21, 1921, at Dedham, Norfolk County. The setting of the trial, in the courthouse opposite the old home of Fisher Ames, furnished a striking contrast to the background and antecedents of the prisoners. Dedham is a quiet residential suburb, inhabited by well-to-do Bostonians, with a surviving element of New England

---

[1] In this account of the joint trial of Sacco and Vanzetti the details of Vanzetti's separate trial cannot find a place. But Vanzetti's prosecution for the Bridgewater job was merely a phase of the South Braintree affair.

small farmers. Part of the jury was specially selected by the sheriff's deputies from Masonic gatherings and from persons whom the deputies deemed "representative citizens," "substantial" and "intelligent." The presiding judge was Webster Thayer of Worcester. The chief counsel for these Italians was a Westerner, a radical and a professional defender of radicals. In opinion, as well as in fact, he was an outsider. Unfamiliar with the traditions of the Massachusetts bench, not even a member of the Massachusetts bar, the characteristics of Judge Thayer unknown to him, Fred H. Moore found neither professional nor personal sympathies between himself and the Judge. So far as the relations between court and counsel seriously, even if unconsciously, affect the current of a trial, Moore was a factor of irritation. Sacco and Vanzetti spoke very broken English and their testimony shows how often they misunderstood the questions put to them. In fact, an interpreter had to be used, whose conduct raised such doubts that the defendants brought their own interpreter to check his questions and answers. The trial lasted nearly seven weeks, and on July 14, 1921, Sacco and Vanzetti were found guilty of murder in the first degree.

II

So far as the crime is concerned, we are dealing with a conventional case of pay-roll robbery. At the trial the killing of Parmenter and Berardelli was undisputed. The only issue was the identity of the murderers. Were Sacco and Vanzetti two of the assailants of Parmenter and Berardelli, or were they not?

On this issue there was at the trial a mass of conflicting evidence. Fifty-nine witnesses testified for the Commonwealth and ninety-nine for the defendants. The evidence offered by the Commonwealth was not the same against both defendants. The theory of the prosecution was that Sacco did the actual shooting while Vanzetti sat in the car as one of the collaborators in a conspiracy to murder. Witnesses testified to having seen both defendants in South Braintree on the morning of April 15; they claimed to recognize Sacco as the man who shot the guard Berardelli and to have seen him subsequently escape in the car. Expert testimony (the character of which, in the light of subsequent events, constitutes one of the most important features of the case and will be dealt with later) was offered seeking to connect one of four bullets removed from Berardelli's body with the Colt pistol found on Sacco at the time of his arrest. As to Vanzetti, the Commonwealth adduced evidence placing him in the murder car. Moreover, the Commonwealth introduced the conduct of the defendants, as evinced by pistols found on their persons and lies admittedly told by them when arrested, as further proof of identification, in that such conduct revealed "consciousness of guilt."

The defense met the Commonwealth's eyewitnesses by other eyewitnesses, slightly more numerous and at least as well circumstanced to observe the assailants, who testified that the defendants were not the men they saw. Their testimony was confirmed by witnesses who proved the presence of Sacco and Vanzetti elsewhere at the time of the murder. Other witnesses supported Sacco's testimony that on April 15—the day that he was away from work—he was in Boston seeing about a passport to Italy, whither he was planning shortly to return to visit his recently bereaved father. The truth of that statement was supported by an official of the Italian consulate in Boston who deposed that Sacco visited his consulate at an hour that made it impossible for him to have been one of the Braintree murder gang. The claim of Vanzetti that on April 15 he was pursuing his customary trade as fish peddler was sustained by a number of witnesses who had been his customers that day.

From this summary it must be evident that the trustworthiness of the testimony which placed Sacco and Vanzetti in South Braintree on April 15 is the foundation of the case.

I. As to Sacco:

The character of the testimony of the five witnesses who definitely identified Sacco as in the car or on the spot at the time of the murders demands critical attention. These witnesses were

Mary Splaine, Frances Devlin, Lola Andrews, Louis Pelzer, Carlos E. Goodridge.

1. Splaine and Devlin were working together on the second floor of the Slater and Morrill factory with windows giving on the railroad crossing about sixty feet away. Both heard the shot, ran to the window, and saw an automobile crossing the tracks. Splaine's identification of Sacco as one of the occupants of this escaping car was one of the chief reliances of the prosecution. Viewing the scene from a distance of from sixty to eighty feet, she saw a man previously unknown to her in a car traveling at the rate of from fifteen to eighteen miles per hour, and she saw him only for a distance of about thirty feet—that is to say, for from one and a half to three seconds. Yet after more than a year she testified:

The man that appeared between the back of the front seat and the back seat was a man slightly taller than the witness. He weighed possibly from 140 to 145 pounds. He was muscular, an active-looking man. His left hand was a good-sized hand, a hand that denoted strength. *Q.* So that the hand you said you saw where? *A.* The left hand, that was placed on the back of the front seat. He had a gray, what I thought was a shirt—had a grayish, like navy color, and the face was what we would call clear-cut, clean-cut face. Through here [indicating] was a little narrow, just a little narrow. The forehead was high. The hair was brushed back and it was between, I should think, two inches and two and one-half inches in length and had dark eyebrows, but the complexion was a white, peculiar white that looked greenish. *Q.* Is that the same man you saw at Brockton? *A.* It is. *Q.* Are you sure? *A.* Positive.

The startling acuity of Splaine's vision was, as a matter of fact, the product of a year's reflection. Immediately after Sacco's arrest the police, in violation of approved police methods for the identification of suspects, brought Sacco alone into Splaine's presence. Then followed in about three weeks the preliminary hearing at which Sacco and Vanzetti were bound over for the grand jury. At this hearing—only forty days after the crime—Splaine was unable to identify Sacco.

Q. You don't feel certain enough in your position to say he is the man? *A.* I don't think my opportunity afforded me the right to say he is the man.

When confronted with this contradiction between her uncertainty a month after her observation and her certainty more than a year after her observation, she first took refuge in a claim of inaccuracy in the transcript of the stenographer's minutes. This charge she later withdrew and finally maintained:

From the observation I had of him in the Quincy court and the comparison of the man I saw in the machine, on reflection I was sure he was the same man.

Then followed this cross-examination:

Q. Your answer in the lower court was you didn't have opportunity to observe him. What did you mean when you said you didn't have opportunity sufficient, kindly tell us, you didn't have sufficient opportunity to observe him? *A.* Well, he was passing on the street.

Q. He was passing on the street and you didn't have sufficient opportunity to observe him to enable you to identify him? *A.* That is what I meant.

Q. That is the only opportunity you had? *A.* Yes, sir.

Q. You have had no other opportunity but that one fleeting glance? *A.* The remembrance of that.

Let Dr. Morton Prince, professor of dynamic psychology at Harvard University, comment on this testimony:

I do not hesitate to say that the star witness for the government testified, honestly enough, no doubt, to what was psychologically impossible. Miss Splaine testified, though she had only seen Sacco at the time of the shooting from a distance of about sixty feet for from one and one-half to three seconds in a motor car going at an increasing rate of speed at about fifteen to eighteen miles an hour; that she saw and at the end of a year she remembered and described sixteen different details of his person, even to the size of his hand, the length of his hair as being between two and two and one-half inches long, and the shade of his eyebrows! Such perception and memory under such conditions can be easily proved to be psychologically impossible. Every psychologist knows that—so does Houdini. And what shall we think of the animus and honesty of the state that introduces such testimony to convict, knowing that the jury is too ignorant to disbelieve?

2. Devlin, at Quincy a month after the murder, merely said, "He [Sacco] looks very much like the man that stood up in the back seat shooting."

Q. Do you say positively he is the man? *A.* I don't say positively.

At the trial, over a year later, she had no doubt and when asked, "Have you at any time had any doubt of your identification of this man?" replied, "No." The obvious discrepancy of an identification reaching certainty by lapse of time, without any additional opportunity for verification, she explained thus: "At the time there I had in my own mind that he was the man, but on account of the immensity of the crime and everything, I hated to say right out and out."

The inherent improbability of making any such accurate identification on the basis of a fleeting glimpse of an unknown man in the confusion of a sudden alarm is affirmed by the testimony of two other eyewitnesses. Ferguson and Pierce, from a window above Splaine and Devlin, on the next floor of the factory, had substantially the same view. They found it impossible to make any identification.

3. Pelzer, a young shoe-cutter, swore that when he heard the shooting he pulled up his window, took a glance at the scene, and saw the man who murdered Berardelli.

Q. How long did you stay in the window? *A.* Oh, about—I would say about a minute. . . .

Q. Then what did you do? *A.* I seen everything happen about that time, about in a minute.

This was the foundation for the following identification:

Q. Do you see in the courtroom the man you saw shooting Berardelli that day? *A.* Well, I wouldn't say it was him, but he is a dead image of him.

Witness points out Mr. Sacco.

Q. Have you seen him since that time until you saw him in the court-room? *A.* No, sir.

Witness was shown picture of him by Mr. Williams today.

Q. You say you wouldn't say it is him, but he is the dead image of him? What do you mean by that? *A.* Well, he has got the same appearance.

On cross-examination Pelzer admitted that immediately after Sacco's arrest, on May 6 or 7, he was unable to make any identification. His inability in May, 1920, to make the identification which he made in June, 1921, was confirmed by three fellow workmen. Two of them testified that instead of pulling up the window he took shelter under a bench, and the third in addition said: "I heard him say that he did not see anybody."

Pelzer's tergiversations and falsifications extracted from the District Attorney, Mr. Katzmann, the following eulogy:

He was frank enough here, gentlemen, to own that he had twice falsified before to both sides, treating them equally and alike, and he gave you his reason. I think he added that he had never been in court before. If not, somebody has and I confused him. It is of little consequence. He is big enough and manly enough now to tell you of his prior falsehoods and his reasons for them. If you accept them, gentlemen, give such weight to his testimony as you say should be given.

4. Lola Andrews, a woman of doubtful reputation, testified that at about 11 A.M. on the day of the murders, while in company with a Mrs. Campbell, she saw an automobile standing outside the Slater and Morrill factory. She saw a "very light" man inside the car (concededly neither Sacco nor Vanzetti) and another man "bending over the hood of the car," whom she characterized as a "dark-complexioned man." She went into the factory in search of a job and at the time "had no talk with either of the men." When she came out "fifteen minutes later" the dark man "was down under the car like he was fixing something" and she asked him the way to another factory. He told her. That was the whole conversation between them. After Sacco's arrest she was taken to the Dedham jail and identified Sacco as the dark-complexioned man. She again identified him at the trial.

How came she to connect the dark man under the car with the murders which took place four hours later?

Q. Would you say that the man had a fuller or more slender face [than the man in a photograph shown to the witness]? *A.* I don't know. He had a funny face. . . .

Q. Meaning by that a face that was not a kindly face, a kind of brutal face? *A.* He did not have a real good-looking face.

Q. (by the District Attorney). What came to your mind, if anything, when you learned of the shooting? . . . *A.* Why, the only way I can answer that is this: When I heard of the shooting I somehow associated the man I saw at the car.

Four reputable witnesses completely discredited the Andrews testimony. The following sample must suffice. It is the testimony of a Quincy shopkeeper.

I said to her, "Hello, Lola," and she stopped and she answered me. While she answered me I said, "You look kind of tired." She says, "Yes." She says, "They are bothering the life out of me." I says, "What?" She says, "I just come from jail." I says, "What have you done in jail?" She says, "The government took me down and want me to recognize those men," she says, "and I don't know a thing about them. I have never seen them and I can't recognize them." She says, "Unfortunately I have been down there to get a job and I have seen many men that I don't know and I have never paid any attention to anyone."

Yet the District Attorney not only offered the Andrews testimony for the consideration of the jury, but gave it the weightiest possible personal sponsorship:

And then there is Lola Andrews. I have been in this office, gentlemen, for now more than eleven years. I cannot recall in that too long service for the Commonwealth that ever before I have laid eye or given ear to so convincing a witness as Lola Andrews.

5. Carlos E. Goodridge (who after the trial was discovered to be a fugitive from justice in another state and to have given evidence under a false name) swore that at the time of the shooting he was in a poolroom in South Braintree, heard shots, stepped to

the door, and saw an automobile coming toward him, and that when he got to the sidewalk a man in the automobile "poked a gun over towards him," whereupon he "went back into the pool-room." About seven months later he identified Sacco as the man for the first time and identified him again at the trial.

Four witnesses, including his employer, squarely contradicted Goodridge's belated identification. Even when completely disinterested, identification testimony runs all the grave hazards due to the frailties and fallibilities of human observation and memory. But Goodridge's testimony, in addition to everything else, was tainted with self-interest. At the time he was a witness for the Commonwealth, he was facing jail under an indictment for larceny to which he had pleaded guilty. The case "had been filed" —that is, no sentence had been imposed—and Goodridge had been placed on probation. The Judge did not allow the defense to show that Goodridge's testimony on behalf of the Commonwealth was influenced by leniency previously shown to him by the District Attorney in connection with the confessed charge of larceny and by fear of losing his immunity. In the light of settled principles of the law of evidence, this ruling, though later sustained by the Supreme Court of Massachusetts, is indefensible.

II. As to Vanzetti:

The Commonwealth offered two witnesses who claimed to identify Vanzetti as an occupant of the murder car. Of these one, Dolbeare, claimed to have seen him hours before the murder, leaving only a single individual, LeVangie, who claimed to have seen him on the spot. The Commonwealth sought to piece out the tenuous testimony by the evidence of two other witnesses who claimed to have seen Vanzetti during the day of the murder elsewhere than at Plymouth, but not at South Braintree. One witness, Faulkner, testified to recollecting a fellow passenger on a train going from Cochesett to Boston who got out at East Braintree at 9:54, and identified Vanzetti as that passenger. The basis of Faulkner's recollection was so frail, and was so fully destroyed by three railroad officials, that further recital of his testimony is superfluous. Finally Reed, a crossing tender, purported to recognize Vanzetti as the man sitting on the front seat of a car which he claimed to identify as the murder car. This was at some distance from Braintree, more than an hour after the murders. Reed's testimony placing Vanzetti on the front seat of the car ran counter to the theory of the Commonwealth that Vanzetti was at the rear. Moreover, Reed testified that "the quality of the English [of Vanzetti] was unmistakable and clear," while at the trial Vanzetti's English was found to be so imperfect that an interpreter had to be employed.

1. Harry E. Dolbeare testified that somewhere between 10 and 12 A.M. he saw a car going past him in South Braintree with five people in it, one of whom he identified as Vanzetti:

I felt it was a tough-looking bunch. That is the very feeling that came to my mind at the time. . . . I guess that is all. That is all I recall now.

There is nothing other than what he has already given by which he characterizes these men as a tough-looking bunch. He does not know whether the other two men who sat on the back seat had mustaches or beards of any kind. He does not know what kind of a hat or cap the man in the middle, who leaned forward to speak, wore. He does not know whether this man had a cap with a visor projecting out or whether he had on a slouch hat.

2. LeVangie, the gate tender of the New Haven Railroad, was on duty at the South Braintree grade crossing on the day of the murder. According to his testimony, the murder car drove up to the crossing just as he was lowering the gate, and a man inside forced him at the point of a revolver to let the car through before the advancing train. LeVangie identified Vanzetti as the man who was driving the car. LeVangie's testimony was discredited by the testimony of McCarthy, a locomotive fireman of the New Haven, who testified that three-quarters of an hour after the murders he had the following conversation with LeVangie:

LeVangie said, "There was a shooting affair going on." I says, "Someone shot?" I says, "Who?" "Someone, a fellow got murdered." I said, "Who did it?" He said he did not know. He said there was some fellows went by in an automobile and he heard the shots, and he started to put down the gates, and as he started to put them down one of them pointed a gun at him, and he left the gates alone and ducked in the shanty. I asked him if he knew them. He said, no, he did not. I asked him if he would know them again if he saw them. He said, "No." He said all he could see was the gun and he ducked.

Moreover, LeVangie was discredited by all the other identification witnesses on both sides, who insisted that the driver of the car was a young, small, light-haired man, whereas Vanzetti was middle-aged, dark, with a black mustache. But, though the District Attorney had to repudiate LeVangie, he characteristically held on to LeVangie's identification. The following quotation from the District Attorney's summing up reveals the worthlessness of LeVangie's testimony; it throws no less light on the guiding attitude of the prosecution:

They find fault, gentlemen, with LeVangie. They say that LeVangie is wrong in saying that Vanzetti was driving that car. I agree with them, gentlemen. I would not be trying to do justice to these defendants if I pretended that personally so far as you are concerned about my personal belief on that, that Vanzetti drove that car over the crossing. I do not believe any such thing. You must be overwhelmed with the testimony that when the car started it was driven by a light-haired man who showed every indication of being sickly.

We cannot mold the testimony of witnesses, gentlemen. We have got to take them as they testify on their oath, and we put LeVangie on because necessarily he must have been there. He saw something. He described a light-haired man to some of the witnesses. They produced Carter, the first witness they put on, to say that he said the light-haired man—the driver was a light-haired man. That is true. I believe my brothers will agree with me on that proposition, but he saw the face of Vanzetti in that car, and is his testimony to be rejected if it disagrees with everybody else if you are satisfied he honestly meant to tell the truth?

And can't you reconcile it with the possibility, no, the likelihood, or, more than that, the probability that at that time Vanzetti was directly behind the driver in the quick glance this man LeVangie had of the car going over when they were going up over the crossing? . . .

Right or wrong, we have to take it as it is. And I agree if it depends on the accuracy of the statement that Vanzetti was driving, then it isn't right, because I would have to reject personally the testimony of witnesses for the defense as well as for the Commonwealth who testified to the contrary. I ask you to find as a matter of common sense he was, in the light of other witnesses, in the car, and if on the left side that he may well have been immediately behind the driver.

In other words, obliged to repudiate the testimony of LeVangie that Vanzetti was on the front seat, the Commonwealth urged the jury to find that, although LeVangie said Vanzetti was on the front seat, he meant he was on the back seat.

At the time that he urged on the jury this testimony of LeVangie, the District Attorney had held interviews with, and had in his possession written statements of, the only two persons, Kelly and Kennedy, who had an extended opportunity to observe the driver of the car. The detailed description given by them absolutely excluded Vanzetti. The reliability of these observers and of their statements has not been challenged. Yet they were not called by the District Attorney; instead he called LeVangie. Unfortunately the existence of Kelly and Kennedy was until very recently unknown to the defense, and of course, therefore, their testimony was unavailable for Sacco and Vanzetti at the trial.

The alibi for Vanzetti was overwhelming. Thirty-one eye-witnesses testified positively that no one of the men that they saw in the murder car was Vanzetti. Thirteen witnesses either testified directly that Vanzetti was in Plymouth selling fish on the day of the murder or furnished corroboration of such testimony.

What is the worth of identification testimony even when uncontradicted? The identification of strangers is proverbially untrustworthy. The hazards of this type of testimony are established by a formidable number of instances in the records of English and American trials. These instances are recent—not due to the brutalities of ancient criminal procedure.

In the Sacco-Vanzetti case the elements of uncertainty were intensified. All the identifying witnesses were speaking from casual observation of men they had never seen before, men of foreign race, under circumstances of unusual confusion. Thus, one witness, Cole, "thought at the first glance that the man was a Portuguese fellow named Tony that he knew." Afterward he was sure it was Vanzetti. Nor can we abstain from comment on the methods pursued by the police in eliciting subsequent identification. The recognized procedure is to line up the suspect with others, and so far as possible with individuals of the same race and class, so as not to provoke identification through accentuation. In defiance of these necessary safeguards, Sacco and Vanzetti after their arrest were shown singly to persons brought there for the purposes of identification, not as part of a "parade." Moreover, Sacco and Vanzetti were not even allowed to be their natural selves; they were compelled to simulate the behavior of the Braintree bandits. Under such conditions identification of foreigners is a farce.

After the conviction Judge Thayer himself abandoned the identification of Sacco and Vanzetti as the ground on which the jury's verdict rested. In denying a motion for a new trial, based on the discovery of a new eyewitness with better opportunities for observation than any of the other witnesses on either side, who, in his affidavit, swore that Sacco was not the man in the car, Judge Thayer ruled that this evidence

would simply mean one more piece of evidence of the same kind and directed to the same end, and in my judgment would have no effect whatever upon the verdicts. These verdicts did not rest, in my judgment, upon the testimony of the eyewitnesses, for the defendants, as it was, called more witnesses than the Commonwealth to testify that neither of the defendants were in the bandit car.

The evidence that convicted these defendants was circumstantial and was evidence that is known in law as "consciousness of guilt."

III

"Consciousness of guilt" meant that the conduct of Sacco and Vanzetti after April 15 was the conduct of murderers. This inference of guilt was drawn from their behavior on the night of May 5, before and after arrest, and also from their possession of firearms. It is vital to keep in mind the evidence on which, according to Judge Thayer, these two men are to be sentenced to death. There was no claim whatever at the trial, and none has ever been suggested since, that Sacco and Vanzetti had any prior experience in holdups or any previous association with bandits; no claim that the $16,000 taken from the victims ever found its way into their pockets; no claim that their financial condition or that of Sacco's family (he had a wife and child, and another child was soon to be born) was in any way changed after April 15; no claim that after the murder either Sacco or Vanzetti changed his manner of living or employment. Neither of these men had ever been accused of crime before their arrest. Nor did they during the three weeks between the murder and their arrest behave like men who were concealing the crime of murder. They did not go into hiding; they did not abscond with the spoils; they did not live under assumed names. They maintained their old lodgings; they pursued openly their callings within a few miles of the town where they were supposed to have committed murder in broad daylight; and when arrested Sacco was found to have in his pocket an announcement of a forthcoming meeting at which Vanzetti was to speak. Was this the behavior of men eluding identification?

What, then, was the evidence of guilty conduct against them?

1. Sacco and Vanzetti, as we have already explained, were two of four Italians who called for Boda's car at Johnson's garage on the evening of May 5. Mrs. Johnson gave the pretext of having to fetch some milk and went to a neighbor's house to telephone the police. She testified that the two defendants followed her to the house on the opposite side of the street, and when, after telephoning, she reappeared they followed her back. The men then left without taking the car, having been advised by Mr. Johnson not to run it without the current year's number plate.

Q. Now, Boda came there to get his car, didn't he? *A.* Yes.
Q. There were no 1920 number plates on it? *A.* No.
Q. You advised him not to take the car and run it without the 1920 number plates, didn't you? *A.* Yes.

Q. And he accepted your view? *A.* He seemed to.

Q. He seemed to. And after some conversation went away? *A.* Yes.

This was the whole of the testimony on the strength of which Judge Thayer put the following question to the jury:

Did the defendants, in company with Orciani and Boda, leave the Johnson house because the automobile had no 1920 number plates on it, or because they were conscious of or became suspicious of what Mrs. Johnson did in the Bartlett house? If they left because they had no 1920 number plates on the automobile, then you may say there was no consciousness of guilt in consequence of their sudden departure, but if they left because they were consciously guilty of what was being done by Mrs. Johnson in the Bartlett house, then you may say that is evidence tending to prove consciousness of guilt.

2. Following their departure from the Johnson house, Sacco and Vanzetti were arrested by a policeman who boarded their street car as it was coming into Brockton. Three policemen testified as to their behavior after being taken into custody. The following will serve as a sample:

I told them when we started that the first false move I would put a bullet in them. On the way up to the station Sacco reached his hand to put under his overcoat and I told him to keep his hands outside of his clothes and on his lap.

Q. Will you illustrate to the jury how he placed his hands? *A.* He was sitting down with his hands that way [indicating], and he moved his hand up to put it in under his overcoat.

Q. At what point? *A.* Just about the stomach there, across his waistband, and I says to him, "Have you got a gun there?" He says, "No." He says, "I ain't got no gun." "Well," I says, "keep your hands outside of your clothes." We went along a little further and he done the same thing. I gets up on my knees on the front seat and I reaches over and I puts my hand under his coat, but I did not see any gun. "Now," I says, "Mister, if you put your hand in there again, you are going to get into trouble." He says, "I don't want no trouble."

3. In statements made to the District Attorney and to the Chief of Police at the police station after their arrest, both Sacco and Vanzetti lied. By misstatements they tried to conceal their move-

ments on the day of their arrest, the friends they had been to see, the places they had visited. For instance, Vanzetti denied that he knew Boda.

What of this evidence of "consciousness of guilt"? The testimony of the police that Sacco and Vanzetti were about to draw pistols was emphatically denied by them. These denials, it was urged, were confirmed by the inherent probabilities of the situation. Did Sacco and Vanzetti upon arrest reveal the qualities of the perpetrators of the Braintree murders? Would the ready and ruthless gunmen at Braintree have surrendered themselves so quietly into custody on a capital charge of which they knew themselves to be guilty? If Sacco and Vanzetti were the holdup men of Braintree, why did they not draw upon their expert skill and attempt to make their escape by scattering shots? But, not being gunmen, why should Sacco and Vanzetti have carried guns? The possession of firearms in this country has not at all the significance that it would have, say, in England. The extensive carrying of guns by people who are not "gunmen" is a matter of common knowledge. Sacco acquired the habit of carrying a pistol while a night watchman in the shoe factory, because, as his employer testified, "night watchmen protecting property do have guns." Vanzetti carried a revolver "because it was a very bad time, and I like to have a revolver for self-defense."

Q. How much money did you use to carry around with you? *A.* When I went to Boston for fish, I can carry eighty, one hundred dollars, one hundred and twenty dollars.

There were many crimes, many holdups, many robberies at that time.

The other evidence from which "consciousness of guilt" was drawn the two Italians admitted. They acknowledged that they behaved in the way described by Mrs. Johnson; and freely conceded that when questioned at the police station they told lies. What was their explanation of this conduct? To exculpate themselves of the crime of murder they had to disclose elaborately their guilt of radicalism. In order to meet the significance which the prosecution attached to the incidents at the Johnson house and

those following, it became necessary for the defendants to adver-
tise to the jury their offensive radicalism, and thereby to excite
the deepest prejudices of a Norfolk County jury picked for its
respectability and sitting in judgment upon two men of alien blood
and abhorrent philosophy.

Innocent men, it is suggested, do not lie when picked up by
the police. But Sacco and Vanzetti knew they were not innocent
of the charge on which they supposed themselves arrested, and
about which the police interrogated them. For, when apprehended, Sacco and Vanzetti were not confronted with the charge
of murder; they were not accused of banditry; they were not
given the remotest intimation that the murders of Parmenter and
Berardelli were laid at their door. They were told they were
arrested as "suspicious characters," and the meaning which that
carried to their minds was rendered concrete by the questions that
were put to them.

Q. Tell us all you recall that Stewart, the chief, asked of you? *A.*
He asked me why we were in Bridgewater, how long I knew Sacco,
if I am a radical, if I am an anarchist or Communist, and he asked me
if I believe in the government of the United States.

Q. Did either Chief Stewart at the Brockton police station or Mr.
Katzmann tell you that you were suspected of robberies and murder?
A. No.

Q. Was there any question asked of you or any statement made to
you to indicate to you that you were charged with that crime on April
15? *A.* No.

Q. What did you understand, in view of the questions asked of you,
what did you understand you were being detained for at the Brockton
police station? *A.* I understand they arrested me for a political matter. . . .

Q. . . . . Why did you feel you were being detained for political
opinions? *A.* Because I was asked if I was a Socialist. I said, "Well—"

Q. You mean by reason of the questions asked of you? *A.* Because
I was asked if I am a Socialist, if I am I.W.W., if I am a Communist,
if I am a Radical, if I am a Black Hand.

Plainly their arrest meant to Sacco and Vanzetti arrest for
radicalism.

Boston was one of the worst centers of the lawlessness and hysteria that characterized the campaign of the Department of Justice for the wholesale arrest and deportation of Reds. Its proximity to industrial communities having a large proportion of foreign labor and a history of past industrial conflicts lent to the lawless activities of the government officials the widespread support of influential public opinion. Mr. John F. Moors, himself a banker, has called attention to the fact that "the hysteria against 'the reds' was so great, at the time when these men were convicted, that even the most substantial bankers in this city [Boston] were carried away to the extent of paying for full-page advertisements about the red peril." Sacco and Vanzetti were notorious Reds. They were associates of leading radicals; they had for some time been on the list of suspects of the Department of Justice; and they were especially obnoxious because they were draft-dodgers.

The terrorizing methods of the government had very specific meaning for the two Italians. Two of their friends had already been deported. The arrest of the New York radical Salsedo, and his detention incommunicado by the Department of Justice, had been for some weeks a source of great concern to them. Vanzetti was sent to New York to confer with a committee having charge of the case of Salsedo and other Italian political prisoners. On his return, May 2, he reported to his Boston friends the advice which had been given him: namely, to dispose of their radical literature and thus eliminate the most damaging evidence in the deportation proceedings they feared. The urgency of acting on this advice was intensified by the tragic news of Salsedo's death after Vanzetti's return from New York. Though Salsedo's death was unexplained, to Sacco and Vanzetti it conveyed only one explanation. It was a symbol of their fears and an omen of their own fate.

On the witness stand Sacco and Vanzetti accounted for their movements on April 15. They also accounted for their ambiguous behavior on May 5. Up to the time that Sacco and Vanzetti testified to their radical activities, their pacifism, their flight to Mexico to avoid the draft, the trial was a trial for murder and banditry; with the cross-examination of Sacco and Vanzetti patriotism and radicalism became the dominant emotional issues. Outside the courtroom the Red hysteria was rampant; it was allowed to dominate within. The prosecutor systematically played on the feelings of the jury by exploiting the unpatriotic and despised beliefs of Sacco and Vanzetti, and the judge allowed him thus to divert and pervert the jury's mind.

The opening question in the cross-examination of Vanzetti by the District Attorney discloses a motif that he persistently played upon:

Q. (by Mr. Katzmann). So you left Plymouth, Mr. Vanzetti, in May, 1917, to dodge the draft, did you? *A.* Yes, sir.

Q. When this country was at war, you ran away, so you would not have to fight as a soldier? *A.* Yes.

This method was elaborated when Sacco took the stand:

Q. (by Mr. Katzmann). Did you say yesterday you love a free country? *A.* Yes, sir.

Q. Did you love this country in the month of May, 1917? *A.* I did not say—I don't want to say I did not love this country.

Q. Did you go to Mexico to avoid being a soldier for this country that you loved? *A.* Yes.

Q. And would it be your idea of showing your love for your wife that, when she needed you, you ran away from her? *A.* I did not run away from her.

Q. Don't you think going away from your country is a vulgar thing to do when she needs you? *A.* I don't believe in war.

Q. You don't believe in war? *A.* No, sir.

Q. Do you think it is a cowardly thing to do what you did? *A.* No, sir.

Q. Do you think it is a brave thing to do what you did? *A.* Yes, sir.

Q. Do you think it would be a brave thing to go away from your own wife? *A.* No.

Q. When she needed you? *A.* No.

The Court. All I ask is this one question, and it will simplify matters very much. Is it your claim that in the collection of the literature and the books and papers that that was done in the interest of the United States?

Mr. Jeremiah McAnarney. I make no such broad claim as that. . . .

Mr. Katzmann. Well, he [Sacco] stated in his direct examination yesterday that he loved a free country, and I offer it to attack that statement made in his examination by his own counsel.

The Court. That is what I supposed, and that is what I supposed that remark meant when it was introduced in this cross-examination, but counsel now say they don't make that claim.

Mr. Katzmann. They say they don't make the claim that gathering up the literature on May 5 at West Bridgewater was for the purpose of helping the country, but that is a different matter, not released [*sic*] to May 5.

The Court. I will let you inquire further first as to what he meant by the expression.

Q. What did you mean when you said yesterday you loved a free country? *A.* Give me a chance to explain.

Q. I am asking you to explain now. *A.* When I was in Italy, a boy, I was a Republican, so I always thinking Republican has more chance to manage education, develop, to build some day his family, to raise the child and education, if you could. But that was my opinion; so when I came to this country I saw there was not what I was thinking before, but there was all the difference, because I been working in Italy not so hard as I been work in this country. I could live free there just as well. Work in the same condition but not so hard, about seven or eight hours a day, better food. I mean genuine. Of course, over here is good food, because it is bigger country, to any those who got money to spend, not for the working and laboring class, and in Italy is more opportunity to laborer to eat vegetable, more fresh, and I came in this country. When I been started work here very hard and been work thirteen years, hard worker, I could not been afford much a family the way I did have the idea before. I could not put any money in the bank; I could no push my boy some to go to school and other things. I teach over here men who is with me. The free idea gives any man a chance to profess his own idea, not the supreme idea, not to give any person, not to be like Spain in position, yes, about twenty centuries ago, but to give a chance to print and education, literature, free speech, that I see it was all wrong. I could see the best men, intelligent, education, they been arrested and sent to prison and died in prison for years and years without getting them out, and Debs, one of the great men in his country, he is in prison, still away in prison, because he is a Socialist. He wanted the laboring class to have better conditions and better living, more education, give a push his son if he could have a chance some day, but they threw him in prison. Why? Because the capitalist class, they know, they are against that, because the capitalist class, they don't want our child to go to high school or college or Harvard College. There would be no chance, there would not be no—they don't want the working class educationed; they want the working class to be a low all the times, be underfoot, and not to be up with the head. So, sometimes, you see, the Rockefellers, Morgans, they give fifty—I mean they give five hundred thousand dollars to Harvard College, they give a million dollars for another school. Every day say, "Well, D. Rockefeller is a great man, the best man in the country." I want to ask him who is going to Harvard College? What benefit the working class they will get by those million dollars they give by Rockefeller, D. Rockefellers. They won't get, the poor class, they won't have no chance to go to Harvard College because men who is getting $21 a week or $30 a week, I don't care if he gets $80 a week, if he gets a family of five children he can't live and send his child and go to Harvard College if he wants to eat everything nature will give him. If he wants to eat like a cow, and that is the best thing, but I want men to live like men. I like men to get everything that nature will give best, because they belong—we are not the friend of any other place, but we are belong to nations. So that is why my idea has been changed. So that is why I love people who labor and work and see better conditions every day develop, makes no more war. We no want fight by the gun, and we don't want to destroy young men. The mother has been suffering for building the young man. Some day need a little more bread, so when the time the mother get some bread or profit out of that boy, the Rockefellers, Morgans, and some of the peoples, high class, they send to war. Why? What is war? The war is not shoots like Abraham Lincoln's and Abe Jefferson, to fight for the free country, for the better education to give chance to any other peoples, not the white people but the black and the others, because they believe and know they are mens like the rest, but they are war for the great millionaire. No war for the civilization of men. They are war for business, million dollars come on the side. What right we have to kill each other? I been work for the Irish. I have been working with the German fellow, with the French, many other peoples. I love them people just as I could love my wife, and my people for that did receive me. Why should I go kill them men? What he done to me? He never done anything, so I don't believe in no war. I want to destroy those guns. All I can say, the government put the literature, give us educations. I remember in Italy, a long time ago, about sixty years ago, I should say, yes, about sixty years ago, the government they could not control very much those two—devilment went on, and robbery, so one of the government in the cabinet he says, "If you want to destroy those devilments, if you want to take off all those criminals, you ought to give a chance to Socialist literature, education of people, emancipation. That is why I destroy governments, boys." That is why my idea I love Socialists. That is why I like people who want education and living, building, who is good, just as much as they could. That is all.

Q. And that is why you love the United States of America? A. Yes.

Q. She is back more than twenty centuries like Spain, is she? A. At the time of the war they do it.

Q. So without the light of knowledge on that subject, you are condemning even Harvard University, are you, as being a place for rich men? . . .

Q. Did you intend to condemn Harvard College? (Objection overruled.) A. No, sir.

Q. Were you ready to say none but the rich could go there without knowing about offering scholarships? (Objection overruled.)

Q. The question is this: As far as you understood Fruzetti's views, were yours the same? (Objection overruled.)

Q. Answer, please. A. (through the interpreter). I cannot say yes or no.

Q. Is it because you can't or because you don't want to? A. (through the interpreter). Because it is a very delicate question.

Q. It is very delicate, isn't it, because he was deported for his views?

Q. Do you know why Fruzetti was deported? A. (through the interpreter). Yes.

Q. Was it because he was of anarchistic opinions?

The Interpreter. He says he understands it now.

Q. Was it because Fruzetti entertained anarchistic opinions? A. One reason, he was an anarchist. Another reason, Fruzetti been writing all the time on the newspapers, and I am not sure why the reason he been deported.

Q. And the books which you intended to collect were books relating to anarchy, weren't they? A. Not all of them.

Q. How many of them? A. Well, all together. We are Socialists, democratic, any other socialistic information, Socialists, Syndicalists, Anarchists, any paper.

Q. Bolshevist? *A.* I do not know what Bolshevism means.

Q. Soviet? *A.* I do not know what Soviet means.

Q. Communism? *A.* Yes. I got some on astronomy too.

Q. You weren't going to destroy them? *A.* I was going to keep them.

Q. You were going to keep them and when the time was over, you were going to bring them out again, weren't you? *A.* Yes.

In the Anglo-American system of criminal procedure the rôle of a public prosecutor is very different from that of an advocate in a private cause. In the words of a leading New York case:

> Language which might be permitted to counsel in summing up a civil action cannot with propriety be used by a public prosecutor, who is a *quasi*-judicial officer, representing the people of the state, and presumed to act impartially in the interest only of justice. If he lays aside the impartiality that should characterize his official action to become a heated partisan, and by vituperation of the prisoner and appeals to prejudice seeks to procure a conviction at all hazards, he ceases to properly represent the public interest, which demands no victim, and asks no conviction through the aid of passion, sympathy, or resentment.

In 1921 the temper of the times made it the special duty of a prosecutor and a court engaged in trying two Italian radicals before a jury of native New Englanders to keep the instruments of justice free from the infection of passion or prejudice. In the case of Sacco and Vanzetti no such restraints were respected. By systematic exploitation of the defendants' alien blood, their imperfect knowledge of English, their unpopular social views, and their opposition to the war, the District Attorney invoked against them a riot of political passion and patriotic sentiment; and the trial judge connived at—one had almost written, co-operated in—the process. To quote the argument of Mr. William G. Thompson:

> The persistent attempt of the court in the presence of the jury to suggest that the defendants were claiming that the suppression of the Socialist literature was "in the interest of the United States," to which exception was taken, was even more objectionable and prejudicial. It

seems incredible that the court could have believed from any testimony that had been given by Vanzetti or Sacco that their purpose in collecting and suppressing the Socialist literature had anything to do with the interest of the United States. *If anything had been made plain, it was that they were actuated by personal fear of sharing the fate of Salsedo, not merely deportation, but death by violence while awaiting deportation.* Yet the court eight times, in the face of as many explicit disclaimers from Mr. McAnarney, suggested that that was the defendants' claim. Had that claim been made it would, of course, have been the grossest hypocrisy, and might well have sealed the fate of both defendants with the jury. The repeated suggestion of the court in the presence of the jury that that *was* the claim amounted to a violation by the court of the defendants' elementary constitutional right to a fair and impartial trial. It was not cured by the court's disclaimer made immediately after the exception was taken to the effect that he did not intend "to prejudice the rights of either of these defendants." Whatever the court intended, he had fatally prejudiced their right to a fair trial, and no general disclaimer could undo the harm.

That the real purpose of this line of the prosecutor's cross-examination was to inflame the jury's passions is suggested by the professed ground on which, with the court's sanction, it was conducted. The Commonwealth claimed that the alleged anxiety of Sacco and Vanzetti on the evening of their arrest and the lies they told could be explained only by the fact that they were the murderers of Parmenter and Berardelli. The defense replied that their conduct was clearly accounted for by the fact that the men were Reds in terror of the Department of Justice. To test the credibility of this answer the District Attorney proposed to examine Sacco and Vanzetti to find out whether they were really radicals or only pretending to be. In effect the Commonwealth undertook to show that the defendants were impostors, that they were spurious Reds. This it made not the least attempt to do. It never disputed their radicalism. Instead of undermining the claim of the defendants by which their conduct was explained, the District Attorney adopted their confession of radicalism, exaggerated and exploited it. He thereby wholly destroyed the basis of his original claim, for what reason was there any longer to suppose that the "consciousness of guilt" was consciousness of murder rather than of radicalism?

I V

The deliberate effort to excite the emotions of jurors still in the grip of war fever is not unparalleled in the legal history of the times. During the year 1918-19 in the United States, forty-four convictions were reversed by appellate courts for misconduct of the trial judge or the public prosecutor; thirty-three of them for inflammatory appeals made by the district attorney on matters not properly before the jury. Appellate courts interfere reluctantly in such cases and only where there has been a flagrant abuse, so that we may safely assume the above figures indicate an even more widespread evil. What *is* unparalleled is that such an abuse should have succeeded in a Massachusetts court.

As things were, what wonder the jury convicted? The last words left with them by Mr. Katzmann were an appeal to their solidarity against the alien: "Gentlemen of the jury, do your duty. Do it like men. Stand together, you men of Norfolk." The first words of Judge Thayer's charge revived their memories of the war and sharpened their indignation against the two draft-dodgers whose fate lay in their hands. "The Commonwealth of Massachusetts called upon you to render a most important service. Although you knew that such service would be arduous, painful, and tiresome, yet you, like the true soldier, responded to that call in the spirit of supreme American loyalty. There is no better word in the English language than 'loyalty.'" It had been to the accompaniment of this same war motif that the jurors were first initiated into the case; by the license allowed to the prosecution it had remained continuously in their ears throughout the trial; and now by the final and authoritative voice of the court it was a soldier's loyalty which was made the measure of their duty.

The function of a judge's charge is to enable the jury to find its way through the maze of conflicting testimony, to sift the relevant from the irrelevant, to weigh wisely, and to judge dispassionately. A trial judge is not expected to rehearse all the testimony; in Massachusetts he is not allowed to express his own opinion on it. But in drawing the disconnected threads of evidence and marshaling the claims on both sides he must exercise a scrupulous regard for relevance and proportion. Misplaced emphasis here and omission there may work more damage than any outspoken comment. By his summing up a judge reveals his estimate of relative importance. Judge Thayer's charge directs the emotions only too clearly. What guidance does he give to the mind? The charge occupies twenty-four pages; of these, fourteen are consumed in abstract legal generalities and moral exhortations. Having allowed the minds of the jurors to be impregnated with war feeling, Judge Thayer now invited them to breathe "a purer atmosphere of unyielding impartiality and absolute fairness." Unfortunately the passion and prejudice instilled during the course of a long trial cannot be exorcised by the general, placid language of a charge after the mischief is done. Every experienced lawyer knows that it is idle to ask jurors to dismiss from their memory what has been deposited in their feelings.

In this case the vital issue was identification. That the whole mass of conflicting identification testimony is dismissed in two pages out of twenty-four is a fair measure of the distorted perspective in which the Judge placed the case. He dealt with identification in abstract terms and without mentioning the name of any witness on either side. The alibi testimony he likewise dismissed in two paragraphs, again without reference to specific witnesses. In striking contrast to this sterile treatment of the issue whether or not Sacco and Vanzetti were in South Braintree on April 15 was his concrete and elaborate treatment of the inferences which might be drawn from the character of their conduct on the night of their arrest. Five pages of the charge are given over to "consciousness of guilt," set forth in great detail and with specific mention of the testimony given by the various police officials and by Mr. and Mrs. Johnson. The disproportionate consideration which Judge Thayer gave to this issue, in the light of his comments during the trial, must have left the impression that the case turned on "consciousness of guilt." As we have seen, Judge Thayer himself did in fact so interpret the jury's verdict afterward.

As to motive, the court expatiated for more than a page on his legal conception and the undisputed claim of the Commonwealth that the motive of the murder of Parmenter and Berardelli was robbery, but made no comment whatever on the complete failure of the Commonwealth to trace any of the stolen money to either defendant or to connect them with the art of robbery. Undoubtedly, great weight must have been attached by the jury, as it was by the court, to the identification of the fatal bullet taken from Berardelli's body as having passed through Sacco's pistol. The court instructed the jury that Captain Proctor and another expert had testified that "it was his [Sacco's] pistol that fired the bullet that caused the death of Berardelli," when in fact that was not Captain Proctor's testimony. Of course, if the jury believed Proctor's testimony as interpreted by Judge Thayer, Sacco certainly was doomed. In view of the temper of the times, the nature of the accusation, the opinions of the accused, the tactics of the prosecution, and the conduct of the Judge, no wonder the "men of Norfolk" convicted Sacco and Vanzetti!

Hitherto the methods pursued by the prosecution, which explain the convictions, rested on inferences, however compelling. But recently facts have been disclosed, and not denied by the prosecution, to indicate that the case against these Italians for murder was part of a collusive effort between the District Attorney and agents of the Department of Justice to rid the country of Sacco and Vanzetti because of their Red activities. In proof of this we have the affidavits of two former officers of the government, one of whom served as post-office inspector for twenty-five years, and both of whom are now in honorable civil employment. Sacco's and Vanzetti's names were on the files of the Department of Justice "as radicals to be watched"; the Department was eager for their deportation, but had not evidence enough to secure it; and inasmuch as the United States District Court for Massachusetts had checked abuses in deportation proceedings, the Department had become chary of resorting to deportation without adequate legal basis. The arrest of Sacco and Vanzetti, on the mistaken theory of Chief Stewart, furnished the agents of the Department their opportunity. Although the opinion of the agents working on the case was that "the South Braintree crime was the work of professionals," and that Sacco and Vanzetti, "although anarchists and agitators, were not highway robbers, and had nothing to do with the South Braintree crime," yet they collaborated with the District Attorney in the prosecution of Sacco and Vanzetti for murder. For "it was the opinion of the Department agents here that a conviction of Sacco and Vanzetti for murder would be one way of disposing of these two men." Here, to be sure, is a startling allegation. But it is made by a man of long years of important service in the government's employ. It is supported by the now admitted installation of a government spy in a cell adjoining Sacco's with a view to "obtaining whatever incriminating evidence he could . . . after winning his confidence"; by the insinuation of an "undercover man" into the councils of the Sacco-Vanzetti Defense Committee; by the proposed placement of another spy as a lodger in Mrs. Sacco's house; and by the supplying of information about the radical activities of Sacco and Vanzetti to the District Attorney by the agents of the Department of Justice.

These joint labors between Boston agents of the Department of Justice and the District Attorney led to a great deal of correspondence between the agent in charge and the District Attorney and to reports between the agents of the Department and Washington. These records have not been made available, nor has their absence been accounted for. An appeal to Attorney-General Sargent proved fruitless, although supported by Senator Butler of Massachusetts, requesting that Mr. West, the then agent in charge, "be authorized to talk with counsel for Sacco and Vanzetti and to disclose whatever documents and correspondence are on file in his office dealing with the investigation made by the Boston agents before, during, and after the trial of Sacco and Vanzetti." The facts upon which this appeal was made stand uncontradicted. West made no denial whatever and the District Attorney only emphasized his failure to deny the facts charged by the two former agents of the Department of Justice by an affidavit confined to a denial of some of the statements of a former government spy. The charge that the principal agent of the Department of Justice in Boston and the District Attorney collaborated to secure the conviction of Sacco and Vanzetti is denied neither by the agent nor by the District Attorney. Chief Stewart of Bridgewater takes it upon himself to say that the officials of the Department "had nothing whatsoever to do with the preparation of this case for trial." Instead of making a full disclosure of the facts, the representative of the Commonwealth indulged in vituperation against the former officers of the Department of Justice as men who were guilty of "a breach of loyalty" because they violated the watchword of the Department of Justice, "Do not betray the secrets of your departments." To which Mr. Thompson rightly replies, "What are the secrets which they admit? . . . A government which has come to value its own secrets more than it does the lives of its citizens has become a tyranny. . . . Secrets, secrets! And he says you should abstain from touching this verdict of your jury because it is so sacred. Would they not have liked to know something about the secrets? The case is admitted by that inadvertent concession. There are, then, secrets to be admitted." Yet Judge Thayer found in these circumstances only opportunity to make innuendo against a former official of the government well known for his long and honorable service, and an elaborate denial of a claim that was never made. Not less than twelve times Judge Thayer ridicules the charge of a conspiracy between "these two great governments—that of the United States and the Commonwealth of Massachusetts"! He indulges in much patriotic protestation, but is wholly silent about the specific acts of wrongdoing and lawlessness connected with the Red raids of 1920. The historian who relied on this opinion would have to assume that the charge of lawlessness and misconduct in the deportations of outlawed radicals was the traitorous invention of a diseased mind.

The verdict of guilty was brought in on July 14, 1921. The exceptions which had been taken to rulings at the trial were made the basis of an application for a new trial, which Judge Thayer refused. Subsequently a great mass of new evidence was unearthed by the defense, and made the subject of other motions for a new trial, all heard before Judge Thayer and all denied by him. The hearing on the later motions took place on October 1, 1923, and was the occasion of the entry into the case of Mr. William G. Thompson, a powerful advocate bred in the traditions of the Massachusetts courts. The espousal of the Sacco-Vanzetti cause by a man of Mr. Thompson's professional prestige at once gave it a new complexion and has been its mainstay ever since. For he has brought to the case, not only his great ability as a lawyer, but the strength of his conviction that these two men are innocent and that their trial was not characterized by those high standards which are the pride of Massachusetts justice.

We have now reached a stage of the case the details of which shake one's confidence in the whole course of the proceedings and reveal a situation which undermines the respect usually to be accorded to a jury's verdict. By prearrangement the prosecution brought before the jury a piece of evidence apparently most damaging to the defendants, when in fact the full truth concerning this evidence was very favorable to them. Vital to the identification of Sacco and Vanzetti as the murderers was the identification of one of the fatal bullets as a bullet coming from Sacco's pistol. The evidence excluded the possibility that five other bullets found in the dead bodies were fired by either Sacco or Vanzetti. When Judge Thayer placed the case in the jury's hands for judgment he charged them that the Commonwealth had introduced the testimony of two experts, Proctor and Van Amburgh, to the effect that the fatal bullet went through Sacco's pistol.

Such was not the belief of Proctor; he refused to accede to this view in the course of the preparation of the case, and the District

Attorney knew that such was not intended to be his testimony. These startling statements call for detailed proof.

Proctor at the time of his testimony was head of the State Police and had been in the Department of Public Safety for twenty-three years. On the witness stand he was qualified at length as an expert who had for twenty years been making examination of, and experiments with, bullets and revolvers and had testified in over a hundred capital cases. His testimony was thus offered by the state as entitled to the greatest weight. If the jury could be convinced that the bullet found in Berardelli's body came out of Sacco's pistol, the state's case was invincible. On this crucial issue Captain Proctor testified as follows at the trial:

Q. Have you an opinion as to whether bullet Number 3 (Exhibit 18) was fired from the Colt automatic, which is in evidence? *A*. I have.
Q. And what is your opinion? *A*. My opinion is that it is consistent with being fired from that pistol.

The government placed chief reliance on his expert testimony. In his closing argument the District Attorney told the jury, "You might disregard all the identification testimony, and base your verdict on the testimony of these experts." It weighed heavily in the court's charge. In simple English he interpreted the evidence to mean that

it was his [Sacco's] pistol that fired the bullet that caused the death of Berardelli. To this effect the Commonwealth introduced the testimony of two witnesses, Messrs. Proctor and Van Amburgh.

Naturally the court's interpretation became the jury's. By their silence the District Attorney and the counsel for the defense acquiesced in the court's interpretation, showing that counsel for both sides apparently attached the same meaning to this testimony. After the conviction Proctor in an affidavit swore to the following account of his true views and the manner in which they were phrased for purposes of the trial. After giving his experience and the fact that he had had the custody of the bullets, cartridges, shells, and pistols in the case, he swore that one of the bullets was, as I then testified and still believe, fired from a Colt automatic pistol of .32 caliber. During the preparation for the trial, my attention was repeatedly called by the District Attorney and his assistants to the question: whether I could find any evidence which would justify the opinion that the particular bullet taken from the body of Berardelli, which came from a Colt automatic pistol, came from the particular Colt automatic pistol taken from Sacco. I used every means available to me for forming an opinion on this subject. I conducted, with Captain Van Amburgh, certain tests at Lowell, about which I testified, consisting in firing certain cartridges through Sacco's pistol. At no time was I able to find any evidence whatever which tended to convince me that the particular model bullet found in Berardelli's body, which came from *a* Colt automatic pistol, which I think was numbered 3 and had some other exhibit number, came from Sacco's pistol, and I so informed the District Attorney and his assistant before the trial. This bullet was what is commonly called a full metal-patch bullet and although I repeatedly talked over with Captain Van Amburgh the scratch or scratches which he claimed tended to identify this bullet as one that must have gone through Sacco's pistol, his statements concerning the identifying marks seemed to me entirely unconvincing.

At the trial, the District Attorney did not ask me whether I had found any evidence that the so-called mortal bullet which I have referred to as Number 3 passed through Sacco's pistol, nor was I asked that question on cross-examination. The District Attorney desired to ask me that question, but I had repeatedly told him that if he did I should be obliged to answer in the negative; consequently, he put to me this question: Q. Have you an opinion as to whether bullet Number 3 was fired from the Colt automatic which is in evidence? To which I answered, "I have." He then proceeded. Q. And what is your opinion? A. My opinion is that it is consistent with being fired by that pistol.

He proceeded to state that he is still of the same opinion:

But I do not intend by that answer to imply that I had found any evidence that the so-called mortal bullet had passed through this particular Colt automatic pistol and the District Attorney well knew that I did not so intend and framed his question accordingly. Had I been asked the direct question: whether I had found any affirmative evidence whatever that this so-called mortal bullet had passed through this particular Sacco's pistol, I should have answered then, as I do now without hesitation, in the negative.

This affidavit of Proctor's was made the basis of Mr. Thompson's motion for a new trial before Judge Thayer. Here was a charge going to the vitals of the case made by a high official of the police agencies of the state. How did the District Attorney meet it? Mr. Katzmann and his assistant, Mr. Williams, filed affidavits in reply. Did they contradict Proctor? They could not deny his testimony or the weight that the prosecution and the court had attached to it. These were matters of record. Did they deny the pre-arrangement which he charged? Did they deny that he told them he was unable to identify the mortal bullet as Sacco's bullet? Katzmann's affidavit stated that

prior to his testifying, Captain Proctor told me that he was prepared to testify that the mortal bullet was consistent with having been fired from the Sacco pistol; that I did not *repeatedly* ask him whether he had found any evidence that the mortal bullet had passed through the Sacco pistol, nor did he *repeatedly* tell me that if I did ask him that question he would be obliged to reply in the negative. [Italics ours.]

Williams's affidavit, after setting forth that Captain Proctor told him before the trial that comparisons of the mortal bullet with bullets "pushed by him through various types of pistols" showed that "the mortal bullet had been fired in *a* Colt automatic pistol," proceeded:

He said that all he could do was to determine the width of the land-marks upon the bullet. His attention was not *repeatedly* called to the question, whether he could find any evidence which would justify the opinion that this bullet came from the Sacco pistol. I conducted the direct examination of Captain Proctor at the trial and asked him the question quoted in his affidavit, "Have you an opinion as to whether bullet Number 3 was fired from the Colt automatic which is in evidence?"

This question was suggested by Captain Proctor himself as best calculated to give him an opportunity to tell what opinion he had respecting the mortal bullet and its connection with the Sacco pistol. His answer in court was the same answer he had given me personally before.

Proctor's disclosures remain uncontradicted: he was unable to identify the murder bullet as Sacco's bullet; he told Katzmann and Williams that he was unable to do it; he told them if he were asked the question on the witness stand he would have to testify that he could not make the identification; a form of words was therefore found by which, without committing perjury, he could convey the impression that he had testified to the identification. The only contradiction by Katzmann and Williams of Proctor's account affects the number of times that he told them that he was unable to make the identification, he having sworn that he told them "repeatedly" and they denying that he told them "repeatedly." Yet Judge Thayer found no warrant in the Proctor incident for directing a new trial. And why?

The Judge quotes the Proctor questions and answers and argues that the questions were clear and must have been perfectly understood by Captain Proctor. Of course the questions were clear and clearly understood by Proctor. The whole meaning of Captain Proctor's affidavit was that the questions and answers were prearranged and that by this prearrangement court and jury were misled with terrible harm to the defendants.

The Judge is extraordinarily versatile in misinterpreting the true purport of the Proctor affidavit. Thus he seriously asks why, if Captain Proctor at the trial was "desirous of expressing his true opinion," he used the phrase "consistent with," language selected by himself. The crux of the matter is that Captain Proctor at the trial was not "desirous of expressing his true opinion," that the District Attorney was very desirous that he should not do so, and that between them they agreed on a form of words to avoid it.

The Judge next attempts to belittle the weight of Proctor's testimony two years after he was offered by the Commonwealth with elaborate reliance as a most important expert. We must dwell on one amazing statement of the court: "With his limited knowledge," says Judge Thayer, "Captain Proctor did not testify that the mortal bullet did pass through Sacco's pistol, but that from his examination of the facts it was simply consistent with it." Why did not Judge Thayer say this to the jury when he charged them with determining the guilt or innocence of Sacco? Why did the Judge charge the jury that Captain Proctor *did* testify that the mortal pullet passed through Sacco's pistol? And why, having in October, 1924, for the purpose of denying the Proctor motion, minimized the Proctor testimony by saying that Proctor testified that the passing of the mortal bullet through Sacco's pistol was "simply consistent with" the facts, does he two years later, in order to show how strong the case was at the original trial, state that the "experts testified in their judgment it [the mortal bullet] was *perfectly* consistent with" having been fired through the Sacco pistol? In charging the jury Judge Thayer misled them by maximizing the Proctor testimony as the prearrangement intended that it should be maximized. When the prearrangement was discovered and made the basis of a motion for a new trial, Judge Thayer depreciated Proctor's qualifications as an expert and minimized Proctor's actual testimony. Finally, when confronted with new evidence pointing seriously to guilt for the Berardelli murder, not only away from Sacco and Vanzetti, but positively in another direction, in order to give the appearance of impressiveness to the facts before the jury Judge Thayer again relies upon the weightiness of Proctor's expert testimony and maximizes Proctor's evidence at the trial, but not to the extent that he did in charging the jury, because Proctor's affidavit now prevents him from doing so!

This is the attitude of mind which has guided the conduct of this case from the beginning; this is the judge who has for all practical purposes sat in judgment upon his own conduct.

English criminal justice is constantly held up to us, and rightly so, as an example. One ventures confidently to say that conduct like that revealed by the Proctor incident is inconceivable in an English prosecution. But if it did take place, there is no possible doubt that the corrective resources of the English courts would not allow a verdict secured by such means to stand. Such behavior surely violates the standards which the Massachusetts Supreme Judicial Court has laid down for district attorneys:

The powers of a district attorney under our laws are very extensive. They affect to a high degree the liberty of the individual, the good order of society, and the safety of the community. His natural influence with the grand jury, and the confidence commonly reposed in his recommendations by judges, afford to the unscrupulous, the weak or the wicked incumbent of the office vast opportunity to oppress the innocent and to shield the guilty, to trouble his enemies and to protect his friends, and to make the interest of the public subservient to his personal desires, his individual ambitions, and his private advantage. . . . Powers so great impose responsibilities correspondingly grave. They demand character incorruptible, reputation unsullied, a high standard of professional ethics, and sound judgment of no mean order.

If the Proctor situation does not come within the condemnation of these requirements, language certainly has strange meaning. Yet the Massachusetts Supreme Court held that Judge Thayer's decision could not "as a matter of law" be reversed.

V I

On May 12, 1926, the Supreme Court of Massachusetts found "no error" in any of the rulings of Judge Thayer. The guilt or innocence of the defendants was not retried in the Supreme Court. That court could not inquire whether the facts as set forth in the printed record justified the verdict. Such would have been the scope of judicial review had the case come before the New York Court of Appeals or the English Court of Criminal Appeal. In those jurisdictions a judgment upon the facts as well as upon the law is open, and their courts decide whether convictions should stand in view of the whole record. A much more limited scope in reviewing convictions prevails in Massachusetts. What is reviewed in effect is the conduct of the trial judge; only so-called questions of law are open.

The merits of the legal questions raised by the exceptions cannot be discussed here. Suffice it to say, with deference, that some of the Supreme Court rulings are puzzling in the extreme. One question of law, however, can be explained within small compass,

and that is the question which is the crux of the case: Did Judge
Thayer observe the standards of Anglo-American justice? In legal parlance, was there abuse of "judicial discretion" by Judge
Thayer? What, then, is "judicial discretion"? Is it a legal abra-
cadabra, or does it imply standards of conduct within the compre-
hension of the laity in whose interests they are enforced? The
present Chief Justice of Massachusetts has given an authoritative
definition:

> Discretion in this connection means a sound judicial discretion, en-
> lightened by intelligence and learning, controlled by sound principles of
> law, of firm courage combined with the calmness of a cool mind, free
> from partiality, not swayed by sympathy nor warped by prejudice nor
> moved by any kind of influence save alone the overwhelming passion
> to do that which is just. It may be assumed that conduct manifesting
> abuse of judicial discretion will be reviewed and some relief afforded.

This is the test by which Judge Thayer's conduct must be measured. The Supreme Court found no abuse of judicial discretion on
the record presented at the first hearing before it. In other words,
the court was satisfied that throughout the conduct of the trial and
the proceedings that followed it Judge Thayer was governed by
"the calmness of a cool mind, free from partiality, not swayed by
sympathy nor warped by prejudice nor moved by any kind of influence save alone the overwhelming passion to do that which is
just."

The reader has now had placed before him fairly, it is hoped,
however briefly, the means of forming a judgment. Let him judge
for himself!

V I I

Hitherto the defense has maintained that the circumstances of
the case all pointed away from Sacco and Vanzetti. But the deaths
of Parmenter and Berardelli have remained unexplained. Now
the defense has adduced new proof, not only that Sacco and Vanzetti did *not* commit the murders, but also, positively, that a well-
known gang of professional criminals *did* commit them. Hitherto

a new trial has been pressed because of the character of the original trial. Now a new trial has been demanded because an impressive body of evidence tends to establish the guilt of others.

Celestino F. Madeiros, a young Portuguese with a bad criminal record, was in 1925 confined in the same prison with Sacco. On November 18, while his appeal from a conviction of murder committed in an attempt at bank robbery was pending in the Supreme Court, he sent to Sacco through a jail messenger the following note:

I hear by confess to being in the South Braintree shoe company crime and Sacco and Vanzetti was not in said crime.

CELESTINO F. MADEIROS

The confession of a criminal assuming guilt for a crime laid at another's door is always suspect and rightly so. But, as we cannot too strongly insist, the new evidence is not *contained in* the Madeiros confession. His note to Sacco was only the starting point which enabled the defense to weave the network of independent evidence implicating the Morelli gang of Providence.

As soon as Sacco's counsel was apprized of this note he began a searching investigation of Madeiros' claim. It then appeared that Madeiros had tried several times previously to tell Sacco that he knew the real perpetrators of the Braintree job, but Sacco, fearing he was a spy, had disregarded what he said. An interview with Madeiros revealed such circumstantiality of detail that an examination of Madeiros, both by the defense and by the Commonwealth, was plainly called for. The various affidavits given by Madeiros and the deposition of one hundred pages, in which he was cross-examined by the District Attorney, tell the following story.

In 1920 Madeiros, then eighteen years old, was living in Providence. He already had a criminal record and was associated with a gang of Italians engaged in robbing freight cars. One evening, when they were talking together in a saloon in Providence, some members of the gang invited him to join them in a pay-roll robbery at South Braintree. A holdup was a new form of criminal enterprise for him, but they told him "they had done lots of jobs of this kind" and persuaded him to come along. As an eighteen-year-old novice he was to be given only a subordinate part. He was to sit in the back of a car with a revolver and "help hold back the crowd in case they made a rush." Accordingly a few days later, on April 15, 1920, the plan was carried into execution. In the party, besides Madeiros, were three Italians and a "kind of a slim fellow with light hair," who drove the car. In order to prevent identification they adopted the familiar device of using two cars. They started out in a Hudson, driving to some woods near Randolph. They then exchanged the Hudson for a Buick brought them by another member of the gang. In the Buick they proceeded to South Braintree, arriving there about noon. When the time came the actual shooting was done by the oldest of the Italians, a man about forty, and one other. The rest of the party remained near by in the automobile. As the crime was being committed they drove up, took aboard the murderers and the money, and made off. They drove back to the Randolph woods, exchanged the Buick again for the Hudson, and returned to Providence. The arrangement was that Madeiros should meet the others in a saloon at Providence the following night to divide the spoils. Whether this arrangement was kept and whether he got any of the Braintree loot Madeiros persistently refused to say.

This refusal was in pursuance of Madeiros' avowed policy. From the outset he announced his determination not to reveal the identity of his associates in the Braintree job, while holding back nothing which seemed to implicate himself alone. To shield them he obstinately declined to answer questions and, if necessary, frankly resorted to lies. Thus, examination could not extort from him the surnames of the gang, and he further sought to cover up their identity by giving some of them false Christian names. Madeiros showed considerable astuteness in evading what he wanted to conceal. But in undertaking to tell the story of the crime without revealing the criminals he set himself an impossible task. In spite of his efforts, a lawyer as resourceful as Mr. Thompson was able to elicit facts which, when followed up, established the identity of the gang and also strongly corroborated the story of Madeiros.

Madeiros said that the gang "had been engaged in robbing freight cars in Providence." Was there such a gang? There was the Morelli gang, well known to the police of Providence and New Bedford as professional criminals, several of whom at the time of the Braintree murders were actually under indictment in the United States District Court for Rhode Island for stealing from freight cars. Five out of nine indictments charging shoe thefts were for stealing consignments from *Slater and Morrill at South Braintree* and from Rice and Hutchins, the factory next door. In view of their method of operations, the gang must have had a confederate at South Braintree to spot shipments for them. The Slater and Morrill factory was about one hundred yards from the South Braintree railroad station and an accomplice spotting shipments would be passed by the paymaster on his weekly trip. It will be recalled that the pay roll was that of the Slater and Morrill factory and that the murder and the robbery occurred in front of these two factories. The Morellis under indictment were out of jail awaiting trial. They needed money for their defense; their only source of income was crime. They were at large until May 25, when they were convicted and sent to Atlanta.

Madeiros did not name the gang, but described the men who were with him at South Braintree. How did his descriptions fit the Morelli gang? The leader of the gang was Joe, aged thirty-nine. His brothers were Mike, Patsy, Butsy, and Fred. Other members were Bibba Barone, Gyp the Blood, Mancini, and Steve the Pole. Bibba Barone and Fred Morelli were in jail on April 15, 1920. According to Madeiros there were five, including himself, in the murder car, three of whom were Italians, and the driver "Polish or Finland or something northern Europe." The shooting was done by the oldest of the Italians, a man of about forty, and another called Bill. A fourth Italian brought up the Buick car for exchange at Randolph. As far as his descriptions carry, Madeiros' party fits the members of the Morelli gang. But the testimony of independent witnesses corroborates Madeiros and makes the identification decisive. One of the gravest difficulties of the prosecution's case against Sacco and Vanzetti was the collapse of the government's attempt to identify the driver of the murder car as Vanzetti. The District Attorney told the jury that "they must be overwhelmed with the testimony that when the car started it was driven by a light-haired man, who gave every appearance of being sickly." Steve the Pole satisfies Madeiros' description of the driver as well as the testimony at the trial. To set the matter beyond a doubt, two women who were working in the Slater and Morrill factory identified Steve the Pole as the man they saw standing for half an hour by a car outside their window on that day. Two witnesses who testified at the trial identified Joe Morelli as one of the men who did the shooting and another identified Mancini. The Morellis were American-born, which will explain the testimony at the trial that one of the bandits spoke clear and unmistakable English, a thing impossible to Sacco and Vanzetti.

Plainly the personnel of the Morelli gang fits the Braintree crime. What of other details? The mortal bullet came out of a .32 Colt; Joe Morelli had a .32 Colt at this time. Mancini's pistol was of a type and caliber to account for the other five bullets found in the victims. The "murder car" at the trial was a Buick. Madeiros said a Buick was used; and Mike Morelli, according to the New Bedford police, at this time was driving a Buick, which disappeared immediately after April 15, 1920. In fact, the police of New Bedford, where the Morelli gang had been operating, suspected them of the Braintree crime, but dropped the matter after the arrest of Sacco and Vanzetti. Shortly after the Braintree job, Madeiros was imprisoned for five months for larceny of an amount less than $100. But immediately after his release he had about $2,800 in bank, which enabled him to go on a pleasure trip to the West and Mexico. The $2,800 is unaccounted for otherwise than as his share of the Braintree booty. Joe Morelli, as we know, was sent to Atlanta for his share in the robbery of the Slater and Morrill shoes. While confined he made an arrangement with a fellow prisoner whereby the latter was to furnish him with an alibi, in case of need, for April 15, 1920, placing Morelli in New York.

Even so compressed a précis of the evidence of many witnesses will have made it clear that the defense has built up a powerful case, without the resources at the command of the state in criminal investigations. The witnesses other than Madeiros of themselves afford strong probability of the guilt of the Morellis. What of the intrinsic credibility of Madeiros' confession, which, if believed, settles the matter? A criminal's confession, as we have noted, must be scrutinized with the utmost skepticism. A man who assumes guilt for one crime while about to undergo the penalty of death for another does not carry the least conviction. The circumstances of Madeiros' confession, however, free it from suspicion and furnish assurances of its trustworthiness. Far from having nothing to lose by making the confession, Madeiros stood to jeopardize his life. For while, to be sure, at the time of his confession he was under sentence for another murder, an appeal from this conviction was pending, which was in fact successful in getting him a new trial. Could anything be more prejudicial to an effort to reverse conviction for one crime than to admit guilt for another? So clearly prejudicial, in fact, was his confession that by arrangement with the District Attorney it was kept secret until after the outcome of his appeal and the new trial which followed it. Moreover, the note of confession sent by Madeiros to Sacco on November 18 was not, as we have seen, his first communication to Sacco. Nor was it his first explicit confession. The murder for which he had been convicted, together with a man named Weeks—the Wrentham bank crime—was a holdup like the Braintree job. Weeks, under life sentence in another jail, when questioned revealed that in planning the Wrentham job Madeiros drew on his experience at South Braintree. During their partnership Madeiros had frequently referred to the Braintree job, saying it was arranged by the Morelli gang (whom Weeks knew), and at one time identifying a speak-easy in which they found themselves as the one the gang visited before the Braintree holdup. In planning the Wrentham job Madeiros further told Weeks that he "had had enough of the Buick in the South Braintree job." Before the Wrentham crime he had talked to the couple who kept the roadhouse where for a time he was a "bouncer" of his part in the Braintree crime and said "that he would like to save Sacco and Vanzetti because he knew they were perfectly innocent."

These earlier disclosures by Madeiros completely refute the theory that he was led to make his latest confession in 1925 by the hope of getting money. It is suggested that in November, 1925, he had seen the financial statement of the Sacco-Vanzetti Defense Committee. But in the first place there is no proof that Madeiros saw this statement before he made the confession. Secondly, he could not have had knowledge of this statement before he talked to Weeks and the others and when he attempted the prior communications to Sacco, because it was not then in existence. It is incredible that a man fighting for his life on a charge for one murder would, in the hope of getting money, falsely accuse himself of another murder. Madeiros knew the danger of a confession, for his conviction in the Wrentham case largely rested upon confessions made by him. Why should he be believed and suffer death when he confesses one crime and not be believed when he confesses another of the same character? Is not his own statement in accordance with the motives even of a murderer?

I seen Sacco's wife come up here with the kids and I felt sorry for the kids.

Let us compare the two hypotheses. The Morelli theory accounts for all members of the Braintree murder gang; the Sacco-Vanzetti theory for only two, for it is conceded that, if Madeiros was there, Sacco and Vanzetti were not. The Morelli theory accounts for all the bullets found in the dead men; the Sacco-Vanzetti theory for only one out of six. The Morelli explanation settles the motive, for the Morelli gang were criminals desperately in need of money for legal expenses pending their trial for felonies, whereas the Sacco-Vanzetti theory is unsupported by any motive. Moreover, Madeiros' possession of $2,800 accounts for his share of the booty, whereas not a penny has ever been traced to anybody or accounted for on the Sacco-Vanzetti theory. The Morelli story is not subject to the absurd premise that professional holdup men who stole automobiles at will and who had recently made a haul of nearly $16,000 would devote an evening, as did Sacco and Vanzetti the night of their arrest, to riding around on suburban street cars to borrow a friend's six-year-old Overland. The character of the Morelli gang fits the opinion of police investigators and the inherent facts of the situation, which tended to prove that the crime was the work of professionals, whereas the past character and record of Sacco and Vanzetti have always made it inherently incredible that they should spontaneously become perpetrators of a bold murder, executed with the utmost expertness. A good mechanic, regularly employed at his trade, but away from work on a particular day which is clearly accounted for, and a dreamy fish peddler, openly engaged in political propaganda, neither do nor can suddenly commit an isolated job of highly professional banditry.

Can the situation be put more conservatively than this? Every reasonable probability points away from Sacco and Vanzetti; every reasonable probability points toward the Morelli gang.

How did these facts appear to Judge Thayer?

VIII

At the outset the scope of Judge Thayer's duty toward the motion for a new trial based upon this new evidence must be kept in mind. It was not for him to determine the guilt of the Morellis or the innocence of Sacco and Vanzetti; it was not for him to weigh the new evidence as though he were a jury, determining what is true and what is false. Judge Thayer's duty was the very narrow one of ascertaining whether here was new material fit for a new jury's judgment. May honest minds, capable of dealing with evidence, reach a different conclusion, because of the new evidence, from that of the first jury? Do the new facts raise debatable issues? Could another jury, conscious of its oath and conscientiously obedient to it, be sufficiently impressed with the new evidence to reach a verdict contrary to the one that was reached on a record wholly different from the present, in view of evidence recently discovered and not adduceable by the defense at the time of the original trial? To all these questions Judge Thayer says, "No." This amazing conclusion he reached after studying the motion "for several weeks without interruption" and set forth in an opinion of 25,000 words! We wish for nothing more than that every reader who has proceeded thus far should study the full text of this latest Thayer opinion. Space precludes its detailed treatment here. To quote it, to analyze it, adequately to comment upon it would require a book. Having now put the materials for detailed judgment at the disposal of readers, we are compelled to confine ourselves to a few brief observations. By what is left out and by what is put in, the uninformed reader of Judge Thayer's opinion would be wholly misled as to the real facts of the case. Speaking from a considerable experience as a prosecuting officer, whose special task for a time it was to sustain on appeal convictions for the government, and whose scientific duties since have led to the examination of a great number of records and the opinions based thereon, I assert with deep regret, but without the slightest fear of disproof, that certainly in modern times Judge Thayer's opinion stands unmatched for discrepancies between what the record discloses and what the opinion conveys. His 25,000-word document cannot accurately be described otherwise than as a farrago of misquotations, misrepresentation, suppressions, and mutilations. The disinterested inquirer could not possibly derive from it a true knowledge of the new evidence that was submitted to him as the basis for a new trial. The opinion is literally honey-combed with demonstrable errors, and a spirit alien to judicial utterance permeates the whole. A study of the opinion in the light of the record led the conservative Boston *Herald*, which long held the view that the sentence against these men should be carried out, to a frank reversal of its position.

Dr. Morton Prince writes that any expert psychologist reading the Thayer opinion "could not fail to find evidences that portray strong personal feeling, poorly concealed, that should have no place in a judicial document." One or two illustrations must suffice. William G. Thompson is one of the leaders of the Boston bar. Yet Judge Thayer thus characterized Mr. Thompson's activities in behalf of these two Italians:

> Since the trial before the jury of these cases a new type of disease would seem to have developed. It might be called "lego-psychic neurosis" or hysteria, which means: "A belief in the existence of something which in fact and truth has no such existence."

And this from a judge who gives meretricious authority to his self-justification by speaking of the verdict which convicted these men as "approved by the Supreme Judicial Court of this Commonwealth." The Supreme Court never approved the verdict; nor did it pretend to do so. The Supreme Court passed on technical claims of error, and, "finding no error, the verdicts are to stand." Judge Thayer knows this, but laymen may not. Yet Judge Thayer refers to the verdict as "approved by the Supreme Judicial Court."

No wonder that Judge Thayer's opinion has confirmed old doubts as to the guilt of these two Italians and aroused new anxieties concerning the resources of our law to avoid grave miscarriage of justice. The courageous stand taken by the Boston *Herald* has enlisted the support of some of the most distinguished citizens of Massachusetts. The *Independent* has thus epitomized this demand:

> Because of the increasing doubt that surrounds the question of the guilt of these men, springing from the intrinsic character of Judge Thayer's decision, and instanced by the judgment of the *Herald* editorial writer and other observers whose impartiality is unquestioned, we strongly hope that a new trial will be granted. It is important to note that the appeal is being made on the basis of new evidence never passed on before the Supreme Court.

No narrow, merely technical, question is thus presented. The Supreme Court of Massachusetts will be called upon to search the whole record in order to determine whether Judge Thayer duly observed the traditional standards of fairness and reason which govern the conduct of an Anglo-American judge, particularly in a capital case. This court has given us the requirements by which

Judge Thayer's decision is to be measured and the tests which it will use in determining whether a new trial shall be granted:

> The various statements of the extent of the power and of limitations upon the right to grant new trials . . . must yield to the fundamental test, in aid of which most rules have been formulated, that such motions ought not to be granted unless on a survey of the whole case it appears to the judicial conscience and judgment that otherwise a miscarriage of justice will result.

Nor must a new trial be withheld where in justice it is called for because thereby encouragement will be given to improper demands for a new trial. For, as the Chief Justice of Massachusetts has announced, courts cannot close "their eyes to injustice on account of facility of abuse."

With these legal canons as a guide, the outcome ought not to be in doubt.

The Supreme Court Writes a Chapter
on Man's Rights

No less than that of Sacco and Vanzetti, the Scottsboro case has achieved a symbolic significance beyond the importance of the individuals involved. Seven Negro boys were arrested in 1930, and charged with the rape of two white girls on a freight train near Scottsboro, Alabama. They were convicted. Their conviction was upheld by the highest court of Alabama. Eventually the Supreme Court held that they had been tried without due process of law. They were again convicted, and the Supreme Court held that, by excluding Negroes from jury service, Alabama had again deprived them of their liberty unconstitutionally. Once again, some of them were convicted, and are still serving life sentences. The rest pled guilty to minor offenses, and served short prison terms. Mr. Frankfurter's article deals with the first Supreme Court decision in their favor. It appeared in the New York Times for November 13, 1932.

THE RAGS and tags of cases that excite public interest usually draw the headlines. But even lay comment upon the Scottsboro decision was alive to a significance that went beyond a respite from death for seven illiterate Negro boys. In truth, the Supreme Court last Monday wrote a notable chapter in the history of liberty, emphasized perhaps in importance because it was conveyed through the sober language of a judicial opinion. The evolution of our constitutional law is the work of the initiate. But its ultimate sway depends upon its acceptance by the thought of the nation. The meaning of Supreme Court decisions ought not therefore to be shrouded in esoteric mystery. It ought to be possible to make clear to lay understanding the exact scope of constitutional doctrines that underlie decisions like the Scottsboro case.

The seven vagrant Negro youths involved in the Scottsboro case were convicted of the crime most abhorrent of all others to the community in which they found themselves. The conviction was sustained by the Supreme Court of Alabama, but over the vigorous dissent of the chief justice of the state. Thereafter leave was asked and granted for a review of the case by the Supreme Court of the United States. There the denial by the Alabama courts of fundamental rights under the federal Constitution was urged.

Specifically, it was claimed that: "(1) they were not given a fair, impartial and deliberate trial; (2) they were denied the right of counsel, with the accustomed incidents of consultation and opportunity of preparation for trial; and (3) they were tried before juries from which qualified members of their own race were systematically excluded." The court, through Mr. Justice Sutherland, without considering the first and third claims, sustained the second, reversed the judgment of the Alabama court and ordered a new trial, in which the denied safeguard would have to be assured.

A rapid summary of the circumstances of the trial, as given by Mr. Justice Sutherland, is a necessary preliminary to the discussion of the legal issues. The defendants were non-residents of Alabama, riding through the state in an open freight car on which were also several white boys and two white girls. A fight ensued in which the white boys were thrown off the train. Upon the complaint of these boys the train was stopped at a station down the line. There the girls accused the Negroes of assault. They were arrested and taken to Scottsboro, the county seat, where a large crowd had already gathered. Six days later indictments were returned. In six days more—the defendants, without families or friends in the state, having meanwhile been closely confined under military guard—the trial began.

"No one answered for the defendants or appeared to represent or defend them." The trial judge stated that he had designated generally the entire local bar for the purpose of arraigning the defendants, "and then, of course, I anticipated them to continue to help them if no counsel appears." A Tennessee lawyer, acting at the suggestion of unnamed "persons interested" but not in their employ, addressed the court; he stated that he had not had opportunity to prepare the case and was unfamiliar with local practice, but offered to appear with such local counsel as the court might appoint. An attorney expressed his willingness to serve under those conditions: "I will go ahead and help, do anything I can do." "The Court—All right."

"And in this casual fashion," writes Mr. Justice Sutherland, "the matter of counsel in a capital case was disposed of. . . . The defendants, young, ignorant, illiterate, surrounded by hostile sentiment, haled back and forth under guard of soldiers, charged with an atrocious crime regarded with especial horror in the community where they were to be tried, were thus put in peril of their lives within a few moments after counsel for the first time charged with any degree of responsibility began to represent them. . . . We think the failure of the trial court to give them reasonable time and opportunity to secure counsel was a clear denial of due process. . . . We are of opinion that . . . the necessity of counsel was so vital and imperative that the failure of the trial court to make an effective appointment of counsel was likewise a denial of due process within the meaning of the Fourteenth Amendment."

From this conclusion only Mr. Justice Butler and Mr. Justice McReynolds dissented.

The stock offenses of American criminal law, it must be remembered—murder, arson, rape, theft—are violations of state law and prosecuted solely through the state courts. As a generality, these are matters wholly outside the concern of the federal judiciary. Understanding of this division of function as to criminal matters between the states and the nation is essential to an appreciation of the Scottsboro decision. It is no part of the Supreme Court's duty to correct errors inevitable to every administration of criminal justice. Erroneous applications of law, the admission of prejudicial evidence, disregard of the conventional niceties of procedure—all these infringements of common right, if they are to be remedied at all, must be remedied in the highest courts of the states. The Scottsboro decision works no impairment of these fundamental assumptions of our constitutional system.

But upon the freedom of all state action the federal Constitution imposes a broad limitation, applicable to criminal as well as to civil proceedings, to judicial as well as to legislative acts. This is accomplished by the Fourteenth Amendment, which provides that no state shall "deprive any person of life, liberty, or property without due process of law." The assertion of that limitation is a study of the federal judiciary, and a right of defendants under the federal Constitution. In its application of this prohibition in the review of the conduct of a state criminal trial, the significance of the Scottsboro decision resides.

The words of the amendment are words of "convenient vagueness," definable only by the cumulative process of judicial inclusion and exclusion. In matters affecting property rights, and notably the regulation of economic enterprise, they have come to be the foundation of a large body of doctrine often interposing irksome barriers to restrictive legislation. Only last year they served Mr. Justice Sutherland in the famous Oklahoma Ice case as a touchstone for the invalidity of a statute which authorized the State Corporation Commission to deny to any person the right to enter the business of manufacturing ice in a community where in its opinion the existing facilities made such entrance injurious to the public. Now, in the hands of the same Justice, they return to their more immediate purpose of protecting black men from oppressive and unequal treatment by whites.

In the illuminating phrase of Judge Learned Hand, due process "represents a mood rather than a command." The mood of the Supreme Court in subjecting the conduct of state criminal trials to the measure of the Fourteenth Amendment has been insistently cautious. Properly so, for the amendment is not the basis of a uniform code of criminal procedure federally imposed. Alternative modes of arriving at truth are not—they must not be—forever frozen. There is room for growth and vitality, for adaptation to shifting necessities, for wide differences of reasonable convenience in method.

Thus it was long ago settled that proceedings in state criminal actions need not be initiated by indictment of a grand jury, albeit the common law so required. Trial by a jury of twelve is not imperative in state courts. The administration of local justice knows no such rigid federal fetters. Here, too, freedom must be left for new, perhaps improved, methods "in the insulated chambers afforded by the several states."

But—and this is of the essence—certain things are basic to the integrity of the judicial process. One of them is a proper tribunal, impartial and uncoerced. In the memorable case of *Moore* v. *Dempsey*, concerning, like the Scottsboro case, the trial of a Negro in a Southern community inflamed by racial hysteria, it was held that a court surrounded by a howling mob threatening vengeance if a conviction were not returned was no court at all, and the case was remanded for retrial under conditions more likely to conduce to the substantial ends of justice. Until the Scottsboro case, this decision stood virtually alone. Counsel for the Scottsboro defendants sought to bring their case within its authority. But the court, instead of reviewing the circumstances of the trial and finding that in substance there was no trial because reason was barred, seized upon a different aspect of the case and enunciated another fundamental requisite of the judicial process.

Not only must there be a court free from coercion, but the accused must be furnished with means of presenting his defense. For this the assistance of counsel is essential. Time for investigation and for the production of evidence is imperative. Especially is this true in a capital case. The more heinous the charge the more important the safeguards which the experience of centuries has shown to be essential to the ascertainment of even fallible truth. Never is it more so than in a case of rape, turning heavily upon the testimony of the alleged victim and requiring to be defended largely by evidence of circumstance and character.

The Scottsboro case announces the doctrine that to every defendant must be assured the minimum conditions for an ordered and reasoned investigation of the charges against him—a proper and a heartening guarantee of fundamental law. The history of liberty, Mr. Justice Brandeis has reminded us, cannot be dissociated from the history of procedural observances. In no sense is the Supreme Court a general tribunal for the correction of criminal errors, such as the Court of Criminal Appeal in England. On a continent peopled by 120,000,000 that would be an impossible task; in a federal system it would be a function debilitating to the responsibility of state and local agencies. But the Court, though it will continue to act with hesitation, will not suffer, in its own scathing phrase, "judicial murder." Here lies perhaps the deepest significance of the case.

Thus the judgment of the Court transcends the fate of the seven pitiful defendants concerned. It leaves that fate ultimately untouched. Upon the question of guilt or innocence it bears not even remotely. That question remains to be determined in normal course by the constituted tribunals of Alabama. The Supreme Court has declared only that the determination must be made with due observance of the decencies of civilized procedure.

Can the Supreme Court Guarantee Toleration?

This selection appeared as an unsigned editorial in the **New Republic** *for June 17, 1925.*

IN 1922 Oregon passed an Education Act with "the manifest purpose," in the language of the Supreme Court of the United States, "to compel general attendance at public schools by normal children, between eight and sixteen, who have not completed the eighth grade." The Act was to become effective September 1, 1926. Two years before the new dispensation became operative, two private schools—a Catholic institution and a military academy—sought to enjoin the future enforcement of the Act. This was the legal machinery by which the Supreme Court was enabled to invalidate the notorious Oregon legislation. . . .

The offense of the law was a . . . far-reaching one. It is summed up in the following sentence of Mr. Justice McReynolds' opinion: "The fundamental theory of liberty upon which all governments in this union repose excludes any general power of the state to standardize its children by forcing them to accept instruction from public teachers only." Thus comes to an end the effort to regiment the mental life of Americans through coerced public school instruction. Two years ago the Supreme Court invalidated legislation ultimately rooted in the same attitude of intolerance, which led Nebraska, Iowa, and Ohio to prohibit the teaching of any other modern language except English in any school, public or private, during the tender years of youth. And perhaps within two years the Supreme Court will exercise its veto against the

Bryan movement already embodied in Tennessee law which finds
the test of truth in Bible stories.

.   .   .   .

Great argument is drawn from both the Oregon and the earlier
Nebraska case for the beneficent value inhering in the scope of
judicial review over the social legislation of the states by the
United States Supreme Court. But, of course, the Oregon case
alone does not tell the tale. It is only one in a series, which has
been spun profusely out of the fateful words of the Fourteenth
Amendment. "No state shall . . . deprive any person of life, liberty, or property without due process of law," are the vague words
which hold the power of life and death over state action. These
words mean what the shifting personnel of the United States Supreme Court from time to time makes them mean. The inclination
of a single Justice, the tip of his mind—or his fears—determines
the opportunity of a much-needed social experiment to survive,
or frustrates, at least for a long time, intelligent attempt to deal
with a social evil. Equally, of course, these words may be availed
of, as is shown in the Oregon case, to stifle certainly for the moment the recrudescence of intolerance. Before one can find in the
Oregon case proof of the social value of the Supreme Court's scope
of judicial review a balance must be struck of all the cases that
have been decided under the Fourteenth Amendment. In rejoicing
over the Nebraska and the Oregon cases, we must not forget that a
heavy price has to be paid for these occasional services to liberalism. The New York bakeshop case, the invalidation of anti-trade
union laws, the sanctification of the injunction in labor cases, the
veto of minimum wage legislation, are not wiped out by the
Oregon decision. They weigh heavily in any full accounting of
the gains and losses to our national life due to the Supreme
Court's control of legislation by the states that does not involve
an arbitrament between state and national powers, such as arises
when purely state legislation encroaches upon the commerce
powers of the federal government. No calculus has yet been invented to make such a precise accounting.

For ourselves, we regard the cost of this power of the Supreme

Court on the whole as greater than its gains. After all, the hysteria and chauvinism that forbade the teaching of German in Nebraska schools may subside, and with its subsidence bring repeal of the silly measure; the narrow margin by which the Oregon law was carried in 1922 may, with invigorated effort on the part of the liberal forces, result in its repeal, at least by a narrow margin. But when the Supreme Court strikes down legislation directed against trade unions, or enshrines the labor injunction into the Constitution, or denies to women in industry the meager protection of minimum wage legislation, we are faced with action more far-reaching, because ever so much more durable and authoritative than even the most mischievous of repealable state legislation.

And this brings us to consider the intrinsic promotion of the liberal spirit by the Supreme Court's invalidation of illiberal legislation. It must never be forgotten that our constant preoccupation with the constitutionality of legislation rather than its wisdom tends to preoccupation of the American mind with a false value. Even the most rampant worshiper of judicial supremacy admits that wisdom and justice are not the tests of constitutionality. Even the extreme right of the Supreme Court occasionally sustain laws which they abominate. But the tendency of focusing attention on constitutionality is to make constitutionality synonymous with propriety; to regard a law as all right so long as it is "constitutional." Such an attitude is a great enemy of liberalism. Particularly in legislation affecting freedom of thought and freedom of speech much that is highly illiberal would be clearly constitutional. . . . Here is ample room for the patrioteers to roll in their Trojan horses. And here is ample warning to the liberal forces that the real battles of liberalism are not won in the Supreme Court. To a large extent the Supreme Court, under the guise of constitutional interpretation of words whose contents are derived from the disposition of the Justices, is the reflector of that impalpable but controlling thing, the general drift of public opinion. Only a persistent, positive translation of the liberal faith into the thoughts and acts of the community is the real reliance against the unabated temptation to straitjacket the human mind.

America and the Immigrant

In April, 1938, Mr. Frankfurter received an award from the National Institute for Immigrant Welfare. The following selection is his speech of acceptance.

SINCE your gracious award, though it might more fittingly have gone to others, has fallen to me, it gives me pleasure to accept it in the representative rôle in which, of course, it is offered. Gratitude is one of the least articulate of the emotions, especially when it is deep. I can express with very limited adequacy the passionate devotion to this land that possesses millions of our people, born, like myself, under other skies, for the privilege that this country has bestowed in allowing them to partake of its fellowship.

It has bestowed this privilege from the beginning. The unfolding of our republic is the story of the most significant racial admixture in history. Of the fifty-six signers of the Declaration of Independence, eighteen were of non-English stock. It deserves to be recalled that, when the Continental Congress chose John Adams, Franklin, and Jefferson as a committee to devise the national emblem, they recommended a seal containing the national emblems of England, Scotland, Ireland, France, Germany, and Holland as representing "the countries from which these states have been peopled."

. . . .

Foreign-born citizens from these and other countries fought in the War for Independence, helped to save the Union, and responded to the appeals for democracy in the World War. No less is our cultural history—the sciences and the arts—the fusion of the genius and labors of men and women who came to these shores from all the corners of the globe. The very Constitution of the United States was made, in the classic language of the Supreme Court, "for an undefined and expanding future, and for a people gathered and to be gathered from many nations and of many tongues."

If one faith can be said to unite a great people, surely the ideal that holds us together beyond any other is our belief in the moral worth of the common man, whatever his race or religion. In this faith America was founded, to this faith have her poets and seers and statesmen and the unknown millions, generation after generation, devoted their lives.

Nothing is more uniquely American than this hospitality to the human spirit, whatever its source. It has found permanent expression in the words by Emma Lazarus inscribed in bronze on the Statue of Liberty:

> Not like the brazen giant of Greek fame,
> With conquering limbs astride from land to land;
> Here at our sea-washed, sunset gates shall stand
> A mighty woman with a torch, whose flame
> Is the imprisoned lightning, and her name
> Mother of Exiles. From her beacon-hand
> Glows world-wide welcome; her mild eyes command
> The air-bridged harbor that twin cities frame.
> "Keep, ancient lands, your storied pomp!" cries she
> With silent lips. "Give me your tired, your poor,
> Your huddled masses yearning to breathe free,
> The wretched refuse of your teeming shore.
> Send these, the homeless, tempest-tossed, to me,
> I lift my lamp beside the golden door!"

To this haven of opportunity came millions before me and millions thereafter. What they have made of this opportunity, which is an obligation, it is not for me to say. Perhaps you will let me quote the judgment of the President of the United States, uttered on the occasion of the fiftieth anniversary of the Statue of Liberty:

I like to think of the men and women who, with the break of dawn off Sandy Hook, have strained their eyes to the West for the first glimpse of the New World.

They came to us speaking many tongues—but a single language, the universal language of human aspiration.

How well their hopes were justified is proved by the record of what they achieved. They not only found freedom in the New World, but by their effort and devotion, they made the New World's freedom safer, richer, more far-reaching, more capable of growth.

.   .   .   .

The volume of this stream of contributions to our country has diminished, but not their longing for us nor our need of them. The times in which we live are bringing to American life doers of great deeds and thinkers of great thoughts, and men and women undistinguished except as the sturdy foundation of every good society.

We should welcome them as generations before us welcomed the pilgrims of '48. For they come not merely because persecution drives them; they come because the American tradition beckons them.

They are men and women like Prof. G. A. Borgese, the distinguished Italian scholar, who only the other day gave exulting voice to his joy on his attainment of American citizenship: "This country has given me the remarkable privilege of creating a new life. It is a gift for which I shall always feel gratitude."

Labor and the Courts

The Eight-Hour Day

The following selection is part of a letter appearing in the Boston Herald *for October 9, 1916. President Wilson, in response to a threatened strike, had recommended legislation to Congress establishing the basic eight-hour day for interstate railroad workers. The Adamson Act, passed shortly afterward, embodied the substance of President Wilson's recommendations.*

Nowhere is it possible to arouse feelings so deeply resentful or prejudiced as in the field of labor problems. Even men otherwise intelligent are apt to become unreasonable when confronted with the questions raised by trade unionism. The explanation is, of course, simple. We are dealing here not with premises or conclusions that are established beyond question, but with the fears and doubts of men. We have as yet no accepted test of right and wrong; and the scientific formulae which are to be the signposts of adequate opinion are as yet wanting. We have not even an adequate fund of experience. So that we are compelled to experiment. In the application of purposeful and probable hypotheses alone can there be the right to hope for knowledge.

What we need is the clarification of our assumptions. To everyone not imbued with a fatal optimism which arrests inquiry, this is simply essential. Anyone at all acquainted with the realities of modern industry, its grinding pressure and spiritual starvation, must feel that wherever the alleviation of its ugliness and injustice may be looked for, there must due search be made. The crucial fact of modern industry is its failure to use the creative qualities of men, its deadening monotony and its excessive fatigue. Nowhere, save in directive or professional work, is there the opportunity for individual expression which was characteristic of the medieval handicraft. The result is to ensure a stunted citizenship, since only in a really adequate leisure and a training in the facility of its use can the qualities of democratic life be made manifest. For it is very certain that without facilities for the cultivation of the amenities of civilized life the mass of the people will remain incapable of disciplined democracy. In a word, leisure has a real social value, and there is every moral and political reason to seek its increase.

Experience amply demonstrates that men, women, and children work too long, from the point of view of the quality of the resulting citizenship. The history of the lowering of the standards of military requirement, the serious disclosure in England after the Boer War as to the deterioration of English factory workers, the testimony of General Gorgas—the most successful health administrator of the world—that poverty, rooted in low wages and long hours, is the greatest enemy to health, are all there to read for him who wants to be informed. This is not, however, merely a humanitarian plea; this is not sentimental talk. The experience of money-making business is that while an eight-hour day may mean increased total labor cost, it does not mean an increased unit labor cost. In other words, experience shows that shorter working hours make for increased production, and therefore more wealth. The apparent paradox is easily explained. Shorter hours result in increased human efficiency, by the reactive effect on the individual; they also provoke inventiveness, all kinds of savings; they secure the stoppage of wastes, just because the utmost value must be obtained from the shorter hours. In a word, they operate as an inducement to greater human competence; they thus increase money values no less than human values.

Of course there is a limit to this decrease in the hours of labor. It is a shallow logic, however, which argues if eight hours, why not six, if six, why not four. That is unreason, not human logic. Human logic is the balancing of opposing needs and forces—the need for work and for creating wealth over against the need for leisure to be able to work and to enjoy rightly the uses of wealth.

We do not say that eight hours is a flat level. We hope for a gradual reduction beyond that—by inventions, by a more orderly industrial system, by a less blind relation between population and resources. Even now we know that in certain occupations men work and should work less than eight hours. Tea tasters and judges and writers are not steadily active at their work more than five or six hours for long with competence. But we do know enough to say that eight hours is a rough minimum—below that we ought to secure scientific knowledge of the boundaries of fatigue for each special industry.

Therefore the President was right in urging the eight-hour day as one that had behind it "the judgment of society." He was right in adopting that as a policy for legislative action. . . .

Child Labor and the Court

This selection appeared as a signed article in the New Republic *for July 26, 1922.*

T HE RECENT decision of the Supreme Court, invalidating the Federal Child Labor Tax Law, raises two wholly different questions, each of very serious public importance. The first involves judgment upon the Supreme Court's action, and to that extent is part of a process of continuing critique of the functioning of the Supreme Court in our national life. A totally different, and immediately practical, issue is presented by the consequences of the Supreme Court's decision; in other words, what are we going to do about child labor?

Is it just to claim, as its critics do claim, that the Supreme Court's decision is "unjust and inhumane"? So to maintain is to imply that the Supreme Court either approves of, or, at least, is indifferent to the horrors of child labor. Such an accusation is absurd. Four of the Justices have heretofore expressed themselves in no uncertain terms about the evils of stunted childhood, and in the present case the Chief Justice, speaking for the Court, characterized the Federal Child Labor Tax Law as "legislation designed to promote the highest good." It is appropriate also not to forget the services which the Chief Justice, while President, rendered in behalf of child welfare. To call the decision "unjust" implies that the Supreme Court, within the bounds of its duty, should have sustained the federal measure. But such a conclusion cannot be reached out of hand. "Humanity" is not the test of constitutionality. Recognition that a law enacted by Congress seeks to redress monstrous wrongs and to promote the highest good does not dispose of the Supreme Court's duty when the validity of such a law is challenged. So long as we are governed by a written Constitution, distributing different powers of government between the federal government and the states, with the Supreme Court as arbiter of a conflict between them, just so long will there be occasions, from time to time, when a good law will not be a "just" law, because it will violate the bond of union. We must pay a price for federalism—at one time the impotence of the federal government to correct glaring evils unheeded by some of the states, at other times the impotence of states to correct glaring evils unheeded by the federal government.

Let us see how the matter stands with the recent Federal Child Labor Tax Law. In 1918 the Supreme Court, in *Hammer* v. *Dagenhart*, invalidated an act of Congress which prohibited transportation in interstate commerce to child-labor products. This unfortunate decision was rendered by a divided court, and the dissenting opinion of Mr. Justice Holmes, on behalf of four of the Justices, has never been answered. Congress at once set about to circumvent *Hammer* v. *Dagenhart*. It did so by levying a tax of 10 per cent on the net profits, for a year, of any mill or mine employing children below the prohibited age. . . .

It was inevitable that the Court should draw the obvious conclusion as to the aim of this act and its real field of operation:

> In the light of these features of the act, a court must be blind not to see that the so-called tax is imposed to stop the employment of children within the age limits prescribed. Its prohibitory and regulatory effect and purpose are palpable. All others can see and understand this. How can we properly shut our minds to it?

Clearly this was not the usual case involving social legislation before the Supreme Court, where invalidity is based on meanings read into the vague "counsels of moderation" embodied in the "due process" clauses. In such decisions—like the Lochner and the Coppage cases, and the recent *Truax* v. *Corrigan*—there is no question of conflicting jurisdiction between states and nation, but a nullification of state action based on eighteenth-century conceptions of "liberty" and "equality." In the present case, however, the questions before the Court were (1) the dishonest use of the taxing power, and (2) the distribution of power between national and state governments.

These are vital questions, and their disposition could not be evaded by the Court. Whatever a man's social outlook, be he stand-patter or liberal, as a member of the Supreme Court his freedom of action is limited, in good conscience, within the federal framework of the Constitution. Passion for the abolition of child labor burns, probably, as strongly in some, at least, of the Justices, as it does in Samuel Gompers. Only the former happen to be on the Supreme Court and could hardly escape the force of the following conclusion:

> Grant the validity of this law, and all that Congress would need to do, hereafter, in seeking to take over to its control any one of the great number of subjects of public interest, jurisdiction of which the states have never parted with, and which are reserved to them by the Tenth Amendment, would be to enact a detailed measure of complete regulation of the subject and enforce it by a so-called tax upon departures from it. To give such magic to the word "tax" would be to break down all constitutional limitation of the powers of Congress and completely wipe out the sovereignty of the states.

. . . This decision will doubtless check further sham use of the taxing power—always excepting the tariff!—by Congress; in any event we may expect, in the future, should new instances arise, increasing frankness from the Supreme Court. All this pre-supposes, of course, continuance of the established structure of federal government and states, and the established scope of judicial review.

The door to the federal action having now been twice shut, what are we to do about child labor, particularly in the stubborn black spots of the South? In my judgment further federal legislation, under the existing Constitution, is unavailing and any such proposal as requiring the products of child labor to be branded as a means of notice to the consumer, before acceptance for interstate shipment, would be as futile as, under *Hammer* v. *Dagenhart*, it is clearly unconstitutional. Naturally, therefore, in and out

of Congress, the friends of the child labor movement are pressing
for a constitutional amendment. But a whole brood of questions
at once demands attention as to the form of such an amendment.
Should the amendment deal with children alone, or should Congress be given power to deal with industrial relations? If the
amendment concern itself wholly with the prohibition of child
labor, what means of enforcement should be provided—what
power or what duty of enforcement should be lodged in the
states? Prohibition of child labor presents different elements from
prohibition of liquor; nevertheless, the Eighteenth Amendment
has taught us something as to the limits of effective federal enforcement. At least it has taught us that there *are* limits. These
are questions that call for the most mature consideration, and
should enlist, for their wise solution, not merely devoted hu-
manitarians, but legal specialists equally zealous to abolish the
plague spots of child labor, but also alive to the delicacies of
American constitutional law and to the inherent difficulties of
law enforcement.

One even ventures to express serious doubt of the wisdom of
a constitutional amendment, rather than, as Secretary Hoover
urges, a renewed energetic movement to rouse the states to action.
Such an attitude, I am well aware, will be received with impatience and disdain by those who see nothing but the cruel evils
of child labor to the exclusion of all else. But the method of
dealing with this ancient enemy does present difficulties perhaps
as important as the evil itself. . . .

Of course child labor is of national concern, and some benefits
will accrue from national action. But this is true of many other
fields which we have not turned over to Washington, because
such concentration would be self-defeating in its execution and
make for a corresponding paralysis of local responsibility.

Withdrawing children from shop and mine is not enough,
unless provision is made to put the children into schools. Today
no state can plead financial want or the need for aid to discharge
these duties. If these rudimentary tasks are not fulfilled by the
states the fact shows that there is not enough civic understanding

and will, among a sufficiently large number of people, to bring to pass a decent level of citizenship. The deeper statesmanship may well be not to attempt removal from the remote center of this or that glaring evil, but to awaken the community to the need of its removal, for only by such vigorous civic education will an informed public opinion, essential to the enforcement of decent standards, be secured and sustained. Only thus will the national aspirations be translated from mere negative prohibitions into affirmatively good lives of men and women. The mere fact that progress through the states in the past has been slow—which, naturally, tries the devotion of such noble champions of children's lives as Mrs. Florence Kelley—need be no measure of future progress. For a new political instrument is now available—the women's vote. Why should not the League of Women Voters in every state make it the order of the day to put a wise child labor law upon the statute books of every state and—what is almost everywhere forgotten—an adequate and efficient corps of inspectors for enforcement? What possible competition for the women's interest *in action* can there be to that of securing a wholesome and just child life? If it be said that the women are least organized in those states where the evil of child labor is the most flagrant, the simple answer is that nothing will furnish such a stimulant to the cohesive organization of women, for the exercise of their political power, as the procurement of fit lives for children. If the women will it, not only would child labor be prohibited by paper legislation but the enforcement of such laws, and an environment fit for children to be born into and to grow up in, will quickly become the possession of every state in the Union. Indeed, the states would furnish competition. not in child labor, but in child welfare.

Law and Order

For a period during and immediately after the World War, Mr. Frankfurter was Chairman of the War Labor Policies Board, created for the purpose of formulating a national labor policy adequate to meet wartime needs. The following selection is from an article appearing in the Yale Review *for the winter of 1920, copyright Yale University Press.*

Just a bare year ago a glowing picture of our industrial relations was drawn by the authoritative presidential hand:

Our people . . . know their own business, are quick and resourceful at every readjustment, definite in purpose and self-reliant in action. . . . I have heard much counsel as to the plans that should be formed and personally conducted to a happy consummation, but from no quarter have I seen any general scheme of "reconstruction" emerge which I thought it likely we could force our spirited businessmen and self-reliant laborers to accept with due pliancy and obedience.

While the war lasted we set up many agencies by which to direct the industries of the country in the services it was necessary for them to render. . . . But the moment we knew the Armistice to have been signed we took the harness off. . . . It is surprising how fast the process of return to a peace footing has moved in the three weeks since the fighting stopped. It promises to outrun any inquiry that may be instituted and any aid that may be offered. It will not be easy to direct it any better than it will direct itself. The American businessman is of quick initiative.

The contrast today between romantic forecast and stern reality is in everyone's mind and, one cannot but hope, part of every man's anxiety. Pandora's box is open—it is needless to stir feelings by even the most surgeon-like summary of the prevailing unrest. Were the proverbial messenger from Mars to visit this country

he would find—where there is the least reason for it—a veritable
devil's dance, with "law and order" emblazoned on the banners.
"Our spirited businessmen and self-reliant laborers" have indeed
been allowed to "go their own way" and, unless we heed, the
drift of their "going" is taking us all perilously near the direction
of Niagara.

The causes of the present discontent have not been born overnight; they have not been fomented, though doubtless intensified,
by alien propaganda. "Agitators" may have found deep-seated
grievances; they did not invent them. No deeper disloyalty has
ever threatened that body of passionate faith which we call American than the effort to stigmatize the orderly clarification and
correction of these grievances as "un-American." "Patriotism" has
always been sought to be invoked for interests less than the common good. But it would be blighting not only the generous traditions of this country, but also the hopes of the world in this
country, to allow the seams of discontent to go deeper because of
the perversion of patriotism by those who are blind and not sensitive to its quality.

The causes of the industrial unrest are perfectly well known.
Apparently they are not so familiar that Macaulay's "every
schoolboy" knows them—but surely they are familiar to every
student of industrial relations. They have been investigated and reported upon by committees and commissions galore. Time has only
served to confirm the diagnosis, to give sharper outlines to the
problem. Of the multitudinous difficulties two emerge as dominant; from them all the rest flow: the lack of scientific organization in industry, and the feelings due to the contrast between
men's participation in political affairs and their exclusion from
the direction of their economic life.

In view of the great achievements of this country in industry,
it must seem temerarious to insist that about those aspects of
industry which most intimately concern the workers, and thereby
most intimately affect the morale of the country, ignorance and
chaos prevail. Wonders have been achieved in mechanical processes, in making nature subservient to our needs and even our

prodigalities. One might almost think the country's energies have been too preoccupied with these material conquests; for pitiable little has been thought or wrought so that we may have the necessary knowledge for a critique of industry, the necessary knowledge as a basis of judgment and action.

.   .   .   .

Industrial unrest is bound to continue just so long as the present state of mind and feeling of workers is generated by growing disparity between their participation in politics and their exclusion from industrial direction. Modern industry more and more stifles the deep creative impulses of the workers at the same time that it emphasizes how illusory is their political power and how unrelated to economic control. They listen to Mr. Bryan's apostrophe, "Behold! a republic in which every man is a sovereign, yet no one cares to wear a crown," only to reflect that as to the essential circumstances of their lives they are but the instruments of needlessly blind chance under the direction of the heads of industry. It is an old story, but at this time we all of us need "education in the obvious more than investigation of the obscure." The last authoritative inquiry into industrial relations made in this country, with wide opportunities for observation and under the most favoring impulses of war, was thus reported to the President:

Broadly speaking, American industry lacks a healthy basis of relationship between management and men. At bottom this is due to the insistence of employers upon individual dealings with their men. Direct dealings with employees' organizations is still the minority rule in the United States. In the majority of instances there is no joint dealing, and in too many instances employers are in active opposition to labor organizations. This failure to equalize the parties in adjustments of inevitable industrial contests is the central cause of our difficulties. There is a commendable spirit throughout the country to correct specific evil. The leaders in industry must go further; they must help to correct the state of mind on the part of labor; they must aim for the release of normal feelings by enabling labor to take its place as a co-partner in the industrial enterprise. In a word, a conscious attempt must be made to generate a new spirit in industry.

Here is the watershed of all the streams of discontent—all the streams that have rush and sweep and power and that will not be denied. And the vague gropings of workers for a dignified participation in industry, for an adequate utilization of their creative faculties, have, of course, been intensified by the war. Generous ideas and glowing watchwords are highest-power explosives. Statesmen cannot regiment a nation behind the appeal to "democracy, liberty, and justice" without compelling men and women to seek significance for these glorious concepts in their daily lives. The impulses aroused by a war waged to bring a new heaven and a new earth cannot be coerced to be content to have the unloveliness and the misery and the repression of the old earth left wholly unchanged.

This familiar analysis suggests its own familiar remedies.

Public opinion must exert its dormant dominance by a frank recognition that the unrest is not "un-American," is not destructive, should not be hunted like a wild beast or a pickpocket. Nor yet must it be looked upon as "belly philosophy." Of course, there are demands for more wages and less hours, but these are really minor issues. Not until there is a generous acceptance of the spiritual depths behind the present unrest will there be or should there be peace among us. Not until then can these depths attain secure and sensible direction. Must it be left to England first to solve the problem of industrial liberty as it was hers to give to the modern world political liberty? Signs are not wanting that she will be the pioneer, driven, perhaps, by the spur of necessity. . . .

Not until we act on a generous acceptance of the fact that what is at stake is a redistribution of power from the autocratic direction of employers to the responsible participation of all who are involved in industry will we get out of the woods of feud and fury. Responsibility for delay in this peaceful adjustment must be made personal. The community must make itself felt. When President Hadley years ago urged social ostracism for social blindness he was merely invoking the pressure of opinion of those upon whom rests *noblesse oblige*. . . .

We thus see that we must carry over into the field of industry the problems of politics. Government in industry, like unto political government, must be worked out where power and responsibility are shared by all those who are participants in industry as well as the dependent "public." The task is nothing less than devising constant processes by which to achieve an orderly and fruitful way of life.

"Collective bargaining" is the starting point of the solution and not the solution itself. This principle must, of course, receive ungrudging acceptance. It is nothing but belated recognition of economic facts—that the era of romantic individualism is no more. These are not days of Hans Sachs, the village cobbler and artist, man and meistersinger. We are confronted with mass production and mass producers; the individual, in his industrial relations, but a cog in the great collectivity. The collectivity must be represented and must be allowed to choose its representatives. And it is through the collectivity, through enlisting its will and its wisdom, that the necessary increase in production alone will come. Needless energy is wasted, precious time is lost, precious feelings are diverted and disturbed by the necessity of fighting for the acceptance of the principle of collective bargaining instead of working out the means and methods of its application. *There* is the rub—on these "details," on organizing industry with collective bargaining as a principle firmly embedded in its structure, invention and intelligence should be centered in this country, as they are in England and Australia and now on the Continent. These questions are still wholly unsolved; we are still in the field of early experimentation. We should study with alert sympathy every trail that is opened up in this country and abroad, realizing the variations of circumstances; conscious, however, that while human nature does change, it does not change much with geography. And so we should get what help we can from the workings of the Whitley Councils in England, similar councils in this country in the clothing and printing industries, the very hopeful results already achieved by the government through its new methods in the Rock Island Arsenal, where men produce primarily because they want to. Every successful experiment must be explored with the scientist's faith that a promising exception can be made the rule.

In a word, we must see these industrial difficulties as a challenge to social engineering, to be grappled with as the medical and the physical sciences meet their problems. Epidemics were once deemed to be visitations of God, but now Dr. Simon Flexner summons his profession consciously to master epidemics. The Rockefeller Institute by a steady and systematic process first seeks to state the problems of disease and then persists until it finds answers. A transcontinental telephone was not the product of a sudden flash of genius nor the gift of happy accident. On the contrary, it was a task definitely set to mathematicians and physicists. Human will and intelligence and persisting faith achieved the miracle. So it must be in industry. The present obstacles to production—the lack of right human relations, the evocation of the creative impulses in workers—are problems to be solved; for upon their solution depends the quality of our civilization. Unemployment is as blighting upon life as an epidemic—and like an epidemic its causes and its sources must first be known and then overcome. Of course, these are most perplexing questions. One is familiar enough with the difficulties of car shortage and storage facilities resulting in idle mines, and, far worse, idle miners. But thus far no systematic effort has been made to apply invention to their solution. And these difficulties can be met, for similar difficulties have been met. Discontinuity of employment in the coal industry can be overcome, for it has been overcome in other industries. What the genius of W. H. McElwain did for the "seasonal" shoe industry can be achieved in other industries.

The spirit and the inventive ferment of the scientist must be brought to bear in industry. We need the authoritative ascertainment of facts both by the government and by industry itself. Light must be shed on all phases of industry, business must be translated into terms of life and judged by the quality of civilization it fosters or frustrates. A civilization eager for its own security must insist on a critique of all aspects of industrial life. . . .

We need, above all, a change of temper, not merely of "capital and labor" towards one another but of both, and particularly of "the public," towards the nature of the problem. On both sides in this country there is distrust of the scientist, the professional student of industry; on the part of labor it is not so much distrust as fear, born of sad experience. This fear is slowly yielding. . . . We need a new public temper, a fructifying atmosphere of good will and humility. Only thus shall we attain to an understanding of the task and its responsibility—the ardent and patient devotion of science to a common social purpose and a common faith. Only thus shall we still the unrest, through processes of law, and not by incantations of "law and order."

Labor Injunctions Must Go

This selection appeared as an unsigned editorial in the New Republic *for September 27, 1922. It followed the issuance of a sweeping injunction by Judge James H. Wilkerson, of the United States District Court in Chicago, against the railway shopmen's strike.*

NEVER in American history has an appeal by the government to the courts, ostensibly on behalf of "law and order," been received with such widespread condemnation as the injunction granted to Attorney General Daugherty at Chicago. Criticism does not abate with time nor with reflection. And never, to such an extent, have conservative organs like the New York *Times* and the *Journal of Commerce* joined in the outcry. That so powerful and responsible a paper as the New York *World* should deem Mr. Daugherty's conduct plausible ground for urging his impeachment is a measure of the depth to which the Attorney General has outraged American feeling. When it comes to criticism of its own, the legal profession, so far at least as represented by "the leaders of the bar," is a reticent priesthood. But so far as legal opinion has become articulate, it supports the popular condemnation. Senator Borah, himself a distinguished lawyer, voices publicly volumes of private legal protest. We have little doubt but that if the President of the American Bar Association, Mr. John W. Davis, were to take the public into his confidence, we should hear some pretty plain speaking.

Such wide and powerful condemnation, obviously, must be deeply grounded. No mere technical differences of opinion, no merely doubtful exercise of discretion can so fiercely and so abidingly stir public and professional feeling. The New York *Times* is very moderate when it declares that certain parts of the Daugherty injunction "are apparently not warranted by federal law or are in conflict with it," and other "provisions . . . whether legally justified or not, are manifestly absurd and incapable of execution." . . .

It is utterly absurd to claim the Debs case as a precedent. Nothing like the following prohibition in the Daugherty injunction was contained in the decree against Debs:

> Attempting to induce by the use of . . . entreaties, argument, persuasions, rewards, or otherwise . . . any person to abandon the employment of said railway companies. . . .
>
> Assembling . . . numbers of the members of said federated shop crafts . . . in proximity of said railway companies . . . and by . . . persuasion . . . entreaties or arguments or in any other way attempt to prevent any of the employees of the said railway companies . . . from entering upon . . . their duties.
>
> In any manner by letters . . . word of mouth . . . oral persuasion or suggestion . . . or otherwise in any manner whatsoever . . . encouraging any person . . . to abandon the employment of said railway companies.

The plain meaning and intent of such prohibitions is the denial of those means of association and activities which *are* a trade union. To say that trade unions have received "affirmative legal recognition of their existence and usefulness and provisions for their protection"—as the Supreme Court of the United States, speaking through Chief Justice Taft, held last June—and at the same time deny them the very means of life, is to make a hypocrite of law, and an enslaving hypocrite.

The simple truth is that Harry M. Daugherty, Attorney General by grace of political friendship, with the complicity of Judge Wilkerson, has set himself above the Constitution, and by his own fiat has prohibited conduct which Congress deliberately refused to declare illegal. The effort to prohibit peaceful, though concerted, abandonment of "the employment of said railway companies," and concerted refusal to re-enter such employment, was tried, under the leadership of Senator Cummins and others, when the Transportation Act of 1920 went through Congress. That effort, as every lawyer knows, failed. Mr. Daugherty goes beyond even this attempted failure. It is certainly questionable whether Congress itself, in view of the First Amendment of the federal Constitution, could put such curbs on "freedom of speech" as Mr. Daugherty jauntily asked for and Judge Wilkerson obeisantly granted. What's the Constitution between friends!—even though one of them happens to be the Attorney General of the United States and the other a federal judge.

The personal elements of the situation are items of aggravation. There is probably agreement by informed professional opinion that in the history of this country there never has been a more unlearned and professionally less equipped Attorney General than Harry M. Daugherty. The spectacle of this man, unrestrained by the statesman's wisdom or the lawyer's tradition from attempting to write his economic prejudices into the law of the land, has a touch of humor which alone saves it from tragedy. The tragic farce was completed by a compliant judge, who had only a few weeks before been appointed by the President, doubtless upon the usual recommendation of his Minister of Justice. And so we read that Judge Wilkerson at once, without careful scrutiny of what he was signing, granted the prayer of the Attorney General, conveyed in a voluminous document of some fifty pages!

.   .   .   .

For more than thirty years the injunction has been used as a familiar weapon in American industrial conflicts. It does not work. It neither mines coal, nor moves trains, nor makes clothing. As an adjustor of industrial conflict the injunction has been an utter failure. It has been used as a shortcut—but it has not cut anything, except to cut off labor from confidence in the rule of law and of the courts as its impartial organs. No disinterested student of American industry, or of American law, can have the slightest doubt that, beginning with the Debs case, the use of labor injunctions has, predominantly, been a cumulative influence for discord in our national life. Mounting embitterment in masses of men and women has generated the growing conviction that the powers of the government are perverted by, and in aid of, the employers, and that the courts are the instruments of this partisan policy. Such has been the price we have paid for this use of the injunction—and the industrial conflict is uglier than ever.

And this result is inevitable so long as this use of the injunction persists. For the acts which injunctions seek to restrain necessarily involve disputed questions of fact, and disputed questions of fact touching men's feelings and motives and opinions. The traditional Anglo-American method for ascertaining such facts is a jury. The social justification of the jury system lies precisely in its element of popular co-operation in the enforcement of law. In labor controversies, if anywhere, one would suppose, this popular vindication of the law would be resorted to. From the point of view of revivifying respect for law and regaining order, no less than from any attempt towards decent industrial relations, it is of the essence that the curb upon trade union action should be administered by courts only through proceedings in which disputed facts are determined by jury.

And there is no reason whatever in so-called expediency for continuing the disastrous shortcut of the injunction. The responsibility of the union, as such, for wrongful acts has now been established. Civil redress by the employer can now be had and should be had only through action for damages. So far as acts of violence are concerned, the resources of the state are ample in the criminal law—if it be made effective. If trade unions are convicted of wrongful acts by their own representatives—the jury of the vicinage—belief in the fairness of law and the impartiality of courts may be restored.

. . . For the moment we know of no more pressing need for the country's well-being than the restoration of confidence in our courts and respect for law through the abandonment of the abuses of the injunction. And the abuse of injunctions in labor cases can be discontinued only by the discontinuance of their use.

The Labor Injunction

This selection is from an article contributed by Mr. Frankfurter
and Mr. Nathan Greene, the latter of the New York Bar, to the
Encyclopedia of the Social Sciences *in 1932 (Vol. VIII, p. 653)*
and is reprinted by permission of the Macmillan Company, pub-
lishers. Two years earlier the same authors had completed their
book, The Labor Injunction.

T HE USE of the injunction in industrial controversies gives
as striking an illustration as the law affords of the truth
that in the domain of ideas, no less than in the biological
world, an organism cannot be torn from the context of its environment without destroying its meaning. Abstractly the labor injunction is merely the application of a generalized legal idea to particular circumstances. But these introduce social and economic
factors which give the injunction a unique setting and create for it
an essentially new situation.

The injunction is the powerful and staple device of the equity
side of Anglo-American legal administration. The first authoritative resort to this remedy in a controversy between employer
and employees was made by an English court. But the innovation
did not take root in its native soil. Until its recent formal revival
in England the labor injunction has remained a chapter of dis-
tinctively American law. As in other fields of social endeavor
American influence has, however, penetrated into Canada. While
as late as 1896 the chief justice of Massachusetts could say in
opposing a labor injunction sanctioned by his court that the "practice of issuing injunctions in cases of this kind is of very recent
origin" . . . the idea once transplanted to America has burgeoned
exuberantly.

The grounds avowed by courts for resorting to the injunction in labor cases are the actual or threatened damage to property rights and inadequacy of legal remedies. To resort to the criminal law, it is urged, is to lock the barn after the horse is stolen, and suits for money damage are futile because money cannot compensate; too many suits would have to be brought in view of the continuing nature of the menace, and the strikers are financially irresponsible. Despite the novelty of the remedy and the serious differences between a labor controversy and the situations for which the injunctions had been historically employed, the Supreme Court in the Debs case concluded that "the jurisdiction of courts to interfere in such matters by injunction is one recognized from ancient time and by indubitable authority." Contemporary legal scholarship challenges this claim.

The labor injunction derives significance from the mode by which it has operated. What is called procedure determines results. In theory the final injunctive decree alone is an adjudication on the merits; temporary restraining orders and temporary injunctions are nominally provisional. In fact, however, the restraining order and temporary injunction usually register the ultimate disposition of a labor litigation, which seldom persists to a final decree. Lack of resources may frustrate pursuit of the litigation or, as is often the case, the strike has ended before the final stage is reached and ended not infrequently as a result of the injunction. . . .

The theoretical safeguards attending the final decree are therefore largely inoperative. Here as elsewhere in law its formal doctrines tell very little of what law does for those who invoke it or against whom it is invoked. Not the so-called principles governing the "rights" and "duties" of the combatants in a strike, but the procedural characteristics of provisional relief furnish the key to an understanding of the labor injunction in action. The truth of the situation is seldom explored through oral testimony, and the proceeding largely resolves itself into a clash of affidavits. These, because they flow from the passionate partisanship of a labor struggle and are drafted more with an eye to the requisites of legal formula than of truth, are generally contradictory in all important particulars. The judge determines the facts without the aid of a jury, and the usual safeguards for sifting fact from distortions or imaginings—personal appearance of witnesses and cross-examination by opposing counsel—are lacking. Finally, the opportunity to correct error by appeal is extremely narrow and seldom exercised.

To be sure, violence is an incident and too often an ingredient of industrial strife in the United States. Latter-day labor racketeering is still another story. Whatever the cause for this violence— the ready resort to violence generally, the survival of pioneer traditions, the less rooted habits of the American population, the exacerbation of feeling or the actual incitement to violence by agents provocateurs and proprietary police—the injunction serves theoretically as a swift and effective check. Legal theory therefore justifies it in so far as it explicitly restrains illegal conduct. But departures from this theory are abundant and indeed common. The text of the injunction has grown to be an elaborate and complex document—a fearsome and ambiguous instrument reaching far beyond outlawed excesses and snuffing out trade union activities which as a matter of abstract law are deemed legitimate. Injunctions have restrained innocent conduct through fear of violation of general and all-inclusive terms of doubtful meaning. They have restrained conduct that is clearly permissible, like furnishing strike benefits, singing songs, maintaining tent colonies; permissible, that is, on the theory that it is the function of the law merely to keep the peace and maintain the ring between employers and employees according to the prevalent standards of fair economic combat. The dangers of these dragnet decrees have led a few of the more farsighted judges to attempt to define with particularity the line between forbidden and permitted conduct. . . . While the injunction is the result of a judicial proceeding between two litigants, its obligations frequently, especially in the federal courts, attach to the general public. By the easy device of blanket clauses its prohibitions extend to "all persons whomsoever" or "all persons to whom notice of this order shall come." All aware of the injunction must obey it or be punished for contempt.

The practical uses to which the labor injunction has been put have turned it into a persisting political issue. It has maintained itself thus to no small degree because disinterested legal opinion has supported the essential grievances of labor. Some of the most learned scholars of equity procedure have found the labor injunction inconsonant with the traditions and philosophy of the whole equitable process. Ever since the Debs case it has been urged that except under appropriate safeguards and within a defined and restricted area the injunction is not an appropriate intervention in the conflict of forces between employers and employed. The decree places the power of the state upon one side of a complicated social struggle in advance of and frequently altogether without that careful ascertainment of fact which is the traditional protection of the innocent; the injunction invades by indirection constitutional safeguards that speech, press, and assembly shall be free from previous restraints; vague and all-inclusive terminology customarily employed results in sweeping decrees which subject all activity—legitimate no less than illegitimate—to the peril of prosecution for contempt; and therefore the injunction becomes in effect a penal code enacted, interpreted, and enforced by a single judge without the constitutional securities available to persons accused of crime.

The extent to which these consequences of the injunction affect the labor conflict lies almost wholly in the realm of guesswork. There are as yet no dependable data regarding the effect of the injunction upon the progress of unionization in America; and equally meager and inconclusive is the evidence, aside from opinion testimony, of the relation of injunctions to the result of particular strikes. Does interdicted conduct cease or is it intensified? Are injunctions enforced and to what extent and with what consequences? Answers to such questions require an intensive and subtle analysis of the elusive factors of particular controversies in their economic, social, and psychological settings. . . . But considerable evidence has necessarily been gathering upon the effect of the injunction on public opinion, particularly on opinion generated by the feelings of the workers. To the United States Commission on Industrial Relations its director in 1915 reported that ". . . there exists among the workers [of whom there were then said to be twenty-five million] an almost universal conviction that they . . . are denied justice in the enactment, adjudication, and administration of law, that the very instruments of democracy are often used to oppress them and to place obstacles in the way of their movement toward economic, industrial, and political freedom and justice."

Labor's feeling against the use of the injunction has certainly not abated since 1915. Nor has its bitterness been appeased by its own occasional resort to the injunction. Labor has employed the injunction as a weapon in internecine conflicts and has invoked it against employers to enforce collective bargaining agreements, to restrain the operation of black lists or to insure some forms of statutory protection. . . . On the whole, however, opportunities for such relief have heretofore been comparatively restricted and the gains achieved have not outweighed the detriments. Moreover the circumstances to which the injunction applies when invoked by labor do not lend themselves to the procedural abuses that have developed as the normal concomitants of the injunctive process against labor. It is not surprising therefore that according to the American Federation of Labor the use of the injunction by labor is "a snare and a delusion."

The pressure of labor for its own immediate interests has combined with the desires for reform of those who are concerned over the weakened prestige of the judiciary, particularly of the federal judiciary, and the undermined confidence in even-handed administration of the law. From the turn of the century there have been manifold attempts at corrective legislation. In their earlier form they were directed against a modification of the ancient doctrines of conspiracy and restraint of trade as applied to contemporary labor conflicts and later on to the outlawry of agreements by workers not to join or remain members of a union —the so-called yellow dog contracts. Corrective measures did in fact reach the statute books, but were in the main nullified by judicial construction. Reform then addressed itself to the procedural aspects of equity jurisdiction in labor cases, ranging from an outright withdrawal of the injunction in labor controversies to the formulation of restricted details in granting such injunction. Here again the courts largely erased what the legislatures wrote. . . . Arizona sustained such a statute, although it finally foundered in the United States Supreme Court. Since this decision . . . was based on the Fourteenth Amendment it has had far-reaching effect upon the movement for dealing with the labor injunction. By the Clayton Act, Congress in 1914 seemed to confine the activities of the federal courts in the issuance of labor injunctions to such narrow limits that Samuel Gompers hailed the Clayton Act as labor's magna carta. But the Supreme Court construed the ambiguous language of the Clayton Act to be "merely declaratory of what is the best practice always" . . . and not as remedying drastically the evils which gave rise to the Clayton Act. In effect therefore the decisions of the Supreme Court and the actions of the lower federal courts have so confined the Clayton Act as to leave substantially intact—in some respects even to enlarge—the grievances against the labor injunction which led to the Clayton Act.

The Supreme Court was more hospitable to another important provision of the Clayton Act—that granting right to trial by jury in certain cases of contempt for violation of an injunction—holding it not to be "an invasion of the power of the courts as intended by the Constitution." . . . This decision was the more significant in that several state courts, interpreting the doctrine of separation of powers as a narrow, mechanical rule of law rather than as a maxim of political wisdom, had invalidated similar state legislation. But in practice this provision of the Clayton Act was narrowly applied.

The labor troubles in the coal, rail, and steel industries in the period following the World War, coming at a time of general conservatism and "Red" phobia, led to a series of injunctions, some of which made the Debs decree look mild. These excesses in turn stimulated a new effort for corrective legislation. Some states, like Illinois and New Jersey, enacted analogues of the Clayton Act, which local courts, following the decision of the Supreme Court upon the Clayton Act, severely limited by construction. A number of states limited—and New York and Wisconsin abolished—the issuance of ex parte orders. In 1928 the Judiciary Committee of the United States Senate proposed a detailed revision of equity practice in labor litigation which sought to withdraw the aid of the federal courts from the enforcement of anti-union agreements, to correct procedural abuses, define and confine discretionary jurisdiction and to extend the right of jury trial for contempt. This proposal became law upon March 23, 1932, when President Hoover signed a bill embodying it. . . .

Government and Administration

The Task of Administrative Law

One of Mr. Frankfurter's chief interests has been administrative law and the actual administration of public policies. It was as Byrne Professor of Administrative Law that he served on the Harvard Law School faculty. The following selection appeared as an article in the University of Pennsylvania Law Review *for May, 1927 (Vol. 75, p. 614).*

THE WIDENING area of what in effect is law-making authority, exercised by officials whose actions are not subject to ordinary court review, constitutes perhaps the most striking contemporary tendency of the Anglo-American legal order. The massive volumes of Statutory Rules and Orders, published annually since 1890, testify to the pervasive domain of delegated legislation in Great Britain. The formulation and publication of executive orders and rules and regulations are in this country still in a primitive stage, which only serves to render more portentous the operation of these forms of law. But the range of control conferred by Congress and the state legislatures upon subsidiary law-making bodies, variously denominated as heads of departments, commissions and boards, penetrates in the United States, as in Great Britain and the Dominions, the whole gamut of human affairs. Hardly a measure passes Congress the effective execution of which is not conditioned upon rules and regulations emanating from the enforcing authorities. These administrative complements are euphemistically called "filling in the details" of a policy set forth in statutes. But the "details" are of the essence; they give meaning and content to vague contours. The control of banking, insurance, public utilities, finance, industry, the professions, health and morals, in sum, the manifold response of government to the forces and needs of modern society, is building up a body of laws not written by legislatures, and of adjudications not made by courts and not subject to their revision. These powers are lodged in a vast congeries of agencies. We are in the midst of a process, largely unconscious and certainly unscientific, of adjusting the exercise of these powers to the traditional system of Anglo-American law and courts. A systematic scrutiny of these issues and a conscious effort towards their wise solution are the concerns of administrative law. The broad boundaries and far-reaching implications of these problems may be indicated by saying that administrative law deals with the field of legal control exercised by law-administering agencies other than courts, and the field of control exercised by courts over such agencies.

But administrative law is hardly yet given *de jure* recognition by the English-speaking bar although the term has now established itself in the vocabulary of the United States Supreme Court. Until very recently even scholars treated it as an exotic. Thus Dicey in his classic *Law of the Constitution* thanked God like a true Briton that *le droit administratif* of the tyrannized French had no counterpart on English soil. But in his "Introduction" to the last edition, he showed himself painfully aware that the channel which separates tendencies in English law from the system and precepts which the French call *droit administratif* is constantly narrowing. Before that "Introduction" reached the public, he had made still handsomer concessions. Again like a true Briton, facing facts eventually and not forever denying them, Dicey was jolted by the famous Arlidge case[1] into writing an exposition of its deep significance. The very title of his essay— "The Development of Administrative Law in England"—must have aroused many an unsuspecting reader. The development to which Dicey so strikingly directed attention in April, 1915, has since then luxuriantly unfolded, and English writers have analyzed acutely the deep forces it reflects. Yet the Lord Chief Justice only the other day inveighed against it as though it were an alien and wholly avoidable phenomenon!

[1] *Local Government Board* v. *Arlidge* (1915), A.C. 120.

In the United States, the pioneer scholarship of Frank J. Good-
now and Ernst Freund long remained caviar not merely to the
general. Their work was for many years unheeded by bench and
bar, a fact which is not too surprising when it is recalled that
legal education hardly took note of it. But the prophetic scholar
has his amused revenge when practice propounds theory. Necessity *is* the mother of discovery. And so this illegitimate exotic,
administrative law, almost overnight overwhelmed the profession,
which for years had been told of its steady advance by the lonely
watchers in the tower. Hardly a volume of bar association proceedings is now without some reference to this new phenomenon.
Brute fact compels resort to despised philosophy. Isolated cases,
in their multitudinous and varying recurrence, require correlation
and creative direction. Thus we find this weighty recognition of
the exigency of our problem in Senator Root's presidential address
to the American Bar Association for 1916:

There is one special field of law development which has manifestly
become inevitable. . . . The Interstate Commerce Commission, the
state public service commissions, the Federal Trade Commission, the
powers of the Federal Reserve Board, the health departments of the
states, and many other supervisory offices and agencies are familiar illustrations. Before these agencies the old doctrine prohibiting the delega-
tion of legislative power has virtually retired from the field and given
up the fight. There will be no withdrawal from these experiments. We
shall go on; we shall expand them, whether we approve theoretically or
not, because such agencies furnish protection to rights and obstacles to
wrong-doing which under our new social and industrial conditions cannot be practically accomplished by the old and simple procedure of legislatures and courts as in the last generation. Yet the powers that are
committed to these regulating agencies, and which they must have to
do their work, carry with them great and dangerous opportunities of
oppression and wrong. If we are to continue a government of limited
powers, these agencies of regulation must themselves be regulated. The
limits of their power over the citizen must be fixed and determined.
The rights of the citizen against them must be made plain. A system
of administrative law must be developed, and that with us is still in its
infancy, crude and imperfect.

Similar appeals have been made by Charles E. Hughes, Mr. Justice Sutherland and William D. Guthrie. One passage in Mr. Guthrie's address before the New York State Bar Association in 1923 strikingly illustrates how far we have traveled from the conventional conception entertained by English-speaking lawyers of *droit administratif*, as an essential denial of the Rule of Law:

> I am not prepared to say that the time has yet come for the creation of special courts similar to the French administrative courts, although I am convinced that this will ultimately be found to be advisable.

One could hardly find more emphatic evidence than this utterance by a distinguished common law lawyer of the gradual approach of different systems of law in fashioning similar covenants and similar swords in order to regulate similar situations.

It is idle to feel either blind resentment against "government by commission" or sterile longing for a golden past that never was. Profound new forces call for new social inventions, or fresh adaptations of old experience. The "great society," with its permeating influence of technology, large-scale industry, and progressive urbanization, presses its problems; the history of political and social liberty admonishes us of its lessons. Nothing less is our task than fashioning instruments and processes at once adequate for social needs and the protection of individual freedom. The vast changes wrought by industry during the nineteenth century inevitably gave rise to a steady extension of legal control over economic and social interests. At first, state intervention manifested itself largely through specific legislative directions, depending for enforcement generally upon the rigid, cumbersome and ineffective machinery of the criminal law. By the pressure of experience, legislative regulation of economic and social activities has turned to administrative instruments. Inevitably this has greatly widened the field of discretion and thus opened the door to its potential abuse, arbitrariness. In an acute form and along a wide range of action, we are confronted with new aspects of familiar conflicts in the law between rule and discretion.

Because of the danger of arbitrary conduct in the administrative application of legal standards (such as "unreasonable rates," "unfair methods of competition," "undesirable residents of the United States"), our administrative law is inextricably bound up with constitutional law. But after all, the Constitution is a *Constitution,* and not merely a detailed code of prophetic restrictions against the ineptitudes and inadequacies of legislators and administrators. Ultimate protection is to be found in the people themselves, their zeal for liberty, their respect for one another and for the common good—a truth so obviously accepted that its demands in practice are usually overlooked. But safeguards must also be institutionalized through machinery and processes. These safeguards largely depend on a highly professionalized civil service, an adequate technique of administrative application of legal standards, a flexible, appropriate and economical procedure (always remembering that "in the development of our liberty insistence upon procedural regularity has been a large factor"), easy access to public scrutiny, and a constant play of criticism by an informed and spirited bar. They are still to be achieved, for we have hardly begun to realize deeply their need. Particularly in the field of so-called minor interests, administrative technique and traditions demand study and improvement. The vast interests confided to bodies like the Interstate Commerce Commission, the Federal Trade Commission and state public service commissions, just because they are so vast, are not likely to suffer much nor long from incompetence or injustice in our legal system. The incidence of law, . . . is most significant at the lowest point of contact. The experience of the mass of men with law's relation to their small concerns is the most important generator of that confidence in law which is its ultimate sanction.

Undoubtedly, a reading of the current law reports gives a just sense of the confusion and incoherence, of the rampant empiricism, which characterize the present state of administrative law. But we must be on our guard against an undue quest for certainty, born of an eager desire to curb the dangers of discretionary power. For the problem of rule *versus* discretion is far broader than its manifestations in administrative law. There are fields of legal control where certainty—mechanical application of fixed rules—is attainable; there are other fields where law necessarily means the application of standards—a formulated measure of conduct to be applied by a tribunal to the unlimited versatility of circumstance. To be sure, the application of a standard to individual cases opens the door to those abuses of carelessness and caprice and oppression against which we cannot be too alert. But resort to standards avoids the oppression and injustice due to abstractions (*e.g.*, "freedom of contract" instead of a working girl) whereby individual instances are tortured into universal molds which do not fit the infinite variety of life.

In administrative law we are dealing pre-eminently with law in the making; with fluid tendencies and tentative traditions. Here we must be especially wary against the danger of premature synthesis, of sterile generalization unnourished by the realities of "law in action." Administrative law is also markedly influenced by the specific interests entrusted to a particular administrative organ, and by the characteristics—the history, the structure, the enveloping environment—of the administrative to which these interests are entrusted. Thus "judicial review" and "administrative discretion" cannot be studied in isolation. "Judicial review" is not a conception of well-defined scope operative wherever the courts review the action of administrative bodies. The problems subsumed by "judicial review" or "administrative discretion" must be dealt with organically; they must be related to the implications of the particular interest that invokes a "judicial review" or as to which "administrative discretion" is exercised. Therefore, a subject like "judicial review," in any scientific development of administrative law, must be studied not only horizontally, but vertically, *e.g.*, "judicial review" of Federal Trade Commission orders, "judicial review" of postal fraud orders, "judicial review" of deportation warrants. For judicial review in postal cases, for instance, is colored by the whole structure of which it forms a part, just as in land office cases, or in immigration cases, or in utility valuations, or in insurance license revocations, it derives significance from the nature of the subject matter under review as well as from the agency which is reviewed.

What we need, above all else, is to know what is happening by objective demonstration of intensive scientific studies, instead of merely speculating, even wisely speculating, or depending on partisan claims of one sort or another. Research to no small measure is a painful means of proving what the insight of a few suspects or feels. There is need also for a technique of appraising the work of administrative agencies and of establishing the utility of such scientific appraisals. The generalizations, the philosophizing, will gradually emerge from specific studies. Intensive studies of the administrative law of the states and the nation in practice will furnish the necessary prerequisite to an understanding of what administrative law is really doing, so that we may have an adequate guide for what ought to be done. Here, as in other branches of public law, only here probably more so, we must travel outside the covers of lawbooks to understand law.

Only a physiological study of administrative law in action will disclose the processes, the practices, the determining factors, of administrative decisions, and illumine the relation between commissions and courts now left obscure by the printed pages of court opinions. . . . While the tendencies with which we are concerned are new in their pervasiveness and proportions, . . . these seemingly very modern problems are rooted in history. The shaping of our administrative law thus calls for students trained in the common law and familiar with its history. But, in addition, the inquirer must have a sympathetic understanding of the major causes which have led to the emergence of modern administrative law, and must be able to move freely in the world of social and economic facts with which administrative law is largely concerned. Above all, he must have a rigorously scientific temper of mind. For we are seeking the formulation of a body of law based upon objective criteria when, in truth, studies . . . must themselves largely formulate and even create the criteria which scientific inquiry assumes.

The Young Men Go to Washington

This selection appeared as an article in Fortune Magazine *for January, 1936, and is reprinted by courtesy of the editors.*

ABOUT ten years ago, one of the most eminent of Europeans, visiting this country, was disturbed to find a photograph of Mussolini, signed by the Duce himself, occupying a proud place in the studies of a leading banker and of a famous university president. This, to the knowing sniff of a statesman, revealed a change of political climate in high places, an ominous loss of robust faith in the traditional ideals of the United States. Our visitor was indeed correct in finding evidences of influential distrust of democracy. It had become the fashion to deify what was called efficiency, to concentrate on the difficulties of democracy, to compare the practical workings of democratic society with the paper advantages of omniscient dictatorship. As long ago as the third century B.C., Aristotle explained definitively how dictatorships come into being and how they maintain themselves, until chaos and ruin overtake their victims. But we learn very little from books. Old forms of tyranny with new labels, sponsored with blood-and-thunder oratory, began to make alluring appeal to people who were not fired by the realization that democracy, especially in a country like ours, is not an automatic device for good government, but a continuous and exacting demand for the exercise of reason on the most extensive scale.

Men learn little from books, but they respond to experience. Better than if contrived as laboratory experiments for our especial benefit, the last two years have disclosed before our eyes the inevitable operations of dictatorship. They have brought to life the exact fidelity of Aristotle's pictures of tyrannies painted more than two thousand years ago. We have been nauseated by "purges" both in Berlin and in Moscow, and we have recalled—what we had too quickly forgotten—the brutalities and violence which followed the march on Rome. As a result, our democratic faith has been invigorated. Doubts about the validity of our great past, though still vigorous, are by no means universal; perhaps the visitor of ten years ago might not now find Mussolini's photograph in a place of pride even in the studies of the leading banker and the famous university president. One hears from time to time much shallow talk about the elimination of politics, as though politics—the free exchange of opinion regarding the best policy for the life of a society—were not the essence of a free and vigorous people. A dictatorship means precisely the prohibition of politics. Nothing has more vindicated democracy than the unhampered exercise of freedom of discussion, howsoever hostile and misrepresentative, during three years of gigantic effort to meet the greatest economic and social crisis within the framework of the traditional American political system.

Democracy is the only way, rough as that way may be, to a civilization that adequately respects and thereby helps to unfold the richness of human diversity. Men to whom the future is an anxious concern no less than those to whom the past is a treasured heritage have no choice but to make democracy work better. For acceptance of the democratic idea by no means implies exhaustion of the various forms in which the idea can be made to work better. If the depression and the government's attempts to master it have done nothing else they have revealed, as never before, the intimacy between government and the welfare of the individual, have revealed that government is not something outside of or in opposition to the public, but is the expression and agent of society. Bankers and businessmen and railroad executives have as a matter of course come to expect government to finance them in their difficulties. The farmer has dumped his surplus on its doorstep. Men and women in every walk of life have come to assume that government must safeguard economic security and, as a last resort in an economic world too unmanageable for individual mastery, even provide such security. To have aroused this new intensity of interest in government—without which democracy cannot effectively function—may, if sustained, appear in the perspective of history as the most important political achievement of our time.

This interest in government on the part of the general public is both the result and the cause of a shift in the conception of the functions of government from that of a big policeman to that of a powerful promoter of society's welfare. "Governments have come to be engaged," according to that wise student of politics, the late Graham Wallas, "not merely in preventing wrong things from being done, but in bringing it about that right things shall be done. A negative government only requires courage and consistency in its officials; but a positive government requires a constant supply of invention and suggestions." Rugged individualism, in the sense of the fullest possible opportunity for development of American men and women, will, one hopes, always continue to be the ultimate aim of American society. But "rugged individualism," as a theory of political non-action and as a practice of hands off by government, has been dead in England since the days of Gladstone and Disraeli, and in this country was buried by Theodore Roosevelt beyond resurrection even by Harding and Coolidge.

Party slogans are one thing, party actions quite another. The elder Huxley once said that old theories survived long after their brains were knocked out. So, old shibboleths continue to enlist feelings long after they have ceased to correspond to reality. In our day no government, whatever its party livery, can avoid responsibility for insuring minimum economic security. Undoubtedly the arrangements by which this general end is sought will vary from time to time. In the give-and-take of minor issues of political partisanship, the people may in turn prefer the solicitations of different political parties asking for responsibility to execute such a program. Undoubtedly also, in the future as in the past, there will be differences of emphasis in the division of responsibility between the states and the national government in translating our federal tradition into daily practice. But the fact itself, and the

tremendous implication of the existence of an enlarged governmental responsibility for the welfare of the people are—like all
humanitarian advances in the history of the English-speaking peoples—here to stay. Alphabetical agencies will continue, or anal-
phabetical agencies will take their place.

Administratively that means much more than the supervision
of old-age and unemployment benefits. Let us consider aspects of
governmental activity quite outside the field of controversy. As part
of any fundamental effort at economic security, both as a stabiliz-
ing factor upon business and as a necessary public protection, we
are certain to continue the regulation of businesses affected with
a public interest which, for the nation, began with the Interstate
Commerce Act in 1887 and has steadily increased since, as to both
the area and the intensity of regulation. Again, the reports of the
Mississippi Valley Committee and of the National Resources
Board are in direct line of descent from Theodore Roosevelt's
conservation policies. Our national welfare will not long permit
that they remain dust gatherers or unexecuted blueprints. The
economic security of the country as a whole, not any doctrinaire or
sentimental theory, will compel a program for the protection and
utilization of our natural resources which will cast upon government responsibilities that private enterprise could not possibly assume, and may well make of government in this country the
greatest builder of all times.

To translate such general policies into wise legislation is sufficiently difficult. But it is child's play compared with the task of
giving the words on the statute books meaning in action, to translate policy into life. The reality of the words of a statute appears
only in the human administration of the statute and that is especially true of statutes dealing with the large, complicated affairs
which now belong to government. Profound experience in the history of liberty is expressed in the noble words of John Adams in
formulating the American ideal of "government of laws, not of
men." But there can be no government of laws except through
men. Administration of a statute, like the administration of a business, depends on the quality of its administrator. Sensible and hu-

mane government is impossible without well-trained, disciplined, imaginative, modest, energetic, and devoted administrators. Indeed, with its modern tasks, government will need even better talent than that which private enterprise enlists. For with us, not until individual initiative has proved its inability to manage enterprise does government take it over. Nor does government begin new enterprises unless private business cannot undertake them.

If, then, democracy is to work, we must in the future, more than ever before, temper the romantic American political tradition that everyone is competent for everything with the common sense of John Stuart Mill's observation: "Mediocrity ought not to be engaged in the affairs of state." How it would baffle the understanding of Mill and even more the purity of his heart to find men of influence today erecting such mediocrity into a philosophy. A former president of the United States Chamber of Commerce was apparently not indulging in subtle irony when he expressed these views: "The best public servant is the worst one. . . . A thoroughly first-rate man in public service is corrosive. He eats holes in our liberties. The better he is and the longer he stays the greater is the danger." And more recently the following advice was publicly tendered to the President concerning the class of men of unusual ability whom this administration has attracted to Washington: "They are not the typical bureaucrats interested in obeying the routine and holding their jobs as inconspicuously as possible, for as long as possible. They are an active, inventive, pushing bureaucracy with many achievements to their credit that would have been beyond the imagination of an ordinary bureaucracy. But they will become a nuisance to the President if he does not promote the good ones to the status of ordinary officials and send the rest of them home with love and kisses." One is reminded of Mr. Gladstone's superb efforts more than eighty years ago in making the beginnings of the British Civil Service of today. "The effect of such a change," says Lord Morley of Gladstone's share in establishing the great British Civil Service, "has been enormous not only on the efficiency of the service, but on the education of the country, and by a thousand indirect influences, raising and strengthening the social feeling for the immortal maxim that the career should be open to the talents. The lazy doctrine that men are much of a muchness gave way to a higher respect for merit and to more effectual standards of competency." Doubtless Mr. Gladstone's reforms were also characterized by some contemporary as the introduction of an "active, inventive, pushing bureaucracy." They were certainly resented as such. This is the contemporaneous picture of the old system which offered such stubborn resistance to Mr. Gladstone when he sought to put the bureaucracy on the basis of professional competence:

> The existing scores of civil servants do not like the new plan, because the introduction of well-educated, active men will force them to bestir themselves, and because they cannot hope to get their own ill-educated sons appointed under the new system. The old established political families habitually batten on the public patronage—their sons legitimate and illegitimate, their relatives and dependents of every degree, are provided for by the score.

This cult of mediocrity certainly did not commend itself to the New England railroads who urged the reappointment of Mr. Eastman as a member of the Interstate Commerce Commission although they disagreed with his views on vital railroad issues. Fear of brains will not advance the solution of problems that call exigently for solution. "Typical bureaucrats interested in obeying the routine and holding their jobs as inconspicuously as possible for as long as possible" will never solve the intricate problems confronting the Social Securities Board in establishing a system of minimum security for the masses. Nor will they succeed in liquidating without loss the $5,750,000,000 which the Reconstruction Finance Corporation invested to save private industry; nor be able to supervise wisely the chameleon-like financial transactions which the Securities and Exchange Commission has been instructed to protect, in the interests of both the investment market and the public.

Surely the common sense of the American people has become thoroughly aware of that fact. The tide of public conviction favors able and trained men in government, not only among the masses who have hitherto had little feeling of identification with government, but also with the great majority of businessmen, big and little. They would be less than sensible did they think otherwise. Since there had to be an RFC to come to the rescue of business, it is obviously advantageous to the complicated and often desperate circumstances that confront businessmen that the personnel of the RFC be competent, resourceful, and energetic. And since the regulation of capital issues and of the exchanges was bound to come and is bound to stay, it is to the selfish interests of those subject to regulation in this highly technical hair-trigger business that the administrative operations of the SEC be technically informed, skillful, sagacious, flexible, and courageous. Industry and finance, no less than the general public, have been more than fortunate that both of these new agencies of government have managed, by extraordinarily competent leadership, to acquire staffs which, according to a consensus of opinion, compare favorably with the representatives of finance and industry who seek either to cooperate with, or to circumvent them. Whether these commissions, so profoundly important to the economic and social well-being of the country, continue to maintain a high administrative level or sink into ineffective mediocrity will depend largely on the prevailing atmosphere of public opinion regarding public service. The esteem in which government work is held will determine whether men of parts are drawn to governmental posts. The attraction of such posts is not money but the opportunity for men of genuine ability to do really useful work and to try their mettle on problems worthy of their best powers.

Complaints concerning the quality of federal administration are not new, though at the moment more vociferous than usual. The critics echo Mark Twain—"There is no end of the laws and no beginning to the execution of them." Whosoever had come to power on March 4, 1933, would have been confronted overnight with new tasks of overwhelming magnitude for government to assume. A recovering patient never remembers, fortunately perhaps, how devilishly sick he was. It is easy to pick flaws in the administration of the spate of new measures which had to be improvised for emergencies—too easy. But the fair-minded public should keep in mind considerations that will move the historians of our time. It is essential to observe certain canons of criticism that are usually neglected because they are so obvious. Headlines announce the occasional egregious blunder, but day-by-day achievement is unchronicled. The clash of politics, the friction between executive and legislature, the taste for scandal, the preoccupation with personalia, make us know whatever goes wrong in government. It is right that it should be so. The critics of government cannot be too Argus-eyed. But no like conjunction of forces educates the public to a knowledge of the good in government. Virtue is proverbially not news, and appreciation of achievement in government, except when attained on the colossal scale of a Panama Canal or in the dramatized conflict of foreign relations, is all too dependent on dull technical details. The public is therefore surprisingly uninformed of the extent to which its servants contribute to the public good. And so the all-too-common depreciation of men in public service is at once shallow and cruel. It debilitates where it should encourage. A collection of condemnatory comments on the Presidents alone, from Washington down, would make a choice anthology of abuse, but it would be a nonsensical history of the United States.

Take the usual uncritical comparisons between business and government. One need not subscribe to the personal views of Henry Cabot Lodge, shared by his friend Theodore Roosevelt, that "The businessman dealing with a large political question is really a painful sight," nor even to the similar testimony of Lloyd George, as War Prime Minister, about businessmen as administrators. Certainly the undramatic Reports of the United States Supreme Court reveal authoritatively that business and finance have their ample quota of favoritism, sharp practices, incompetence, and failures. Moreover, it is too often overlooked that government as a rule undertakes no services or regulations except after private agencies have proved themselves incapable or unwilling. Under such circumstances, to succeed even measurably is proof of initiative and invention in public enterprise. Hence, in addition to the legitimate criticisms of public administration, there is the much larger fault-finding due to comparing preconceived theories about government with the best practices of business, instead of the *prevailing* practices of government with the *prevailing* practices in business. In a word, government has the benefits as well as the burdens of being subjected to the judgment of higher standards than those which are conventional in private business.

Certainly the student of history will place contemporary administrative problems in the perspective of history. The vital consideration was put by an undisputed leader of the New York bar whose office is very close to Wall Street. He was overheard to say that the central task of the present administration was to correct, overnight, conditions which were allowed to go unattended for twenty or thirty years. The War not only interrupted the execution of Woodrow Wilson's domestic program; it aggravated and enlarged the problems the solution of which was being neglected. With the inevitable growth, in the soil of our political traditions, of administrative duties which the depression created, the wonder is not that administrative difficulties have arisen, but that the improvisations function so well. People talk glibly about "principles of government" as though there were a pharmacopoeia of politics and economics to which one could go for prescriptions. More than a hundred years ago, one of the greatest of the Justices, speaking for the Supreme Court, shattered this illusion of simplicity, and a hundred years have multiplied out of all proportion the intricacy and the novelty of our problems. "The science of government," said Mr. Justice William Johnson, "is the most abstruse of all sciences; if, indeed, that can be called a science, which has but few fixed principles, and practically consists in little more than the exercise of a sound discretion, applied to the exigencies of the state as they arise. It is the science of experiment."

Inevitably, with the problems of administration created by the depression, younger men have found their way into places of great responsibility. The political law of gravitation has operated as it usually operates when new problems call for new endeavor. It was not accident that the founders of the republic were mostly youngish men. Disinterested enthusiasm, freedom from imprisoning dogmatism, capacity for fresh insight, unflagging industry, ardor for difficulties—these are qualities that in the main youthful years must supply. Moreover, except under the romantic and compelling circumstances of war, men who have already succeeded in life seldom can be induced to abandon an assured career or to sever the manifold ties of private life at the call of public service. Of course much valuable part-time work has been done, with fine public spirit, by important business and professional men. But government business, like private business, cannot be conducted effectively except at full time and with undivided allegiance. For various reasons, therefore, it would not have been possible to meet the burdens which the depression thrust on government by recruiting dollar-a-year men as was done during the War.

The tasks of these younger men have been vastly more complicated and diverse than even those that faced the winners of the War, and they have been subjected, as the price of our democracy, to the most bitter partisan criticism, whereas it was deemed unpatriotic to criticize the mistakes and deficiencies of War administrators. By their disinterested contribution of energy, ability, training, and imagination to the public service, hundreds of unknown young men and women have demonstrated beyond doubt that the indispensable step for improving the public service lies in some method of keeping a constant flow of qualified young people attracted to it.

Much of the work of government makes very little demand on that political sense and shrewdness in negotiation which age and experience alone can give. Scientists and lawyers in government work need little of such skill. And as the world becomes more complicated, no man's experience can possibly encompass all the problems of his specialty. Moreover, specialized experience more and more tends to restrict the horizon, to hamper the mind rather than guide it wisely in the disposition of a new combination of factors in interrelated complexities of public problems. A first-rate, well-trained, lively mind of twenty-five is better economy for the government than the services of those who, in the language of Civil Service Commissioner Leonard D. White, "have failed to achieve success in the competitive world, and who in middle life seek refuge in the official world." "I always regard men and women," once said Sir Robert Morant, the greatest of recent British civil servants, "who work at all seriously at things, as falling into two classes roughly—those who leave absolutely no stone unturned to make the thing they are at a success, and those who turn just enough stones to make it just about do." It is the younger official mostly who leaves absolutely no stone unturned, especially when stones to be turned are new. The younger man's enthusiasm and capacity for learning rapidly assimilate the wider field of which his particular routine task is only a part. He is freed from complicated ramifications of private life; he is diverted by a minimum of vanities and jealousies; he is more resilient, more cooperative in taking orders; and his technical preparation for his work is on the whole much better than the equipment of the generation that preceded him.

Under the direction of leadership capable of utilizing energy and imagination and disciplined intelligence in subordinates, a continuous supply of this type of young man would furnish constant renewal of energy and ability and disinterestedness to public administration. To evolve such a system for government would merely imitate the practice of the biggest law offices of this country. Annually these recruit their lower ranks from the best men of the graduating classes of the leading law schools. From such recruits the government could hope to develop at least a portion into permanent public servants of higher grade. Even those who left after a few years would not be completely lost to public service. To the communities where they were engaged in private enterprise they would bring that continuing interest in public affairs which a former public servant seldom loses. From them might come, ten or fifteen years later, the mature leaders of public affairs in their generation. Many of the older able men in the federal government today had a youthful place in the affairs of government fifteen or twenty years ago. In every administration, the occasional really first-class man willing to leave established success in private enterprise for the new risks of an important post on the firing line of governmental affairs has more often than otherwise been one who in his youth tasted the joy of disinterested public service.

How young men of first-rate caliber can, year by year, be won for government service, in periods of calm no less than in days of excitement, and how an adequate proportion of them can be retained permanently, are problems that do not divide parties. They seem unimportant in comparison with the economic and political slogans that rend the air. But upon their answer may well depend the success of whatever economic and social program theoretically prevails.

Government cannot compete with private employers for the most desirable recruits through the ordinary inducements. The best of the annual crop of the good law schools, for instance, will normally be offered places in the great private law offices of New York and other centers with promises of immediate professional opportunity that are exceedingly alluring. The great potential rewards with which business tempts able young lawyers, engineers, and economists serve as a powerful attraction to ambitious youth. Moreover, the impalpable pressure of the conventional standards of achievement is overwhelmingly on the side of private gain. Nevertheless, even before the depression, there was a perceptible drift of interest to the public service. Successful practitioners, distinguished judges, and industrial leaders were eager to see their sons start rather than finish their careers in public life. The depression has given vigorous momentum to this tendency. In no section of public opinion is there greater sensitiveness to the inadequacy of old catchwords and obsolete theories to meet the needs of our day than among the young who have to face life on their own. More and more, the ablest of them—in striking contrast to what was true thirty years ago—are eager for service in government. They find satisfaction in work which aims at the public good and which presents problems that challenge the best ability and courage of man.

Business and the Courts

Public Services and the Public

The following selection was delivered as one of the Dodge Lectures in Government at Yale University in 1930, appeared first as an article in the Yale Review *for the autumn of 1930, and later as a chapter in Mr. Frankfurter's book,* The Public and Its Government *(1930), copyright Yale University Press.*

N O TASK more profoundly tests the capacity of our government, both in nation and state, than its share in securing for society those essential services which are furnished by public utilities. Our whole social structure presupposes satisfactions for which we are dependent upon private economic enterprise. To think of contemporary America without the intricate and pervasive systems which furnish light, heat, power, water, transportation, communication, is to conjure up another world. The needs thus met are today as truly public services as the traditional governmental functions of police and justice. That both law and opinion differentiate from all other economic enterprise the economic undertakings which furnish these newer services is not the slightest paradox. The legal conception of "public utility" is merely the law's acknowledgment of "irreducible and stubborn facts."

The crux of the matter was put sixty years ago by Charles Francis Adams, the younger, in one of his famous reports for the Massachusetts Board of Railroad Commissioners. He laid down this basic principle: "All sums exacted from the community for transportation, whether of persons or of property, constitute an exaction in the nature of a tax—just as much a tax as water rates, or the assessments on property, or the tariff duties on imports. . . . The reduction of this tax to the lowest possible amount paid for the greatest possible service rendered, always observing, of course, the precepts of good faith and the conditions of a sound railroad system—this must be the great object the [railroad] commissioners retain always in view." Railroad regulation was the precursor of the far-flung system of utility control today, and what Charles Francis Adams said about the relation of transportation to the community applies with equal force to more recent utility services.

Indeed, the services rendered by what we now call "public utilities" have been under public supervision of some sort for a century. Regulation of railroad rates by the states began with railroad transportation. From the outset, the special charters by which railroads were authorized prescribed maximum rates or, more frequently, permitted the railroads to fix their charges—subject to limitations upon the amount of net earnings. Provisions like these are found in New York legislation, for instance, as far back as 1828. There were also requirements as to facilities and services. But they were tenuous attempts at control and proved increasingly ineffective. So legislatures began to experiment with early forms of continuous administrative oversight of railroads and, in the wheat regions, of grain elevators. Water and light companies, first gas and then electricity, largely restricted their services during this period to individual communities, and regulation by such localities sufficed. Gradually, the extension of the area of service by the utilities, the political influences they exerted, the technological advances, the feebleness of existing machinery and procedure for control, combined to make the movement for more effective regulation of public utilities perhaps the most significant political tendency in this country at the turn of the century.

Congress had set the states an example in the establishment of the Interstate Commerce Commission in 1887, and Roosevelt made vivid the need for government to counterbalance the powerful economic forces in whose keeping the public services then were. The incapacity of the existing system of regulation to cope with revealed abuses and the emergence of new forms of public services, like pipe lines and power, were texts employed by Roose-

velt with constant reiteration. By arousing the country, he secured
from Congress legislation which energized the enforcement of the
Interstate Commerce Act and greatly extended its scope. Roosevelt was really in the tradition of the Granger Movement, which
in the '70s began "to put teeth" into law for the control of railroads. In a considerable degree he expressed the midwestern emphasis in politics, of which men like the elder La Follette of Wisconsin and Dolliver of Iowa had become the most conspicuous
leaders. But by dramatizing these problems and utilizing to the
full the prestige of the presidency, Roosevelt gave impetus to the
progressive forces within the states to control their utilities. The
modern system of state utility regulation thus coincides with the
efforts of Roosevelt to arm the federal government with powers
adequate to assure interstate public services.

The present systems of state utility regulation have been operative about a quarter of a century. Wisconsin led the way, quickly
followed by New York. Urgent public needs prompted the legislation. Its rationale was public protection through governmental
instrumentalities that should be capable of matching, in power and
in technical resources, the power and resources of the public utilities. The situation was thus put by Governor Hughes in his message to the New York Legislature of 1907, recommending the
passage of a public service commission law:

Proper means for the regulation of the operations of railroad corporations should be supplied. For want of it, pernicious favoritism has been
practiced. Secret rebates have been allowed, and there have been unjust
discriminations in rates and in furnishing facilities for transportation.
Those who have sought to monopolize trade have thus been enabled
to crush competition and to grow in wealth and power by crowding out
their rivals who have been deprived of access to markets upon equal
terms. These abuses are not to be tolerated. Congress has legislated
upon the subject with reference to interstate commerce, where naturally
the evil has been most prominent. But domestic commerce must be
regulated by the state, and the state should exercise its power to secure
impartial treatment to shippers and the maintenance of reasonable rates.
There is also need of regulation and strict supervision to ensure ade-

quate service and due regard for the convenience and safety of the
public. The most practicable way of attaining these ends is for the legislature to confer proper power upon a subordinate administrative body.

Prior to this legislation, the two vital elements in the part
played by utilities in the community's life were the dependence
of the community upon the utilities and the reliance upon the self-
interest of private enterprise in vindicating this public trust. The
new legislation was intended to create governmental instruments
and processes through which sound relations between public utilities and the public could work themselves out. To that end, a non-
political administrative agency was established, presumably expert
and disinterested and equipped with the necessary technical aid,
charged with securing to the public at reasonable charges services
adequate according to modern technological standards, and assur-
ing to the utilities a fair income to make possible these services.

These measures encountered serious constitutional hurdles, as
had the Interstate Commerce Act before them. The obstacles were
narrow conceptions of the doctrines of separation of powers and of
limitation upon legislatures in delegating their authority. So distinguished a lawyer as W. M. Evarts, then Senator from New
York, thought that the Interstate Commerce Act violated the
Constitution. Similarly, Governor Hughes's efforts to fashion effective instruments of regulation were opposed by many of the
leading lawyers. Happily, statesmanship triumphed both in legislation and adjudication. A few judges and an occasional court were
imprisoned by their own dialectic. But the Supreme Court, and
the state courts generally, found these constitutional doctrines
adaptable to the new exigencies of government. They did not read
the Constitution so as to forbid the creation of administrative
devices merely because these exercised functions which, as a matter of logical analysis, partook of all three forms of governmental
power—legislative, executive, and judicial.

Though not wholly unknown to legal history, in their range
and complexity these commissions constituted new political inventions responsive to the pressure of new economic and social facts.
The decade prior to our entry into the World War was the

period of initiation of this new political machinery, its adjustment
to the traditional legal system, the improvisation of its own procedure, and the steady increase of the load which it had to carry.
The commissions' ambit of authority was extended both by subjecting more classes of utilities to their control and by widening
the sphere of oversight. The public interest in rates, services, accounting, finance, organization, with all the intricacies which these
imply, was entrusted to the commissions. With characteristic
American buoyancy, we assumed that we had discovered a panacea
and so made it work overtime. We also assumed that it would
work by itself.

Undoubtedly, much was accomplished during this first period.
The cruder corruption of earlier days was terminated, glaring
practices of unfairness were corrected, the preoccupation with dividends which received its classic epitome in Commodore Vander-
bilt's "the public be damned" had at last a counterpoise. Here
seemed to be real achievement; solid proof that government could
meet needs of society at once the most complicated and fundamental. Thus, when New York came to revise her constitution,
her leading men believed the experiment of regulating utilities by
commission had so proved itself that it should be withdrawn from
the risks of politics and the hazards of legislative repeal. In the
debate on this subject, the chairman of the convention, Senator
Root, intervened, and some of his observations bear reminder:

The method of exercising the jurisdiction of these commissions is still
in the stage of development. But I do not think we should lose the
opportunity to put into the Constitution enough to make it impossible for
any legislature ever to abandon the system of regulating public service
corporations through a commission or commissions whose business it is
to deal with the subject, and to go back to the old method of leaving
public service corporations unregulated, except by the passage of laws
in the legislature. The public service commissions, both in this state and
in other states and in the nation, were created to meet and deal with
very great and real evils. In this state before we had that system, if a
man was unjustly treated by a railroad, he had no recourse, except a

lawsuit that was beyond his means, or a complaint to his representative in the legislature. A lawsuit by a single individual of moderate means against one of these great corporations was hopeless. . . . Many of us can now remember the dreadful days of the Black Horse Cavalry which came as an incident mainly to the performance of this duty by the legislature. . . . The whole system became a scandal and a disgrace, and it was to remedy that here in New York and all over the country that this system of regulation by a commission created by law was established. The results have been most beneficent. No greater reform has been wrought in the public life of our country than has been wrought by the transfer of this attempt to regulate these great corporations from the legislative bodies of the country to public service commissions.

The system thus lauded by Senator Root in 1915 is now, with an exception or two, part of the governmental machinery of every state. Concerning its efficacy, however, pessimism has supplanted the earlier feeling of hope. No doubt this change of temper is partly a reflex of the different price levels before and after the War. When the commissions began to function, rates were widely believed to be unreasonable. To secure their reduction was one of the chief motives for the establishment of commissions. For the pre-War period, this hope was in large measure realized. But even during the War, street railways found themselves in difficulty, and the great rise in prices following the War made the commissions instruments for the increase of utility rates rather than their decrease. In the aspect most immediate and obvious to the public, the utilities and not the public appeared to be the beneficiaries of utility regulation. This was, of course, a very shallow view, and disregarded all the complexities of inflation, gold reserves, and war dislocations behind price movements. The general public did not fathom these complexities. It did know that it was paying more for street-car rides and telephone calls, for gas and electricity. Since the public service commissions ordered these increases, earlier public support of them turned into skepticism and distrust.

But this only partly accounts for a growing discontent with the working of the system during the last decade. Throughout the United States, there has been creaking in the machinery of utility regulation. Conviction has been gathering that not only have the aims for which the commissions were designed not been realized, but that the regulatory system operates to defeat the very purposes for which it was created.

Particularly in the leading industrial states, criticism has been voiced against the failure of utility rates to reflect decreased operating costs due to technological improvements; against the costly futility of rate proceedings which distort the protection intended by law; against failure to exercise skilled initiative in the promotion of the public interest. And all the time the power of the utilities has been increased through versatility in devising intercorporate relations. Partly through devices not subject to law and partly through the ineffectiveness of law in actual administration, the impotence of the individual is increased, and the mastery of law over these enterprises is eluded.

.   .   .   .

Informed opinion is in substantial agreement that the present system is not adequate for the old evils which brought it into being, and is incapable of coping with new problems of greater subtlety and deeper concern to society. In the diagnosis of this situation, there is also common ground among students of utility regulation.

The difficulties will perhaps appear more clearly by analysis of a concrete situation. The New York Telephone case will serve as an illuminating sample of utility regulation in action.

In the winter of 1919, the New York Telephone Company filed with the Public Service Commission for the Second District of New York (the Commission having jurisdiction of telephone rates within the state) more than two hundred separate schedules of rates, nearly all of which included increases in existing rates. Almost every municipality in the state questioned the propriety of such increases, and a hundred and thirty-five separate complaints against such rates were filed. The Commission entered upon hearings in two of these proceedings, one relating to Buffalo, the other to Syracuse.

.   .   .   .

Down to the Special Master's report of last year, the record of this controversy contains 62,864 pages of testimony, and the number of exhibits filed is 4,323—making a shelf of books about ten times as long as President Eliot's famous library! The Company alone has spent $5,000,000 in the fight, but the more significant cost is the bitter feeling which the controversy has engendered between the Telephone Company and the public. And after ten years of regulation, New York and its telephone company are still in the throes of conflict over what the public may fairly be asked to pay for its telephone service and what the Company is fairly entitled to earn for rendering it.

The heart of the difficulty is the current judicial approach to utility valuation. Out of the constitutional provision safeguarding property against deprivation "without due process of law," the Supreme Court has evolved a doctrine that a utility is entitled to a fair return on its present "value," and "value" must be ascertained by giving weight, among other things, to estimates of what it would cost to reproduce the property at the time of the rate hearing. The Supreme Court has not given us a calculus of present value, and it has left in conscious obscurity the amount of weight to be given reproduction cost. Some of its language has, however, induced commissions and lower courts to find that controlling effect should be given to such cost.

The doctrine was originally urged upon the Supreme Court in 1893 by William Jennings Bryan, on behalf of agricultural communities, as a protection against inflated claims based on what were then deemed inflated prices of the past, and in order to justify reduction of railroad rates. It is a matter of history that "insistence upon reproduction cost was the shippers' protest against burdens believed to have resulted from watered stocks, reckless financing, and unconscionable construction contracts. Those were the days before state legislation prohibited the issue of public utility securities without authorization from state officials; before accounting was prescribed and supervised; when outstanding bonds and stocks were hardly an indication of the amount of capital embarked in the enterprise; when depreciation accounts were unknown; and when book values, or property accounts, furnished no trustworthy evidence either of cost or of real value. Estimates of reproduction cost were then offered, largely as a means, either of supplying lacks in the proof of actual cost and investment, or of testing the credibility of evidence adduced, or of showing that the cost of installation had been wasteful." What thus served as an empiric device for preventing swollen returns on fictitious values has in the course of time, but particularly during the last few years, been turned into the most luxuriant means for creating fictitious values. And for this economic legerdemain, constitutional sanction has been sought.

Yet the minimum supposedly fixed by the Constitution is far higher than the earnings of utilities during a period of greatest prosperity. As a matter of "good business judgment," utilities have charged rates which would be confiscatory under the doctrine of a reasonable return on "present value." But these lower rates have been adequate to attract needed new capital and pay good dividends on the common stock.

The determination of utility rates and the ascertainment of the rate base are essentially economic problems. But no judicial pronouncements upon matters fundamentally economic run so counter to the views of economists as do the more recent utterances of the Supreme Court upon present value. They are based upon unrealities, are financially unsound, and lead to uncertainty and speculation. The so-called rules set the regulating agencies an impossible task, for they form a maze of cobwebbery.

The method of valuing the property of a utility by estimates of the cost of reproducing "the congeries of old machinery and equipment called the plant, and the still more fanciful estimates concerning the value of the intangible elements of an established business" is bound to discredit any system charged with its administration. For this method of determining value, in the language of the Michigan Commission, "usually included percentages for engineering services never rendered, hypothetical efficiency of unknown labor, conjectural depreciation, opinion as to the condition of property, the supposed action of the elements; and, of course, its correctness depends upon whether superintendence was or would be wise or foolish; the investment improvident or frugal. It is based upon prophecy instead of reality, and depends so much upon half truths that it bears only a remote resemblance to fact, and rises at best only to the plane of a dignified guess."

The New York Telephone case proves conclusively why the prevalent Supreme Court doctrine does not work; it also proves why, in the vernacular, it is being "worked." The range of "values" in this case reveals that the doctrine of present value is totally devoid of elements for objective tests. For the same property as of July 1, 1926, there were six different estimates of the fair "value" and fair "return" of the New York Telephone Company for rate-making purposes. These were given as follows in the 1930 report of the New York State Commission on the Revision of the Public Service Commission Law:

	Fair Value	Rate (%)	Fair Return
Majority of Public Service Commission	$366,915,493	7	$25,635,000
Federal Court	397,207,925	7	27,804,555
Minority of Public Service Commission	405,502,993	8	32,480,000
Special Master's Report	518,109,584	8	41,448,777
Company claim based on Whittemore appraisal	528,753,738	8	42,300,299
Company claim based on Stone & Webster	615,000,000	8	49,200,000

The estimates of value thus ranged from $366,915,493 to $615,000,000, with a corresponding spread in the return thereon from $25,635,000 to $49,200,000. Between the two valuation estimates by the Company's own experts there was a disparity of $86,246,262. Yet all these estimates purported to be based on the requirement of Supreme Court decisions. And at the end of ten years the final guess is still in doubt! Moreover, much new capital has been added since the date of these estimates, new problems of depreciation have arisen, and indeed, the whole process of valuing the property now in use, must, according to the theory of present value, start all over again.

Undoubtedly, the stakes are high for those who control utilities through very narrow equities which offer great opportunity for speculative gain. But to conservative utility managers and to investors in bonds and preferred stocks, the present scheme of utility valuation must be as unsatisfactory as it is to utility commissions. For it is based fundamentally upon untruths.

But perhaps the social costs are the severest, poisoning as they do the relations between utilities and public and undermining the confidence of the community in the effective capacity of government. This phase of the matter has been put impressively in the famous dissenting opinion of Mr. Justice Brandeis in the Southwestern Bell Telephone case, in which he said:

> The most serious vice of the present rule for fixing the rate base is not the existing uncertainty, but that the method does not lead to certainty. Under it, the value for rate-making purposes must ever be an unstable factor. Instability is a standing menace of renewed controversy. The direct expense to the utility of maintaining an army of experts and of counsel is appalling. The indirect cost is far greater. The attention of officials high and low is, necessarily, diverted from the constructive tasks of efficient operation and of development. The public relations of the utility to the community are apt to become more and more strained. And a victory for the utility may in the end prove more disastrous than defeat would have been.

The doctrines of fanciful valuation have greatly encouraged recent tendencies in financial organization. In turn, the elaborate and mysterious refinements of intercorporate relations have powerfully sustained the efforts by which lawyers and engineers have built up schemes for inflated values. The search for fictitious value —at best a game of blind man's buff—is thus greatly complicated by the intricacies of elaborate corporate arrangements within utility enterprises. Not only is there the excitement of a game fascinating to technicians in law and engineering, but in applying the prevalent judicial doctrines of utility valuation by manipulating intercorporate relations, there are the cruder but more solid temptations of buttressing unreasonable rates by law and securing huge profits through speculative utility holdings.

The characteristic of present-day utilities is the interrelation of the various systems. Recently Massachusetts and New York commissions reported to their legislatures that the basic utilities in their states were controlled by a few great systems, themselves affiliated and tending towards monopoly. These developments are, of course, justified by claims of economic advantage, and because they are types of organization required by technological advances. But other influences are also at work, and these have created social problems and governmental difficulties not at all foreseen by the architects of the present system of utility regulation.

In the consolidation of utilities extremely high prices are paid for the stock of the acquired companies, with consequent pressure for rates high enough to permit profit on the investment. Because of bankers' control of utilities, their policies are largely determined not by utility managers nor with reference to their public obligations. Bankers who finance utilities, naturally enough, look upon them like other investments. "The danger of domination of the [utility] systems by large scale financing is very apparent," reports the Massachusetts Commission, "and the great importance of the investment banking houses must be recognized." Moreover, these systems have organized auxiliary companies for management, construction, purchase, and finance by which services are rendered to affiliated operating companies. "Large profits"—I again quote from the Massachusetts report—"have been made from contracts for such services made between parties under the same control, and so without any equality of bargaining power." All these unreasonable profits are included in the operating expenses for which the public pays.

Here, then, are major aspects of the public services which are either wholly beyond the sphere of utility regulation or outside its competence. For the holding companies, which serve merely as a financial mechanism for controlling operating companies, are practically immune from law, and certainly no state exercises an effective grip upon them. Indeed, attention has recently been called by the Interstate Commerce Commission to the danger of circumvention of the Interstate Commerce Act by means of holding companies. The national policies regarding railroad consolidation, the restriction of railroads to the railroad business, and the promotion of efficiency through absence of conflicting interests, are now threatened by the subtle intrusion into the railroad situation of financial arrangements, through holding companies, investment trusts, and like devices.

Equally beyond the scope of the existing regulatory system are the schemes for draining off "profits surreptitiously in various indirect ways" through adjustment of claims for management, construction, purchasing, and financing among different units within a single system. Such transactions are either outside the bounds of present-day utility regulation or they so complicate the situation as to evade the reach of the administrative authorities. Thus arrangements between the American Telephone and Telegraph Company and the separate operating companies of the Bell System raise intricacies of finance and accounting that call for the highest skill and pertinacity in exploration. In practical result, they may involve differences of many millions in the burdens of the community or the gains of investors; and even more important, perhaps, are the consequences of controversies about such stakes, under existing legal conditions, to the public relations of utilities. In such a conflict Chicago and its telephone company have been embroiled for seven years, and the litigation still awaits final determination.

But the growing utility concentration raises a problem perhaps even more fundamental. The community's interests, as well as the satisfaction of incentives to private enterprise to furnish services for the community, assume civilized standards of fair dealing. It is most difficult to translate these generalities into concrete policies in matters so technical and complicated as those involved in management and regulation of public utilities. Government to be effective must have ample knowledge. That implies capacity on the part of its administrators to attain and use knowledge. But even this is not enough. We must have conditions under which truth and knowledge may flourish and function. Knowledge must be freed from the operation of inhibiting forces, whether those forces

operate through pressure exercised crudely or through atmos-
pheric influence. In order to be free, men must feel free to act.
Therefore, to secure just dealings with public utilities, it is essential that the community conditions be such that those representing
the public are not consciously or unconsciously warped in judgment or enfeebled in will.

In view of the intrinsic difficulty of its problems, the technical
developments, the recent tendencies in organization, the vast and
subtle interests to be composed, utility regulation at its best would
call for fresh accession of energy and newer resources to cope with
the new and greater tasks that now confront it. But the administration of public service laws is nowhere "at its best," and almost
everywhere is meager and ineffective. Even if it were not caught
in the quicksands of the judicial doctrines of valuation, the whole
scheme of utility regulation presupposes men of capacity and prestige, of courage and discernment, to match the powerful resources
of the utilities. Instead, as a matter of blunt truth, there is inequality in expertness, in will, in energy, in imagination, between
the utilities and government.

The men entrusted with the task have almost everywhere been
overburdened with details, inadequately staffed, denied necessary
technical aid, subjected to short tenures, dependent on meager
salaries, and generally restricted to appropriations which produce
humdrum routine. But some of the important states have escaped
the folly of short tenure and niggardliness of compensation. Thus
New York wisely avoided popular election of commissioners, provided for their appointment by the Governor for a term of ten
years, and gave a salary of $15,000. Positions of dignity and pres-
tige were created, which were to attract such men as are attracted
to the important posts in the British civil service, by the exhilara-
tion of steering the state through some of the most treacherous
and uncharted reefs and shoals of politics. But in New York especially, all this hopeful planning went awry. Valuation litigation
has largely absorbed the energies of administrators; and, as we
have seen, to no good purpose. Of course, there have been exceptions; and, without being invidious, one thinks of such men as the

late John M. Eshleman, the first president of the California Railroad Commission; Judge George W. Anderson and Interstate Commerce Commissioner Joseph B. Eastman, both of whom served on the Massachusetts Commission; Milo R. Maltbie, formerly of the Public Service Commission of New York and recently recalled to be its chairman. But, in the main, the public as well as the utilities has suffered from too many mediocre lawyers appointed for political considerations, looking to the public service commissions, not as means for solving difficult problems of government, but as opportunities for political advancement or more profitable future association with the utilities.

Except for occasional men of great capacity and exceptional devotion to the public interest, the technical staffs of the commissions, their engineers and accountants, are also no match for the experts against whom they are pitted. Indeed, the extent to which engineering talent is concentrated on the side of the utilities in these profoundly important public matters is one of the most ominous features of the situation. As a result, the community is not represented by skill, enterprise, determination, and persuasiveness. And when the public and its utilities are in conflict before the courts, there is disparity of resources in the contest.

The sharpest emergence of these problems is due to the widespread development of electric power. Technology, a diminishing coal supply, the growing burden of transportation costs, the resulting stimulation of new forms of cheaper power, the pressure of the World War in accelerating this movement, have all combined to make "the electrical age" an apt characterization of our time. The primitive beginnings of this era lie less than forty years behind us. But probably no influence of applied science has had such pervasive economic and social consequences in so short a time. From small independent plants generating electricity for a limited local market, the art first developed the stage of interconnection, then the further advances of giant power whereby a vast network of generating plants, transmission lines, and distributing stations, heretofore independent in their operations, are combined into a unified system.

Such an integrated system, it has been urged, will make for great social gains by cheapening power, minimizing waste, and checking urbanized congestion by a wide diffusion of industry. That the concentration of the electrical industry is also fraught with grave public dangers is amply attested by the disclosures before the Federal Trade Commission, the reports of the New York and Massachusetts Commissions, the debates over water power at Muscle Shoals and Boulder Dam and on the St. Lawrence. Every student of social economics recognizes the baffling problems raised by modern large-scale industry. The familiar difficulties would be present in intensified form, should monopolized control determine the country's dependence on power.

President Roosevelt gave early warning of these dangers. He thus put the matter in a message to Congress:

The people of the country are threatened by a monopoly far more powerful, because in far closer touch with their domestic and industrial life, than anything known to our experience. A single generation will see the exhaustion of our natural resources of oil and gas and such a rise in the price of coal as will make the price of electrically transmitted water power a controlling factor in transportation, in manufacturing, and in household lighting and heating. Our water power alone, if fully developed and wisely used, is probably sufficient for our present transportation, industrial, municipal, and domestic needs. Most of it is undeveloped and is still in national or state control.

To give away, without conditions, this, one of the greatest of our resources, would be an act of folly.

Roosevelt therefore insisted upon alert safeguarding of the public interest in the development of water power on navigable streams by full utilization of the authority of the federal government to that end. Not until 1920, however, did Congress formulate a comprehensive measure of protection in the disposal of these enormously valuable sources of power. But at the end of a decade the Federal Power Commission, which was the agency for the enforcement of the law, discloses the same defects in administration as I have noted in the state public service commissions. The Federal Power Commission has spent itself in the same

wasteful controversies about valuation, and has been devoid of
the driving force necessary for great enterprise. The members of
that Commission, to be sure, have been men of prestige and ability. For the Secretaries of War, Interior, and Agriculture *ex officio* have constituted it. But that very fact has been one of the
chief sources of the Commission's failure. The responsibility for
the water power policies of the United States and the protection
of the power resources of the country cannot be left to the casual
attention of three members of the cabinet, whose own departmen-
tal duties are sufficient to absorb the time and talents of the most
gifted Secretaries. The work of the Federal Power Commission
has therefore fallen into the hands of subordinates, some of whom
have shown unusual public zeal and discernment. But a few subordinates, subjected to great temptations and with appropriations
from Congress so meager as to starve their efforts, are hardly
equipped to meet complacency and legalisms within the Commission and the pressure of acute and powerful forces without.
Recently, Congress has amended the Federal Power Act so as to
provide for a full-time instead of an *ex officio* commission. The
effectiveness of the new commission will depend upon the quality
of the President's appointees and the adequacy of appropriations
by Congress.

If this picture of our public service problems appears gloomy,
I can only plead a rigorous attempt to be faithful to the scene.
Nor am I a dealer in panaceas, believing deeply that reflection
upon government inadequacies and concern for their improvement furnish the most potent stimulus for devising reforms. Once
the social implications of these public services are grasped and the
failures of utility regulation are traced to their sources, there will
not be lacking power and intelligence, if there be will, to translate
the public interest into public administration.

A few postulates may, however, be ventured. Public regulation
must extricate itself from the present doctrines of judicial valuation. Some such fixed rate base as has recently been proposed by
the Interstate Commerce Commission and by Governor Roosevelt's representatives on the New York Commission is necessary

in the interest of the public as well as that of far-sighted investors. Mr. Owen D. Young's desire "to see a rate base fixed on the actual investment and not on reproductive value," may eventually commend itself to other utility leaders. The drop in the price of commodities far below the prices on which utility developments have been made since 1920 may lead the utilities to realize that a return on prudent investment is their own best safeguard. And the Supreme Court, one believes, will find the Constitution no bar to economic wisdom and to the demands of stability and fair dealing. In any event, the state should not subject water power and other utility resources still within public control to the dangers of current theories of judicial valuation. And municipalities must be given sufficient power to enable them to supply public services where private enterprise fails in its public obligations.

Again, local administration should be charged with responsibility for such matters of essentially local concern as the regulation of local public utilities. The present enfeeblement of utility administration by the states is in no small measure due to interference in administration by the lower federal courts. Gratuitous hostility to the federal courts has thereby been aroused. These utility controversies turn largely on complicated state legislation, on local arrangements, and local contracts peculiarly within the competence of the local tribunals. Deep reasons of regard for state action on policies peculiarly within state control support Senator Wagner's proposal that judicial review of state utility regulation should be restricted to the state courts, leaving the protection of rights under the federal Constitution to the ample reviewing power of the Supreme Court.

Finally, the public service commissions must be made adequate instruments for expressing the social policies that should guide the relations between utilities and public. The complex problems of regulation call for a governmental agency qualified by experience, fortified by technical assistance, free from the pulls and pressures of politics, generating an esteem in the public such as it now entertains for the judiciary—a public esteem which, in its turn, will arouse in these officials enterprise, courage, and devotion to the public good.

The Packers *v.* the Government

This selection appeared as an unsigned editorial in the New
Republic *for May 15, 1932.*

RECALCITRANCY to law has been a dominant characteristic of
the packers for more than a generation. Efforts to confine their greed and curb their aggressions began in
Roosevelt's administration, and the latest chapter in the long story
has just been written by Mr. Justice Cardozo on behalf of the
majority of the Supreme Court. Investigations by congressional
committees, reports of the Commissioner of Corporations and of
the Federal Trade Commission, presidential messages, enforcement of old laws and the enactment of new ones, administrative
control, prosecutions, court decrees, decisions by the lower courts
and half a dozen decisions by the Supreme Court—all the resources open to government have at one time or another been
employed in the thirty years' war of the United States against
the packers. Monopoly for private profit in meat and other foods
has been the stake for which the packers fought.

Early in his first administration, Roosevelt moved against the
beef trust. Dissolution of the Standard Oil, the tobacco and the
beef trusts was the chief objective of Roosevelt's trust-busting.
All three had attained their "evil eminence" by the crude and
ruthless methods of the pioneer days of big business. The refinements of pyramiding and affiliates were not yet in vogue. Suppression of competition both in the purchase of livestock and in
the sale of dressed meat, control of stockyards and terminal railroads, the indispensable instrumentalities for such a combination,
unduly favorable traffic arrangements with carriers—by such
methods was a monopolistic position in the industry largely

attained and a challenge to its power by any foolish individualism successfully resisted. A suit for the dissolution of the combine was instituted by Roosevelt's Attorney General, and criminal prosecutions for rebating were brought. The practical results of these proceedings were meager. Soon the World War intervened, and a steady flow of meat shipments abroad seemed much more important than a little thing like aggrandized economic power in the hands of a few, whatever might be its future effect upon livestock breeders, independent dealers, and the American consumer. These were matters to which one could turn when peace came, and turn to them the government did. In the meantime its resources against the power of combination had been strengthened by the Clayton Act of 1914.

And so, in 1920, the government took action to dissolve the packers' combination. The charge was monopoly achieved by means thus summarized in Justice Cardozo's opinion:

They had attained this evil eminence through agreements apportioning the percentages of livestock to which the members of the combinations were severally entitled; through the acquisition and control of stockyards and stockyard terminal railroads; through the purchase of trade papers and journals whereby cattle raisers were deprived of accurate and unbiased reports of the demand for livestock; and through other devices directed to unified control.

Having eliminated competition in the meat products, the defendants next took cognizance of the competition which might be expected from what was characterized as "substitute foods." To that end, so it was charged, they had set about controlling the supply of "fish, vegetables, either fresh or canned, fruits, cereals, milk, poultry, butter, eggs, cheese and other substitute foods ordinarily handled by wholesale grocers or produce dealers." Through their ownership of refrigerator cars and branch houses as well as other facilities, they were in a position to distribute "substitute foods and other unrelated commodities" with substantially no increase of overhead.

Whenever these advantages were inadequate, they had recourse to the expedient of fixing prices so low over temporary periods of time as to eliminate competition by rivals less favorably situated. Through these and other devices there came about in the view of the government an unlawful monopoly of a large part of the food supply of the nation.

Although asserting "their innocence of any violation of law in fact or intent," but "desiring to avoid every appearance of placing themselves in a position of antagonism to the government," the patriotic packers consented to an injunction subjecting them to restraints which were justified only if the government's charges were true. What the lawyers call a consent decree was entered, sugar-coated by the phrase that such decree shall not "be considered an adjudication that the defendants or any of them have in fact violated any law of the United States." The diplomats have a name for such a formula: they call it face-saving. By this device an especially offensive combination was dismembered. But more was necessary. Remedies to be effective must forestall their circumvention. The past performances of the packers demanded not only dismemberment of the combination but safeguards against future oppressive tactics by the powerful component units. They were therefore enjoined "from (1) holding any interest in public stockyard companies, stockyard terminal railroads or market newspapers, (2) engaging in, or holding any interest in, the business of manufacturing, selling or transporting any of the 114 enumerated food products (principally fish, vegetables, fruit and groceries), and 30 other articles, unrelated to the meat-packing industry; (3) using or permitting others to use their distributive facilities for the handling of any of these enumerated articles, (4) selling meat at retail, (5) holding any interest in any public cold-storage plant, and (6) selling fresh milk or cream."

The desire of the packers "to avoid every appearance of placing themselves in a position of antagonism to the government" was not long-lived. To forgo money-making opportunities in the piping days of Harding normalcy was too quixotic. And so, in 1922, the packers began a series of efforts to get from under the decree to which they had consented. First, they used the California Canneries as their cat's-paw. The Canneries asked to have the decree set aside, claiming that it interfered with performance by Armour of a contract to buy large quantities of California canned fruit. After the Coolidge election, with big business triumphantly in the saddle, the packers launched a direct attack on the consent decree. The decree to which they consented was beyond the court's jurisdiction, insisted the packers. But this was too bald an attempt to make an ass of the law, and in March, 1928, was unanimously rejected by the Supreme Court. In the meantime, however, at the instance of the California Canneries, the operation of the 1920 decree was suspended by the courts of the District of Columbia and not until May, 1929, did the Supreme Court remove the obstacles to its obedience by the packers.

But packers are greedy and lawyers imaginative. Confronted at last with the apparent necessity of obeying restraints, nine years after they so unctuously consented to them, Swift and Armour in April, 1930, sought to modify the consent decree "and to adapt its restraints to the needs of a new day."

The lower court modified the decree and gave the packers permission to deal at wholesale in groceries and other commodities. This decision the Supreme Court has just reversed. A majority of the Court refused to undo the consent decree and held the packers to the restraints to which they assented in 1920. Three of the judges were disqualified. . . . Mr. Justice Butler, with the concurrence of Mr. Justice Van Devanter, dissented, welcoming the packers as competitors against wholesale grocers. Reading his opinion, one would suppose that the packers had no history.

Mr. Justice Cardozo placed the new desire of the packers in the perspective of their past conduct:

Size and past aggressions induced the fear in 1920 that the defendants, if permitted to deal in groceries, would drive their rivals to the wall. Size and past aggressions leave the fear unmoved today. Changes there have been that reduce the likelihood of a monopoly in the business of the sale of meats, but none that bear significantly upon the old-time abuses in the sale of other foods. The question is not whether a modification as to groceries can be made without prejudice to the interests of producers of cattle on the hoof. The question is whether it can be made without prejudice to the interests of the classes whom this particular restraint was intended to protect.

Nor has the rise of chain stores affected the coercive power of the packers. These stores increase rather than curtail the dangers of monopolistic control. Reminding that "size carries with it an opportunity for abuse that is not to be ignored when the opportunity is proved to have been utilized in the past," the court thus keeps the packers within the bounds dictated by experience:

The defendants, the largest packers in the country, will thus hold a post of vantage, as compared with other wholesale grocers, in their dealings with the chains. They will hold a post of vantage in their dealings with others outside the chains. When they add groceries to meats, they will do so, they assure us, with substantially no increase of the existing overhead. Thus in the race of competition they will be able by their own admission to have a handicap on rivals overweighted at the start. The opportunity will be theirs to renew the war of extermination that they waged in years gone by.

Sporadic instances of unfair practices even in the meat business are stated in the findings to have occurred since the monopoly was broken, practices as to which the defendants' officers disclaim responsibility when a business is so huge. They become less plausible when the size of the business is moderate. Responsibility is then centered in a few.

Here is a Supreme Court opinion that deals with economic issues in terms of economic realities. Central control, plus savings in overhead and ability to reduce prices, would be desirable if exercised *in the public interest*. But the whole story of the efforts to curb the packers sheds a searchlight on the anarchic character of our acquisitive society. For our food, we are largely dependent on the wise pursuit of the money motive by very few men. How naïve of us to expect it of them! In the case of the packers, the Supreme Court for a generation has been alert to the public interest. But adequate regulation of such a basic industry through intermittent lawsuits is to ask of courts what they cannot give.

Mr. Hoover on Power Control

This selection appeared as a signed article in the New Republic *for October 17, 1928.*

Thus far in the campaign, Mr. Hoover has maintained complete silence on a problem second to none in importance to the future well-being of the country—how to safeguard the public interest in the development of our electric power resources. Here is a subject within the field of Mr. Hoover's special interest and experience.

Perhaps before the close of the campaign he will choose to educate the public mind upon this problem. The more is this to be wished, since Mr. Hoover's past record on this issue reveals a significant shift of attitude. To this record, then, until he discloses his present mind, attention is invited.

In October, 1923, before the Superpower Conference, Mr. Hoover took this position:

> I am not here to advocate federal super-regulation of interstate movement of power. I believe that power development and distribution would find its greatest solution in co-ordinated state regulation, perhaps with assistance and co-operation of the federal government, rather than in any super-structure of authority such as has been found necessary in transportation unless, of course, necessities of the case cannot be attained otherwise. . . .

These views he elaborated in 1924 in his address before the National Electric Light Association:

> But today through longer transmission and interconnection the state boundaries in power distribution are disappearing. Moreover, the control of much of our water resources lies in the federal government, and

their distribution must move across state lines. . . . We cannot secure superpower development unless there is a free flow of power across state lines. We have thus at once created, at least, a physical and economic interstate question. . . . Federal regulation is not the road to solution of these problems of interstate movement of power. I would regard any federal regulation such as has been found necessary in transportation as a disaster to the development of our power resources. The fact is slowly emerging that the United States will eventually divide itself into several power districts, each with its own problems—problems relating to the origin of power, problems of climate, problems relating to the character of industries and uses. No national regulation can supply that intimate knowledge of local problems which this industry requires. I believe that power development and distribution would find its greatest solution in co-ordinated state regulation, perhaps with voluntary assistance from the federal government in securing this co-ordination. We need interconnection between state utility commissions where conflicting questions arise. . . .

In both these statements, Mr. Hoover's scheme for regulation is that of "co-ordinated state regulation, perhaps with assistance and co-operation of the federal government." This formula derives meaning when placed in the context of contemporary events. It was a time when use of the "compact" provision in the federal Constitution—agreements between states with the consent of Congress—was urged by Governor Pinchot and his "giant power" associates. Mr. Hoover's experience as chairman of the Colorado River Commission, which had formulated the Colorado River Compact, had made him familiar with the legal mechanism of compact. Plainly in his utterances in 1923 and 1924, Mr. Hoover had in mind some such device for securing unified state action. The reference to "assistance and co-operation of the federal government" suggests the consent required of Congress to effective state action through compact. Mr. Hoover was concerned with power regions larger than the individual states, and he was mindful of the need of legal control coterminous with the geographical power regions.

In 1925, speaking to the National Electric Light Association, Mr. Hoover begins to talk differently:

. . . It is my belief from this investigation that the public service commissions with very little just criticism are proving themselves fully adequate to control the situation. *The laws as written in the state statute books are sufficient to protect both the public and the industry, the two parties to the utility contract.* . . . The essence of regulation lies in a tight grip on the concern that actually deals with the consumer. There is the possibility that generating concerns may sell their power wholesale at the state line to distributing companies, thus attempting to make their wholesale prices exempt from the regulation of the consuming state. But that state still regulates the price and service of the distributing company. Most commissions exercise supervision of the contracts for purchase of power. The commissions are unlikely to blindly accept as an item of cost the amount paid to an external transmission company for its power, but rather they will examine the cost and reject it as a basic element if found unfair or excessive or collusive. I commend this view to the careful consideration of the state commissions. The utilities themselves would do well not to oppose it. It would create the only gap justifying federal intervention. For the rest, co-operation between commissions would settle the possible minor questions. . . . Central generation and interconnection do not in any way alter the essential character of regulation. . . . [Italics are mine.]

Later, in October, 1925, addressing the National Association of Railroad and Utilities Commissioners, he was still more emphatic as to the adequacy of existing state regulation, and he rejected the idea of interstate compact. For him now only two types of "legal interstate problems" called for solution. And for these he found ample answer in existing state machinery:

Furthermore, there has been considerable exaggeration of the probable extent of interstate power. For economic reasons these power districts in but few cases will reach across state lines. There will be interconnection between systems of different states, but even including this traffic, the proportion of actual interstate movement in power to the intrastate movement will be comparatively small. At the present time less than 4 per cent of the power developed passes state lines. . . .

Thus we see that 96 per cent of the whole of this interstate bogie can be dismissed upon economic analysis of the facts. The other 4 per cent lies in the legal field. And legal interstate problems can only arise where the activities of the operating companies extend beyond state lines. I am advised by our legal staff there will be two cases of this kind: first, where the same company is engaged in generation and distribution over a district embracing parts of two or more states, and second, where an operating company purchases power generated in a foreign state—the latter instance also embracing the "interconnection" between districts lying in different states. As to the first series of cases to which I have referred, it has been well established by the courts in analogous instances that the state commissions have the power and authority to establish "reasonable rates" to their consumers whether the property may be wholly within the state or not. These cases take care today of the 4 per cent of the total power passing our state line.

Thus we again further reduce this whole assertion by, say, 98 per cent. There remains, therefore, a small fraction of the problem to dispose of, and the second case, where the distributing company buys power by interconnection or otherwise from outside the state. Here the question is simply as to whether the rate paid by the distributing company for the purchased power is reasonable. If unreasonable, the commission may refuse to allow the full amount in settling the rate base for consumers. It is open to the state commission to fix a rate for resale to consumers within its jurisdiction based upon what the commission considers a fair price, the companies having the usual recourse to the courts for redress against injustice.

It is difficult to conceive of a situation which, as far as public interest goes, could not be controlled in this simple and effective manner. It needs no new machinery, no complicated interstate compacts, between each of forty-eight states and its numerous neighbors, requiring sanction by Congress. . . .

Gone is the vision entertained by Secretary Hoover in his Annual Report to Congress in 1924, of a "liquidity of power over whole groups of states," of power distribution spreading "across state lines and into diverse jurisdictions," of the emergence of "new legal problems in states' rights and federal relations to power distribution." . . . No new machinery is needed now or in the recognizable future! These are the Hoover views, so the Federal Trade Commission inquiry has just revealed, which the power lobby widely disseminated.

There was, said Mr. Hoover, "considerable exaggeration of

the probable extent of interstate power." There was exaggeration
—exaggeration by Mr. Hoover as to the limited scope of interstate power. For 1926, the power transmitted across state lines
was about double the amount indicated by Mr. Hoover the year
before. The interstate transmission of power in 1926 amounted
to 9.06 per cent, not including 1,127,073,793 kilowatt hours that
crossed the Canadian and Mexican boundaries. During the same
year, instead of power districts reaching across state lines in few
cases, more than 453 transmission lines crossed state boundaries.
Instead of the greater part of interstate transmission constituting
power of the same company engaged in generation and distribution over a district embracing more than one state, only 26.28 per
cent of the total interstate power involved no change in ownership. Instead of interconnection between different systems in
different states being negligible, *i.e.,* the interchange of power for
special markets created by load demands or generating conditions
of a temporary character, this interchange power represented 16.7
per cent of the interstate power. . . .

Mr. Hoover's proneness to inaccurate statistics, as shown in his
Newark speech figures on unemployment, is further manifested
when he deals with utility earnings. In his 1925 address he gives
the return on investment of electric utility companies as less than
or about 6 per cent during 1924. The report of the Federal Trade
Commission found the rate on the total net investment "7.94 per
cent, or approximately 8 per cent." . . . This difference between
6 per cent and 7.94 per cent is a difference of millions of dollars,
and may be the difference between confiscation and reasonable
return.

Mr. Hoover now sees the problem of control over electric
transmission between states as one limited solely to rate-fixing.
The various problems at which he hinted in 1923 and 1924 have
evaporated. Problems of service, of accounting methods as a basis
of adequate inspection, of standardization for purposes of efficiency, of extended development, of industrial relations, have
now no concern for him. According to the later Mr. Hoover, "It
is difficult to conceive of a situation which, as far as public interest

goes, could not be controlled in this simple and effective manner"
[*i.e.,* existing state regulation]. Those familiar with the legal
problems here involved will be bound to dissent from Mr.
Hoover's assurance. Some of the gravest difficulties of power
regulation have not been, nor can they be, met merely by individual state regulation. . . .

At the very time that Mr. Hoover so confidently relied on the
adequacy of state regulation, court decisions had already demonstrated the incapacity of a single state to control interstate transmission of power. In *Missouri* v. *Kansas Gas Company,* decided
May 26, 1924, . . . the Supreme Court had held that where a
gas company distributed natural gas which it produced and bought
in Oklahoma and Kansas to independent distributing companies
in Kansas and Missouri, neither Kansas nor Missouri could regulate the rates at which the company supplied gas to the independent distributing companies in the respective states. In *Attleboro Steam and Electric Company* v. *Public Utilities Commission,*
the Rhode Island Supreme Court, on June 18, 1925 . . . decided
that the state was without power to regulate the rate charged by
a Rhode Island generating and transmitting company for electricity sold to a distributing Massachusetts company at the state
line, even though the Rhode Island Utilities Commission sought
to compel the increase of this rate so as to enable the Rhode
Island company, by eliminating its losses on the interstate transmission of power, to serve its customers in Rhode Island at reasonable rates. Later, on January 3, 1927, the United States Supreme
Court sustained the Rhode Island Court. . . . That interstate
power must be regulated by agencies transcending existing state
machinery can no longer be open to dispute, except by those who
are opposed to any kind of effective regulation.

But not even within the narrow field of rate regulation, in
which alone Mr. Hoover conceded problems for solution, is the
existing state machinery adequate. His opinion as to the efficacy of
state control, in cases where the same company generates, trans-
mits, and distributes electric power across a state line (which represents less than 27 per cent instead of more than 50 per cent of

power, as he intimates) rests upon the decision of the Supreme Court in *Pennsylvania Gas Company* v. *Public Service Commission*, decided March 1, 1920. . . . That case involved the distribution of interstate natural gas by a Pennsylvania corporation directly to consumers located in several New York towns. The Court upheld regulation of the rates by the New York State Commission for gas furnished to consumers in one of these towns. There are plain differences between such a case and that of interstate electrical power transmission and distribution. The transmission and distribution of natural gas are subject to limitations not applicable to electricity. The area of electrical distribution far exceeds the area of gas distribution. Such differences become decisively significant in constitutional adjudications, where, as in the Pennsylvania Gas case, the basis for state control was found in the fact that the distribution was "local" and "in such a case," the Supreme Court ruled, "the local interest is paramount, and the interference with interstate commerce, if any, indirect and of minor importance."

In the second class of rate regulation for which Mr. Hoover finds state regulation adequate, there seems to be no foundation whatever in authority for the availability of the state control upon which he relies. The state, under the adjudicated cases, has no control over the rate charged by the interstate transmitting company. Neither has the distributing company. It has to pay the rate the former charges. It has no option, for, practically, it cannot purchase from anyone else. How can the state in regulating the rate for distribution reject as an item of cost the rate at which the distributing company has to purchase its power, even though both the state commission and the distributing company regard that rate as unreasonably high? Whether high or not, it does represent an item of cost, and if the state commission rejected this item of cost in its rate-fixing, and proceeded on the basis of a hypothetical item of cost, how long would such rate-fixing stand the test of confiscation under the due-process clause? No legal authority sustains such a proposal. Instead, the Attleboro case, by denying the state any direct control over the rate charged the distributing company, by implication denies the state such indirect control, if, as Mr. Hoover asserts, the indirect control would be just as effective. Furthermore, in the absence of power on the part of a state commission to examine into the conduct of the business of the interstate transmitting company, how can a state commission reach any adequate conclusions as to the reasonableness of the rate charged by it for its service?

But the great defect of Mr. Hoover's later attitude is his failure to recognize that interstate electrical transmission of power has other and deeper problems of control than mere rate regulation. The long-range planning demanded for an adequate superpower system to bring about Mr. Hoover's "liquidity of power over whole groups of states," demands control in the public interest if it is not to be wholly haphazard in character. Without the control of adequate public safeguards, power development will repeat the disastrous history of transportation development—overcapitalization, wasteful competition, needless duplication of equipment, receiverships, undesirable consolidations, instead of a directed development of the generation, transmission, and distribution of power.

In recent years federal *v.* state regulation has greatly agitated the electrical industry. It is uncompromisingly against federal regulation; it is equally opposed to effective state or regional control. The power interests defeated Governor Pinchot's efforts towards wider state regulation in Pennsylvania; they defeated Governor Smith's power program in New York; the Insull interests resisted Governor Brewster's plan for co-operative state regulation in Maine. Whatever may have led to Mr. Hoover's shift of attitude, in result he champions the immunities demanded by the power interests. One thing is clear: instead of Mr. Hoover educating the electrical industry, the power interests have educated Mr. Hoover.

Law and Science

The Conditions for, and the
Aims and Methods of, Legal Research

The following paper was read at the annual meeting of the Association of American Law Schools in December, 1929, and appears in the Iowa Law Review *for February, 1930 (Vol. 15, p. 129).*

WE ARE to discuss this afternoon "the conditions for, and the aims and methods of, legal research," and our president has very kindly asked me to lead the discussion. I shall take at face value President Horack's wish as well as the formulation of our topic. I shall regard this as a discussion, and not subject you to a drowsy, learned or unlearned paper. And not belonging to any theological school of jurisprudence, I shall not avail myself of the theologian's privilege—or is it a right?—to discard the text after announcing it. Let me assume, then, that there are only six of us sitting around the table. I am challenged to say all I have to say about research in law—what it is and what it isn't. What fertilizes it? What distracts it? To what end is it pursued, and how do you go about it? My party gives me the free run of talk to say all I have to say, because they well know that if I keep faith with them I shall engage their ears for not much more than twenty minutes.

Speaking thus to a half dozen familiars, it would be understood, of course, that I am not here to criticize others; I am not here to speak *pro mea domu*, not even *pro mea vita*. If criticism you must find in what I am about to say, it is directed more against my own school than any other institution because, being provincial, I covet most for my school. Nor must you treat me as representative of anything except of the views I sponsor. Naturally, I would hold my tongue against my own family—in public. And I am wholly without authority to speak for it. But let us forget the strife of schools and let all the winds of doctrine blow freely this afternoon. Let us pool our individual hopes and fears, avow our biases and predilections.

I shall disappoint you by trying to define my terms. What is research? I deem it highly important to strip the term of its mysteries and to prick the bubble of its novelty. It happens to be a term of fashion, and a word of fashion all too readily becomes encrusted with conceptions alien and irrelevant to its crucial meaning. There is nothing technical about the meaning of research, and there is nothing new except the currency of the term. Maitland and Ames and Holmes did not talk about research nor did they deem themselves researchers. But eliminate their contributions from the history of modern jurisprudence, and you take away its greatest glories, the most powerful influences in the promotion of the scientific temper in law. I do not mean to deny that the atmosphere is now more electric with desire to attain conquests for the mind concerning those phenomena which we call law, than was true in the days of Maitland and Ames, who would have gloried, as Holmes glories, that a later generation has carried on the work begun more than half a century ago. I merely wish to insist that research is not a recent discovery, nor even one of the post-War moralities.

What is research? It is not a method, it is not an object, it is a behavior. "It is a behavior," writes Dr. Alfred E. Cohn of the Rockefeller Institute, "directed to answering a question concerning something which exists in nature." Research is the systematic indulgence of one's curiosity—that is, the kind of research that I am talking about, for I am concerned with research that aims at the extension of knowledge. Its spring is curiosity; and when systematically pursued for the elucidation of events, we call it science.

I have already said enough to indicate that I shall refresh your recollection with commonplaces. But commonplaces are sometimes neglected and need reviving. Dealing in commonplaces, I shall shelter myself behind high authorities. For the meaning of science I turn to one of Whitehead's essays.

> Science is a permanent record of premises, deductions, and conclusions, verified all along the line by its correspondence with facts.

In passing let me note that such a conception of science resolves the false antithesis between deduction and induction, for it reveals science as a deductive-inductive-deductive process. But what is our science, the science of the law? What are the phenomena and the materials for its study? For the phenomena that are objects condition methods. What it is about which we are trying to gain knowledge determines how we shall go about seeking knowledge.

.   .   .   .

As is to be expected from a parochial Harvard man, I have quoted three Harvard men, and as is to be expected from Harvard men, they disagree with each other. It is just a hundred years ago since Story found the common law a perfect system of deductive demonstration "apart from a few blemishes." Langdell, in the '70s, still conceived of law as a self-contained system, the logical unfolding of relatively few principles whose history and meaning and direction were all immanent in the cases. Undoubtedly Langdell has had an enormous influence upon the whole atmosphere and temper of American education, not merely legal education, during the last fifty years. Story and Langdell symbolize different epochs. For between Story and Langdell there occurred one of the decisive events in the history of thought— the publication, in 1859, of the *Origin of Species*. Plainly, Langdell carried over into the law as a method of study the method pursued by Darwin for the verification of his theory. Langdell's method was inductive, but his outlook was that of a theologian— he was an implacable logician, a brilliant reasoner within a fixed formal framework. The extent to which every law library and every law writer today goes beyond case law for the understanding of cases is the measure of Langdell's preoccupation with formal law—marvelously tough-minded in his preoccupation and serving as a constant admonition against loose talk, but nevertheless too neglectful of "the secret root from which the law draws all the juices of life."

Which brings me, of course, to Holmes, the source, I need hardly tell you, of my last quotations. His thoughts are familiar, for he has achieved the triumph by which novel and originally heretical ideas become catchwords. I venture to remind you that his analysis of the paradox of form and substance in law, tracing its substance to considerations of policy outside the law, was written in the *American Law Review* just fifty years after Story's inaugural, and exactly half a century ago. It may fairly be said that we have been living on Holmes ever since—that the effort of the modern science of law is to investigate law in the perspective in which he has set the problems of law. Take all our present-day slogans and preoccupations—and I speak as a sinner among you, I speak as friend, not as skeptic—and they are all traceable to Holmes's insight into the stuff of law as a task for those who seek to understand it. "Functional approach," "law in books and law in action," "the administration of law as its center of gravity"—these express perhaps the dominant preoccupations of contemporary jurisprudence and the problems which they imply are as intricate and exhilarating as they are still unanswered. We have as yet only a most meager number of active votaries. Pitiably few in number as yet are those whose curiosity has been aroused as a life work to try to give answer to these subtle and obstinate inquiries. But it does not detract from the vast work that has been hardly begun and from the answers that still must be found, that Holmes was the first man to put the essential questions. We are still heady with the wine that we have begun to sip—if you will pardon an anachronistic figure—from the new loving-cup of the social sciences. We are still largely in the social stage of the social sciences. We are mostly only talking about collaboration, and have as yet hardly begun to experiment on the processes by which to "integrate" or "co-ordinate" or "collaborate" with one another. We have hardly got over the discovery that we are members of the same family; we have not yet acquired family habits with one another. But in all this ferment, Mr. Justice Holmes must recall with gladness what he said more than a generation ago and without pedagogic pedantry:

> We must beware of the pitfalls of antiquarianism, and must remember that for our purposes our only interest in the past is for the light it throws upon the present. I look forward to a time when the part played by history in the explanation of dogma shall be very small, and instead of ingenious research we shall spend our energy on a study of the ends sought to be attained and the reasons for desiring them. As a step toward that ideal it seems to me that every lawyer ought to seek an understanding of economics. The present divorce between the schools of political economy and law seems to me an evidence of how much progress in philosophical study still remains to be made.

Law, then, is as broad and deep as those social desires which have behind them or seek to have behind them the coercive will of society—whether that expresses itself through penalties or prisons, through injunctions or public ill-will. To understand these desires, their origin, their intensity, the means of their satisfaction, the cost of consequences of the means—these are the business of the science of law. And the behavior which makes men turn to this business we now call research. But whatever called, only those who have a deep curiosity to inquire into these matters and to seek what little light may be vouchsafed to them, have the necessary equipment for the enterprise and the pertinacity for its quicksands. For research requires the poetic quality of imagination that sees significance and relation where others are indifferent or find unrelatedness; the synthetic quality of fusing items theretofore in isolation; above all the prophetic quality of piercing the future by knowing what questions to put and what direction to give to inquiry.

This brings me to another age-old and futile antithesis between theory and practice. Again I shall let Whitehead speak for me:

> Science is a river with two sources: the practical source and the theoretical source. The practical source is the desire to direct our actions to achieve predetermined ends. . . . The theoretical source is the de-

sire to understand. Now I am going to emphasize the importance of theory in science. But to avoid misconception I most emphatically state that I do not consider one source as in any sense nobler than the other, or intrinsically more interesting. . . .

The importance, even in practice, of the theoretical side of science arises from the fact that action must be immediate, and takes place under circumstances which are excessively complicated. . . . Success in practice depends on theorists who, led by other motives of exploration, have been there before, and by some good chance have hit upon the relevant ideas. By a theorist I do not mean a man who is up in the clouds, but a man whose motive for thought is the desire to formulate correctly the rules according to which events occur. A successful theorist should be excessively interested in immediate events, otherwise he is not at all likely to formulate correctly anything about them.

I emphasize the importance of theory in legal science because in the balance of culture, particularly in the culture of our present-day civilization, we have far too little theory—the odds are all against its pursuit. Sir Frederick Pollock very recently touched on this theme, in his paper on "Judicial Caution and Valour." "The balance," he said, "is weighted against speculation by the fact that it needs a share of energy, intelligence, and imagination beyond the average allowance of educated citizens, and still more by the constant passive resistance of mere inertia." I venture to believe that even more powerful forces weight the balance against theoretical science—the push and pressure of our times for quick and immediately practical results and the high rewards that go for the immediate and practical, rewards of comfort as well as rewards of public esteem. Our moral climate is against the pursuit of science as a systematic effort at understanding.

I deem it fundamental to the advance of the research about which I have been talking that we differentiate two distinct stages in the progress of ideas: namely, their invention and their acceptance. Significant advance in the social sciences requires that we keep rigorously apart the modes by which we arrive at tentative truths and working hypotheses, and the process of securing their acceptance with such modification and qualification as a world of compromise requires. To borrow, as is the custom these days, the language of the business world, it is vital not to confuse the production of ideas with their distribution. The two involve different processes, different methods, different atmospheres, above all, different temperaments. It is, I believe, fatal to the development of new ideas to pursue them in an atmosphere and with processes that predominantly reflect a desire to "put over" ideas. Those who have the aptitude for discovery, for invention, for fashioning new hypotheses are seldom equipped to secure their practical applications. An indispensable condition for fruitful theoretical research is the right kind of intellectual climate for important ideas to come to life. That means a total lack of the urgencies of the immediate and a freedom from worry about all the accommodations and compromises that become pertinent when ideas are to be translated into action or to be formulated for acceptance. This may all sound very abstract, but it expresses the deepest conviction I have regarding the most concretely indispensable condition for seminal or even significant thinking in law. There must be freedom from pressure for results, for approval by committees or conferences or foundations, for satisfying this hope and allaying that fear, which necessarily and properly condition the whole psychological atmosphere under which the work of securing acceptance for ideas proceeds.

By way of illustration, I am sorry to see that the scientific inquiry which has just been undertaken with presidential blessing into the "social trends" resulting from our great technological developments, should be promptly followed with a statement that this inquiry is expected to lead to "constructive action." If researches have to satisfy expectations of practical results which they arouse, it will affect the course of their inquiries and influence the formulation of their findings. Thus they will be subject to all those pulls and pressures and will be making all those compromises which are appropriate when one comes to apply knowledge, but are wholly irrelevant to seekers for understanding. This is a long way of saying, you will say to yourself, that the work of the thinker is quiet and unhurried work, with complete indifference to a predetermined output or a predetermined public. That is *all* I am saying. But if it be true that these are the conditions of effective scholarship, then we must insist upon them and offer what resistance we can to all the distractions and diversions that beset research in an age which professes as never before to worship it.

The success of the *Origin* may, I think, be attributed in large part to my having long before written two condensed sketches, and to my having finally abstracted a much larger manuscript, which was itself an abstract. By this means, I was enabled to select the more striking facts and conclusions. I had, also, during many years, followed a golden rule, namely, that whenever a published fact, a new observation or thought came across me, which was opposed to my general results, to make a memorandum of it without fail and at once; for I had found by experience that such facts and thoughts were far more apt to escape from the memory than favorable ones. Owing to this habit, very few objections were raised against my views which I had not at least noticed and attempted to answer.[1]

The story is familiar to you but it will bear recalling in Darwin's own words:

I gained much [he continues] by my delay in publishing from about 1839, when the theory was clearly conceived, to 1859; and I lost nothing by it, for I cared very little whether men attributed most originality to me or Wallace; and his essay no doubt aided in the reception of the theory.

I will not labor the point. But please do not brush Darwin and his example aside as irrelevant or as a counsel of perfection. To be sure, his was monumental work. Much important work is done on a much smaller scale and does not need twenty years of incubation after insight has conquered. But the conditions under which Darwin worked and the standards to which he subjected himself, govern all enduring work in the domain of theoretical science.

I avouch very practical authority for the dependence of civiliza-

---

[1] Darwin, *Life of Darwin* (1892), 42.

tion upon theoretic research and the dangers to which it is at present exposed.

Every practical advantage gained in utilizing natural forces for the benefit of mankind can be traced back to a necessary basis established through fundamental research in pure science by men who had no other object than to ascertain the truth.

These are the words of Elihu Root. And our engineer President is even more explicit:

The sudden growth of industrial research laboratories has in itself endangered fundamental research by drafting the personnel of pure science into their ranks. Applied science itself will dry up unless we maintain the sources of pure sciences. We must add to knowledge, both for the intellectual and spiritual satisfaction that comes from widening the range of human understanding, and for the direct practical utilization of these fundamental discoveries.

The research laboratories of industry have done more than deplete the available human resources for theoretical research. They have largely set the psychologic pace for scientific endeavor. The aims and methods, the assumptions and the atmosphere of present-day highly organized industry are steadily, though unconsciously, associated with the purposes and the methods of research. Organization is at present exerting dominant influence. And nothing is more hostile to the progress of new ideas. Origination must precede organization of thought, and must remain constantly free. Let me draw upon one of the natural sciences and quote from the opening address of Professor Krogh at the International Physiological Congress last August:

The catchword of our post-War times is organization. . . . The individual freedom is our chief asset, the mainspring of the really new ideas, the guarantee of progress. Physiology does not go forward as an ordered line of battle on a continuous front, but must be carried on, as someone has aptly said, as a guerrilla warfare against the unknown, conducted single-handed or by quite small units. There is no need for an extensive organization of research, but there is much need for voluntary co-operation on a limited scale between individuals and laboratories.

There are many problems which can only be successfully attacked when experimental physiologists co-operate with histologists, with chemists or physicists or with clinicians, and some problems will require the combined efforts of several of these groups, but the affair is always one of local and voluntary co-operation and does not concern us here.

While I have no faith in the organization on a large scale of research I think there is a wide and fruitful field for organization of what we might term the services behind the front.

By these services behind the front, Professor Krogh of course means the familiar tools of indices to periodicals and the like. This may include gathering of data once we know exactly what data we want to gather. But we must beware of the ambiguities that lurk in data nor can we expect mere technicians and fact-gatherers to bring forth the Promethean spark of illumination that only comes from working with material at first hand. I once heard Wallace Notestein say that an historian must get his own fingers dirty with the documents. First-hand contact is necessary. And skill is needed as well as sincerity, deftness as well as detachment. As a result of getting his own fingers dirty, Notestein is responsible for a reconsideration of the whole constitutional history of the Tudor period and is giving us profoundly new insight into the significance of procedure in the attainment of parliamentary government in Great Britain. Men like Maitland and Notestein read documents with a poet's mind. In them, as in all first-class researchers, science and art are wedded.

These considerations are of special moment to us in the law. The ultimate concern of the social sciences, law among them, is the conquest of knowledge leading, one hopes, eventually to new and important insights into the good life of society. But we are still at the very beginning of this effort and the methods, the criteria, even the aims of the social sciences are still at large and still unshapen. There must be every inducement, every encouragement, towards originality, spontaneity and variety, always provided that men of real capacity are engaged in the enterprise. Correspondingly, with scope and encouragement men of capacity will be drawn to the enterprise. These are considerations decisive also for the form and atmosphere which should determine graduate work. I would not divide a faculty into rigid departments or institutes nor have any formal director of research nor formal organs of research, but depend upon the free collaboration of scholars who are colleagues to share in the furthering of intellectual effort no less disciplined and directed because self-directed and self-disciplined, not organized as business is organized. That means a very small number of rigorously selected graduate students. For no man can explore the unknown, track new knowledge, with more than a handful of students. Graduate work implies a personal relation between two students, one of whom is a professor. If there is not common intellectual enterprise between professors and graduate students, there may be facilities for giving degrees but not graduate work in any fruitful meaning of the term.

As for methods—there are no sovereign answers and no sovereign methods. Methods must attend problems. If a significant inquiry is pursued on a significant level, it will suggest to a man eager for discovery and familiar with its history the various modes of attack. There should be much flexibility as to method. Once the central issues of a problem are apprehended the imagination should not be confined by a paper program. Cavalry attacks will be needed again and again, and many reconnoitering parties will have to be sent into the unknown territory. Freely must we utilize all the allies there are—statistics, history, anthropology, psychology. But let us beware of their limitations and particularly of our own. Addressing students of economics, a distinguished mathematical economist admonished them that "when you take a complex tool from the mathematical statistician and start using it yourself, don't expect it to do everything for you, or swallow anything it may tell you, without critical inspection and reservation."

So we have to be constantly on our guard lest psychology be more unequivocal in her wisdom when she speaks to lawyers than when she speaks to psychologists. In the treacherous domain of the social sciences we must be wary lest we live on one another's washing—lest we prove an unknown in one field by an unknown in another.

By all means let us use all the aids and all the insights that other workers in the kingdom of the mind put at our disposal. Let us not disperse our very limited resources by controversy over superiorities. There are more roads to wisdom than are trodden. There are more roads to wisdom than we know of. Let us not engage in wasteful conflict over primacy, particularly over primacy of method, nor lose ourselves in pride of place. Let us avoid the strife of formal theories, untested by experience, except in so far as even such strife makes for illumination. The whole of truth is never even remotely in sight. Let us labor humbly but passionately, gaining here an insight, revising there an assumption, jettisoning one error now and perhaps taking aboard a bit of weighty cargo later.

English Law Schools and American

The following book review of Annual Survey of English Law, 1930, *London School of Economics and Political Science, Department of Law, appeared in the* Harvard Law Review *for January, 1932 (Vol. 45, p. 536).*

NOW THAT the country is in a mood of deep self-searching, it might not be superfluous for the law-teaching profession to take stock of its accomplishments and directions. One of our national complacencies is the conviction of superiority of American over English legal education, a notion which English scholars have at times encouraged, partly through their subtler politeness and partly to foster schemes of educational reform in England. Surely the proof of the pudding of legal education is the quality of bench and bar and of legal scholarship. There is considerable ferment in the law schools today. But, after all, the glories of scholarship are durable additions to intellectual capital. Of this, in the form of books or essays, there is pitiably little in proportion to the number of law teachers and the enormous resources devoted to legal education. One fears that the overshadowing influence of business psychology—quick results and many of them—have subtly, and sometimes not too subtly, exerted a powerful undertow influence upon law schools. Intellectual product of a high order, foundation work like James Bradley Thayer's for the law of evidence requires brooding reflection, long-term inquiry, and a high indifference to immediate practicality. Our law reviews multiply like rabbits, but how much of their content is worth reading two years after publication?

When we turn to bench and bar, England has nothing to fear by comparison with us. We have, of course, a few giants, particu-

larly on the bench. But the run of the mill is a poor run. If painful devotion on earth will move St. Peter's challenge, those who
are condemned to the systematic reading of the current law reports—barring the opinions of the Supreme Court, those of the
New York Court of Appeals, and some of the lower federal
courts, and those of an occasional judge here and there—ought
to have an excellent chance of being admitted by the gateman of
heaven. That the average of arguments and briefs in our appellate
courts is extremely low is common ground among our best judges.
A much more civilized atmosphere dominates the whole process
of legal administration in England. Their barristers and judges
move on a higher intellectual level than is true of the legal scene
in the United States. It would, of course, be absurd to credit the
more cultivated characteristics of English legal life to their mode
of legal education or to charge all our inadequacies to our law
schools. Each is a product of different historical development, and
it is always dangerous to compare the conditions of a small island
with those of a continent. But, when all is said and done, the law
schools ought to have, if they have not, dominant influence in
the directions pursued by the bar, and in fashioning the standards
which lawyers observe and not merely profess. And the bench
fundamentally is always an offspring of the bar. Not the least
function of law schools, and of the profession which they nurture,
is the influence which they ought to exert on lay opinion regarding the requirements of legal administration and the qualities that
ought to be demanded for the judicial office.

All of which is much too fat a sermon to hang on the text of
this volume. But it is the nature of sermons to be related only
remotely to texts, and the third issue of the *Annual Survey of
English Law,* a collaborative product of the Departments of Law
and International Studies at the London School of Economics, is
an achievement of English law teachers which we may well envy.

English legal journals, like our own, have notes on the rulings
of diverse tribunals, comment on new legislation, and review contemporary legal literature. But such attention to current legal
events is necessarily piecemeal and fragmentary, is concerned with

trees which do not always convey the woods. To give the law of the year in retrospect and to place the items in the perspective of the whole, promotes reflective understanding, enables one to see what is episodic and what more permanently significant. It also furthers that ordering of the harum-scarum outpour of the legal mills which is certainly one duty of scholars. Moreover, by bringing together the various manifestations of law-making and law-shaping, emphasis is secured where it should be placed, upon the significance of all the influences that go to make up the coercions, whether of force or of opinion, by which the affairs of men are finally settled. To speak thus may merely reveal a brummagem mind. To speak thus is perhaps to evade hoary juristic issues regarding "law" and the "sources of law," whether legislation is "law" or law fit for the rarefied atmosphere of law schools, and the numerous other threshings of old straw. But, then, the life of the law is brummagem and full of evasions.

In any event, the aims which English legal scholars have set themselves in this series is again admirably fulfilled in the *Survey* for 1930. Within the covers of a book we have a critical account for 1930 of the important legislation, delegated as well as parliamentary, the case law and literature, articles and official reports, as well as books, in the various domains in the great kingdom of the law. I am, of course, not competent to judge the quality of the work in all these fields. In the particular areas of the law about which I am least ignorant, the legislation and the cases have been summarized with care and are placed in appropriate perspective, the literature is subjected to a penetrating judgment which escapes the twin vices of much American book-reviewing— shallowness and back-scratching.

I am sufficiently chauvinistic to covet such an *Annual Survey* for American law by American scholars. I am not unaware that we have fifty or more jurisdictions, not one, and that the United States is bigger than England. All the more reason for trying to see the woods for the trees and making a systematic effort to interpret the individual instance in its interrelations. The short-lived "Progress of the Law" series in this *Review*, and the steady labors of Thomas Reed Powell in his analysis of Supreme Court decisions, show what can be done and how valuable such efforts are. Why should not the American Association of Law Schools charge itself for this country with the task which the London School of Economics so admirably achieves for England? It might be done, perhaps, by dividing the country into appropriate regional studies. Here is common labor that may put an end to the useless strife of schools and still the sound of shibboleths that at present often too emptily fill the air. Once we are made to realize, for instance, that statutes and rules and ordinances play an important rôle even in such pure fields of private law as torts, and that an American book comparable, say, to *The Age of the Chartists* by the Hammonds, is as relevant to the understanding of industrial and administrative law as decisions of a high court, or that if such a book is not in existence it ought to be written, then perhaps we shall be so busy contributing something to insight and to the vindication of law's purposes that there will be little time left for preoccupation with any juristic sect or even for descanting on "methodology."

A Political Autobiography

Herbert Croly and
American Political Opinion

Herbert Croly (1869-1929) exercised a profound effect upon Mr. Frankfurter, as he did upon all young "progressives" who came of age during the "Bull Moose" days. His Promise of American Life, *published in 1909, just when the "progressive" movement became articulate, was one of the books which, by Mr. Frankfurter's own testimony, most influenced his political thinking. From the foundation of the* New Republic *until Mr. Croly's death they were intimately associated. This piece was contributed to a commemorative issue of the* New Republic *which appeared on July 16, 1930.*

THE ILLUSION of fresh stirrings possesses every generation. Certainty that an old tradition has become inadequate may merely prove the strength of the illusion. Yet a quarter-century ought to correct the blind vanity of youth. In any event, those of us who came to maturity in the Roosevelt era are still confident that new questionings and confusions and conflicts were beginning then to push their way to the surface of American society. The raucous voices and pugnacities of the Roosevelt days were not merely reflexes of his personality. Rather does Theodore Roosevelt appear to have been a function of his time—the first President to express the need for adjusting our political system to the changes resulting from the practical cessation of pioneer conditions and the increasing concentration of economic power. To be sure, the conflict between the Western farmer and the Eastern capitalist had already registered itself in the '70s in successive agricultural movements; the assertion of national authority against railroad control wrote itself into legislation in 1887; and in 1890 the Sherman Law began its career of futile resistance to the power of economic monopoly.

In truth history *is* a seamless web. For at the every birth of the American republic there begins to unfold, with the inevitability of a Greek drama, the conflict between a society of rustic simplicity and that of industrial capitalism. But in history also the emphasis makes the song, and what was episodic, tentative, and subordinate in the decades before Roosevelt, after the Spanish War emerged with central significance. Sectional and abortive movements of the past attained enduring national scope. Proposals of heretics and outcasts became presidential policies. Behind the diverse and discordant movements for reform to which Roosevelt gave voice lay the assumption that the traditional hopes of American democracy had been defeated and its purposes subverted by social and economic forces not contemplated by the founders of our nation. But there was lacking a thoroughgoing critical analysis of the ways in which Americanism had become merely a formal creed and a "combination of optimism, fatalism, and conservativism." Roosevelt's exhilarating vitality readily lent a feeling of coherence to these motley elements of skepticism and reform. And his optimism suited the American tradition in evading rather than exposing the conscious transformation required of American opinion, if American democracy was to practice with success the art of self-government under changed conditions.

Standpattism had been challenged largely by slogans. The rallying cry was progressivism, and in Herbert Croly it found its philosopher. The progressive movement really came to its full tide after Roosevelt left the White House. Roosevelt himself made the most radical critique of the traditional system not while President, but when in opposition. In 1914, during the Wilson administration, Croly could write with strict accuracy, "For the first time in four generations American conservatism was confronted by a pervasive progressivism, which began by being dangerously indignant and ended by being far more dangerously inquisitive." And to the "thoroughgoing curiosity" which conservatives themselves had provoked, Croly made the most powerful single intellectual contribution. His *Promise of American Life* was published in November, 1909, and reprinted the following June. Its total sales amounted only to about 7,500 copies. Those were the days before book clubs, but it is hard to think of this book at any time as "the book of the month." Croly never was meant for mass readers.

But the *Promise* is one of those books which prove that the influence of ideas is not to be measured by sales. To omit Croly's *Promise* from any list of half a dozen books on American politics since 1900 would be grotesque. It became a reservoir for all political writing after its publication. Roosevelt's *New Nationalism* was countered by Wilson's *New Freedom,* but both derived from Croly. Very little political literature ever survives its day, and the devastation of the World War was especially fatal to the political speculation which preceded it. But Croly's thinking cut below episodes and incidents. He had an avid interest in the shifting scenes of contemporary politics and in its fleeting personalities. But for him, politics floated in the stream of history and was significant only in so far as it fulfilled the possibilities of man's nature. For years he was a student of philosophy, nurtured by William James and Royce and Santayana; for years also he soaked himself in European as well as American history. Unlike almost all American pre-war writers on politics (with the notable exception of Captain Mahan, because of his special interest in navalism) Croly saw the American situation with its international implications. Thus, when American political writers generally were unconcerned with America's relation to the world, he wrote, "A decent guarantee of international peace would be precisely the political condition which would enable the European nations to release the springs of democracy; and the Americanism which was indifferent or suspicious of the spread of democracy in Europe would incur and deserve the enmity of the European peoples."

And so it comes about that the vitality of the *Promise* has survived even the World War. Of course not all of it, and not in its details. Already in 1914, in his *Progressive Democracy,* he had

made additions and subtractions. But no student of American politics can now reread *The Promise of American Life* without assent-
ing to its essential analysis. The book runs the whole gamut of
American political problems and faces them unflinchingly. Croly's
writing is organic and does not readily lend itself to pithy quotations. He subjected himself to the painful labor of thought, and
spared the reader little in going over his own journey. Yet perhaps a few paragraphs will indicate the task which he set for himself in the *Promise* and the temper in which he approached it.

Croly challenged the state of mind of the ordinary American
who considered himself the member of a chosen people, whose
success was guaranteed by Manifest Destiny. His book was concerned with defining our destiny in terms of national purposes:

> When the Promise of American life is conceived as a national idea,
> whose fulfillment is a matter of artful and laborious work, the effect
> thereof is substantially to identify the national purpose with the social
> problem. What the American people of the present and the future have
> really been promised by our patriotic prophecies is an attempt to solve
> that problem. They have been promised on American soil comfort, pros-
> perity, and the opportunity for self-improvement; and the lesson of the
> existing crisis is that such a promise can never be redeemed by an indis-
> criminate individual scramble for wealth. The individual competition,
> even when it starts under fair conditions and rules, results, not only, as
> it should, in the triumph of the strongest, but in the attempt to perpetu-
> ate the victory; and it is this attempt which must be recognized and
> forestalled in the interest of the American national purpose. The way
> to realize a purpose is, not to leave it to chance, but to keep it loyally in
> mind and adopt means proper to the importance and the difficulty of
> the task. No voluntary association of individuals, resourceful and dis-
> interested though they be, is competent to assume the responsibility. The
> problem belongs to the American national democracy, and its solution
> must be attempted chiefly by means of official national action.

After the War, Croly saw more clearly than ever the extent to
which democracy must vindicate itself otherwise than through political action—the extent to which political action is itself an aspect
of mature education and co-operative living. But at no time did he

minimize the implications of democracy or maximize political reliances. With him humanism was always central. Not the sectarian
humanism that is now having its day, not the humanism of negation, but the joyous humanism that is an affirmation of the latent
possibilities of human nature. Such was the culminating note of
the *Promise:*

> For better or worse, democracy cannot be disentangled from an
> aspiration toward human perfectibility, and hence from the adoption of
> measures looking in the direction of realizing such an aspiration. It may
> be that the attempt will not be seriously made, or that, if it is, nothing
> will come of it. Mr. George Santayana concludes a chapter on "Democ-
> racy" in his *Reason in Society* with the following words: "For such ex-
> cellence to grow general mankind must be notably transformed. If a
> noble and civilized democracy is to subsist, the common citizen must be
> something of a saint and something of a hero. We see, therefore, how
> justly flattering and profound, and at the same time how ominous, was
> Montesquieu's saying that the principle of democracy is virtue." The
> principle of democracy *is* virtue, and when we consider the condition of
> contemporary democracies, the saying may seem to be more ominous
> than flattering. But if a few hundred years from now it seems less omi-
> nous, the threat will be removed in only one way. The common citizen
> can become something of a saint and something of a hero, not by grow-
> ing to heroic proportions in his own person, but by the sincere and en-
> thusiastic imitation of heroes and saints, and whether or not he will ever
> come to such imitation will depend upon the ability of his exceptional
> fellow-countrymen to offer him acceptable examples of heroism and
> saintliness.

This was not merely rhetoric, for in the most eloquent pages of
the book he had analyzed Lincoln as a transcendent democrat:

> The average Western American of Lincoln's generation was funda-
> mentally a man who subordinated his intelligence to certain dominant
> practical interests and purposes. . . . Lincoln, on the contrary, much
> as he was a man of his own time and people, was precisely an example
> of high and disinterested intellectual culture. During all the formative
> years in which his life did not superficially differ from that of his associ-
> ates, he was in point of fact using every chance which the material of
> Western life afforded to discipline and inform his mind. . . . While

still remaining one of a body of men who, all unconsciously, impoverished their minds in order to increase the momentum of their practical energy, he none the less achieved for himself a mutually helpful relation between a firm will and a luminous intelligence. His intelligence served to enlighten his will, and his will to establish the mature decisions of his intelligence. . . . Just because his actions were instinct with sympathy and understanding, Lincoln was certainly the most humane statesman who ever guided a nation through a great crisis. . . . In the midst of that hideous civil contest which was provoked, perhaps unnecessarily, by hatred, irresponsibility, passion, and disloyalty, and which has been the fruitful cause of national disloyalty down to the present day, Lincoln did not for a moment cherish a bitter or unjust feeling against the national enemy. . . . Lincoln had abandoned the illusion of his own peculiar personal importance. He had become profoundly and sincerely humble, and his humility was as far as possible from being either a conventional pose or a matter of nervous self-distrust. . . . His humility, that is, was precisely an example of moral vitality and insight rather than of moral awkwardness and enfeeblement. It was the fruit of reflection on his own personal experience—the supreme instance of his ability to attain moral truth both in discipline and in idea; and in its aspect of a moral truth it obtained a more explicit expression than did some other of his finer personal attributes. His practice of cherishing and repeating the plaintive little verses which inquire monotonously whether the spirit of mortal has any right to be proud indicates the depth and the highly conscious character of this fundamental moral conviction. He is not only humble himself, but he feels and declares that men have no right to be anything but humble; and he thereby enters into possession of the most fruitful and the most universal of all religious ideas.

The *Promise* may fairly be called seminal for American political thinking. The seeds it scattered bore one concrete and wholly unexpected fruit. The *New Republic* was the direct offspring of the book. Croly himself has told the story of its founding in his characteristic modest and impersonal way. In the ardent and public-spirited minds of Willard and Dorothy Straight, the *Promise* stirred ambition to promote the endeavor towards a humane and self-conscious America as sketched by the book. And so in October, 1914, the *New Republic* was launched. Others must tell the romance and the difficulties of the enterprise, the wisdom and humility, the endurance and generosity required of the leader of a group of highly gifted temperaments. It is, however, appropriate to recall Croly's conception of the purpose of a "journal of opinion":

> We called it a journal of opinion. Its object was less to inform or entertain its readers than to start little insurrections in the realm of their convictions. Opinions are the currency by which the citizens of a democracy exchange spiritual values. But just because they pass through many hands, serve so many doubtful purposes, and are accepted at their face value by undiscriminating tradesmen, they tend to become dull, shopworn, and even debased. . . . We wished to prick or even goad public opinion into being more vigilant and hospitable, into considering its convictions more carefully and into attaching to them a higher intrinsic value.

The function of the editorial writer, according to Croly, was that of social mediation. But his acutely sensitive integrity made him uncommonly aware of the pitfalls of self-deception to which the purveyor of opinion was exposed. With surgeon-like candor, he analyzed the dangers of that very dogmatism against which the *New Republic* was to serve as a ferment:

> It is, I think, useful to compare editorials to the petty currency of social intercourse, but the comparison interprets only part of what takes place in the minds of the writers and readers of editorials. Editorials rarely stimulate either one or the other to seek some better approximation to the truth for themselves. When I write an editorial, I am not conversing with my readers; I am usually telling them what is what. To be sure they hand me a penny for my thoughts, but how often do I believe that my pearls of opinion are worth no more than a penny? On the other hand, if I succeed in being honest with myself, how can I protect my readers from expecting too much from me? [The editor's] natural desire to play his part bravely almost forces him into magnifying the pretensions of his job. He parades under the veil of anonymity the valor of ignorance. He makes sounds as if his editorials issued like an oracle from some divinely subsidized source, and they sound sonorous in his own ears. . . . What we editors need is a method of cutting opinions to suit the rapidly changing body of an editor's problems without depriving our own minds of continuity and integrity and without

pretending to ourselves and others that in this business fine feathers make fine birds.

Croly thus stated what in recent years became more and more the central problem of his thinking: how to adjust one's life in its social relations, how to contribute the experience gained from a conscious direction of the individual to the social fund of experience. More and more he was seeking illumination for the problems of politics from the slow accretions of insight into human behavior. He had no fixed system and was wholly committed to the fact that the findings of science are tentative, particularly the findings of scientific observation of human conduct. He was constantly striving towards a synthesis, but he realized that true insight depends on the interaction of an analytic-synthetic process. He would frequently talk of the "purging of personality from opinion." By this he meant an "inveterate curiosity about life," which included in the sphere of curiosity the thoughts and actions of one's own life. The effort was nothing less than to be actor and observer at the same time. This highly complicated self-conscious process he attempted to formulate at once as a confession and as a faith:

Instead of treating the world as the permanent possibility of being edified by my virtuous opinions, I am treating it as something which must primarily be inspected through the eyeglasses of my own feelings and interests, but always with the deliberate intention of separating what I observe from the coloring which my personality gives it. There seems to be a chance that in this way I may build up within myself a vision of the world and of my relation to it whose reports are not tainted at their source. In order to have any power of edifying or co-ordinating worldly processes and activities for the benefit of my readers, I must begin by co-ordinating the instinctive, emotional, and intellectual activities which make up my life. Co-ordination, like charity, must find a home in the individual spirit, or it will have to satisfy itself with a habitation in churches, states and other institutons; and it is absurd even to seek the kind of co-ordination which we editorial writers among others need unless we can learn how to purify, stretch, and intensify individual consciousness.

In fair weather and foul he lived his faith with extraordinary fidelity. Though highly sensitive and strong-willed, he maintained his intellectual and emotional rectitude with unruffled serenity. He was a Spartan, but the more Spartan because he wanted a world of joy and beauty and could revel in their exercise. I have never known a worldly man who was more just, nor one of tenacious will more gentle and forbearing. He cared passionately for the fulfillment of the promise of American life, and because he so cared, he labored with an almost heroic perseverance to bring his own life into the greatest possible accord with the insight that was vouchsafed him. He was as far removed from a prig as the poles are asunder; nothing therefore could have been farther from his mind than to serve as an exemplar. But if he had been consciously designed as a model of brave and sincere and generous living, he could not have been fashioned more appropriately.

Why I Shall Vote for La Follette

This selection appeared in the New Republic *for October 22, 1924.*

I CANNOT say that I am in the slightest degree impressed," Huxley told this country at Johns Hopkins in 1876, "by your bigness, or your material resources, as such. Size is not grandeur, and territory does not make a nation. The great issue, about which hangs a true sublimity and the terror of overhanging fate, is, What are you going to do with all these things?" Fifty years of the most feverish preoccupation with material development in the world's history, with its accompaniment of appalling social and industrial problems, have made Huxley's prescient inquiry the most pervasive and exigent question in American politics. Not that politics alone should be expected to furnish relief; not even that political action can supply the chief forces for the making of a truly civilized commonwealth. But politics must be looked to for a good deal, not so much through the specific acts of government as in the ideals which it pursues and the spiritual atmosphere which it helps to generate. And the instruments of politics are parties.

I belong to the increasing body of Americans who cannot forget that parties are instruments, because we are not tied to parties by bonds as obstinate and irrational as ties of church. For us, during the last two decades, each presidential election has brought with increasing emphasis the question: To what ends are the two old parties instruments? Bryce asked this question with his inveterate persistence. Listen to the answer:

Neither party has, as a party, anything definite to say on these issues [which one hears discussed in the country as seriously involving its welfare]; neither party has any cleancut principles, any distinctive tenets. Both have traditions. Both claim to have tendencies. Both have certainly war cries, organizations, interests enlisted in their support. But those interests are in the main the interests of getting or keeping the patronage of the government. Distinctive tenets and policies, points of political doctrine and points of political practice have all but vanished. They have not been thrown away, but have been stripped away by time and the progress of events, fulfilling some policies, blotting out others. All has been lost except office or the hope of it.

No candid student of American politics would gainsay this picture except to paint it even darker than it was when Bryce wrote. As a believer in a two-party system I want two parties which will correspond to basic political realities which divide men, broadly speaking, into those who think things are substantially all right or fear to change them, and those who are greatly perturbed by the present-day economic and social tendencies of this country and are eager for the high adventure of bringing society through slow, persistent, disciplined thinking and action nearer to what things ought to be.

The true principle of a free and popular government would seem to be so to construct it as to give to all, or at least to a very great majority, an interest in its preservation; to found it, as other things are founded, on men's interest. . . . The freest government, if it could exist, would not be long acceptable, if the tendency of the laws was to create a rapid accumulation of property in few hands, and to render the great mass of the population dependent and penniless. . . . Universal suffrage, for example, could not long exist in a community where there was great inequality of property.

So wrote Daniel Webster in 1820. A hundred years later "great inequality of property" is the most significant characteristic of our social-economic life. Its most devastating consequence is the permeation of the whole American life with material standards and material preoccupations. The federal statistics of income drily tell the tale, but only partly, as figures do. Out of 6,787,481 who filed income tax returns for 1922 (the last available year) 5,003,-155 reported incomes below $3,000, and 6,193,270 incomes below $5,000; while 4,031 had incomes above $100,000, 1,860 over $150,000, 537 above $300,000, 228 above $500,000, and 67 above $1,000,000 per year. Beneath these quiet figures lie the most pulsating problems of American society.

I do not know the answers to these problems, but I do know there *are* answers. I also know that the indispensable step to the solution of a problem is the recognition that there is a problem. Neither, for instance, of the two parties, however, faces the issues. Neither has a conception of social aims through taxation. The Republican party is frankly standpat—things are all right. To the Democracy, also, things are all right, only those who administer them are not. What the country needs is "honest" Democrats and, doubtless, William J. Bryan would add, "deserving Democrats." The Republican and Democratic parties do not face the issues because there are no differences in realities cutting across the two parties. They each represent unreal cohesions, because they are both organized appetites kept alive by the emotional warmth of past traditions. The "solid South" is at once the single greatest cohesive factor of the Democratic party and in turn explains the outworn survival of the G.O.P. The "solid South" is thus the greatest immoral factor of American politics, and to the extent that Northerners help to perpetuate it they are accomplices in all the evils that flow from it. But with the rapid industrialization of the South, the increasing migration of Negroes to the North, with our new immigration policy and its inevitable repercussions upon politics and industry, one need not be foolish or fanciful to look for a realignment in political affairs which will, in Woodrow Wilson's phrase, "uncover realities."

At all events, one's duty is to make the effort and not wait to join the winning team. If it had not been for the Frémont campaign in 1856, there could have been no Lincoln in 1860. If it had not been for Keir Hardie and the work of the Fabians, there could have been no British Labor party, but there might have been disastrous revolutionary interludes in England. The La Follette candidacy represents a determined effort to secure adequate attention for the great interests of the workers and of agriculture in those economic and social compromises which, in the last analysis, underlie all national action. "Different interests necessarily exist in different classes of citizens," the Fathers wrote in the *Federalist*, and the security of the state depends upon fair representation as a basis of fair adjustment of the various interests. Labor and agriculture require more consideration and a better understanding, not because any class is to be coddled, but only because thus will national needs be satisfied. Adequate regard for the men and women who make up what we glibly call "labor" and "agriculture," and for the whole national economy that lies behind them, does not at all mean amelioration through legislation. Much more important are the influences which will flow from educating public opinion, generally, to the claims and needs of labor and agriculture by recognizing their just position in the state. The greatest source of hope behind the La Follette candidacy is that unlike the Progressive campaign of 1912 which was after all the reflex of a great personality, the present Third party movement was impelled by the insistencies of great bodies both of labor and of agriculture. It is rightly founded, as Webster put it, "on men's interest."

Foreign policies cannot be dissociated from the ideals and policies of a country at home. International relations mean international neighborliness. A national policy that will avoid the irritations, the injustices, the suspicions which create the atmosphere of hostility which breeds war is the surest international policy for peace. Both the Republican and the Democratic parties have failed in this respect because they have both pursued unworthy material interests in unworthy ways. Inevitably, the Democratic candidate has adopted "the silent treatment," to which he objects in the President, when it comes to our conduct towards Latin America, because both parties have an identic record of economic imperialism. This country under the guidance of both the Republican and Democratic parties has proved itself an exploiting neighbor because of the false economic emphasis of our international policy. The Democratic candidate, who is silent about Mexico, Haiti and Santo Domingo, and oil in foreign parts, is greatly disturbed that "the English guns definitely outrange ours," and that our fleet is only as big as Japan's and smaller than the British! Did Mr. Davis learn something as ambassador to Great Britain that makes him want to arm us against her? Surely, we have here the revelation of a mind characteristically conventional. War with Great Britain will be avoided only if we are determined in the very marrow of our bones that war is an intolerable and therefore inadmissible mode for settling inevitable controversies. Is it seriously tenable that the hopes and the interests which are behind La Follette are, to put it mildly, less likely agencies for peace than those represented by the governing forces in the two old parties?

But what of La Follette himself? I am not voting for him for his sake. I do not regard him as a messiah. Belief in political messiahs is one of the greatest drawbacks to realizing that we ourselves, the man and woman in the street, must come to grips with our difficulties. But I welcome La Follette as a fit symbol of the movement which he leads. I do not believe in all his specifics; I am indifferent to others. But specifics by a party out of power are really unimportant because necessarily they are somewhat academic and artificial. Behind such proposals is lacking the vivifying impact of responsibility. What matters in a statesman is his direction, his general emphasis and outlook. Senator La Follette's direction is revealed by forty years of public service. His aim has been consistently to give deeper meaning and scope to the masses of men, to make the commonwealth more secure and enduring by resting it on a broad basis of independent, trained, and contented citizens. These are his aims. He has pursued them with unflagging devotion to the resources of reason. Nowhere does the university so permeate the life of a state as it does in Wisconsin. That is an achievement of which Senator La Follette was the guiding spirit. Probably no other man in public life today compares with La Follette in the extent of his reliance on disinterested expertness in the solution of economic and social questions.

Those of us who have no particular economic bias and who are least preoccupied with economic interests owe it most to bend our disinterestedness and our intellectual discipline to the solution of pressing economic-social problems. It is peculiarly up to us to supply the temper of good will and the courageous persistence of the inquirer. This election is important, more because of the forces in our national life that may permanently be encouraged or discouraged, than because of any specific acts of the next administration. If clarification of American politics through the formation of a new party is required to make our politics more honest and more real, then all the talk of "throwing one's vote away" is the cowardly philosophy of the band-wagon. Our duty is to help give cohesion and direction to the groping forces behind La Follette. The road ahead is long and steep; the goal is in the dim distance. When we attain it, others from there will start for a new goal.

Why I Am for Smith

The following selection appeared in the New Republic *for October 31, 1928.*

IT IS midnight, Tuesday, November 6, and the next day's papers must go to press with the election undecided. Not until the early afternoon of Wednesday is the uncertainty lifted and Smith's electoral majority decisively established, though by the narrowest of margins. The commentators upon the result in Thursday's papers have thus had more than the usual time allowed journalists for reflection upon the meaning of events. What interpretation will the American correspondents of important European dailies place upon so lively a change in public feeling, compared with the vote in 1924, as is implied by the election of Governor Smith? How are the observers for the London *Times* and the *Manchester Guardian* likely to explain to English readers Governor Smith's victory and Mr. Hoover's defeat? They will doubtless discern confused and conflicting impulses registered in the result, the play of obscure currents and cross-currents, the operation of many minor and local causes expressed in the nation's choice. But, surely, analysis of the deeper influences in the election of Governor Smith will run somewhat along these lines:

First and foremost, Governor Smith's election implies an unequivocal rejection of any sectarian allegiance as a disqualification for the presidency. Inasmuch as the issue had been so decisively raised, Smith's election is vindication of the principle that fitness to rule over the United States is determined by relevant qualities of character and ability and experience. Proof was required that the presidency is a function of no creed. The appeal to Methodists will not soon again be resorted to by a high official of the government and of the Republican party; the appeal to Presbyterians by their Moderator "to vote and pray" for the Republican candidate will not be imitated by his successor in the reasonable future. Even more important, were such sectarianism again to raise its head, future candidates for the presidency would quickly and effectively combat such divisive forces in our national life as one of the most urgent duties of statesmanship. Hereafter, belated, formal, and abstract disavowals of intolerance would not be deemed sufficient resistance to the exploitation of religious loyalties and sectarian passions in the interest of one seeking the office which symbolizes the good will and the common aspirations of the nation.

By the persuasiveness of a living personality in the White House, Alfred E. Smith will help to soften and displace the pernicious abstractions of religious fanaticism. Adapted to the spiritual ills and disorders of our own day, he will, as truly as Lincoln did in his, help to bind up the wounds of the nation. Whole sections of the United States are at present the prey of religious strife. The dominant political issue in those sections, and a powerful influence everywhere, was Governor Smith's Catholicism; not the specific claim that his Catholicism would improperly affect his Mexican policy or his labor policy or his farm policy, but his Catholicism as such. It will greatly strengthen America as a fellowship and promote our inner security to have in the White House a Catholic like Alfred E. Smith. Our politics will regain its rightful function as the pursuit of those ideals and traditions which have always blended a country of diverse races and religions into a single people. Sectarianism will again confine itself to the awful problems of the ways of God to man.

Second. Governor Smith's election is a rejection of a recurring attempt in the United States to attach false values to social distinction. It cannot be too often repeated that the President is much more significant as a symbol, as an educational influence upon the feelings and ideals of our people, particularly of youth, than as a promoter of this or that economic policy. He is the most powerful teacher in the country. What he says, what he does, what he is, reaches the eyes and the ears and touches the imagination beyond the influence of any other person. Governor Smith again proves the social fluidity of America, its vitality and spiritual freshness, precisely because we have a tradition against social stratification. A marshal's baton in every private's knapsack may be a romantic ideal, but of such ideals are great armies and great nations made. In essence, it embodies a profound ethical truth: respect for the intrinsic qualities of a human being and rejection of the snobbish accentuation of surface conventions and surface refinements that are so largely the product of early material opportunities. Jackson and Lincoln with their own ill-mannered and "unrefined" characteristics gave meaning to Emerson's proud boast that America means opportunity—opportunity for fruition of character and of talent not always appearing in the habiliments of sedate taste and drawing-room restraint.

In a country without traditional aristocracies, social distinctions are largely dependent upon differences in wealth. Especially in a democracy must we resist the subtle danger of stereotyping social distinction into political significance. To do so is a rank betrayal of the democratic principle. Here again, Alfred E. Smith will serve as a symbol. The lowliness of his origin, his lack of cultural opportunities, and his esthetic limitations will fall into their proper places in the perspective of his whole personality. More and more it will become manifest that his character is an achievement and not a gift of circumstances. His election is thus a stimulus to honorable and brave and truthful living, despite the pressure of an environment which leads other men to yield to easy acquiescence, petty compromise, and ignoble self-pursuit.

Third. Smith's election registers a profound conviction that it is the essence of every experiment in government, even of a "noble experiment," to be freely tested by its results and not to be erected into a religious dogma entrusted to the zealous keeping of the Church. A social policy the adoption of which was opposed by two Presidents of the United States because fraught with public disaster cannot be immune from reconsideration. That prohibition has been a potent ally of crime and a promoter of the most widespread political corruption is evidenced by judicial records throughout the country. The corrosive influences of prohibition are as widespread in the home state of Secretary Mellon, who has charge of prohibition enforcement, and in the District of Columbia, governed by President Coolidge's appointees, as in the New York of Governor Smith. Former Senator Wadsworth justly pointed out that the Republican party is committed, not to prohibition, but to "law enforcement," and law enforcement is merely public lip-service to a dogma flagrantly violated in practice. To what extent the feeling for all law is attenuated by nation-wide disregard of one law no man can measure. That the integrity of American social life is tarnished and confused by the permeating hypocrisies due to prohibition only fanatics will deny.

Governor Smith's election is not a ratification of his specific program for relief. The Eighteenth Amendment has enmeshed the country in difficulties from which it cannot quickly or easily be disentangled. Measures for reform will have to be achieved slowly and experimentally. But Smith's election is a mandate for inquiry, for courageous and candid re-examination into ways and means to work ourselves out of the morass of corruption and crime. It is a rejection of prohibition as a shirt of Nessus. Guided by the tests of social utility, of workability under a federal system spanning a continent, the United States will not be wanting in legal and administrative resources to bring law into conformity with truth and with the diverse needs of a hundred and ten millions of people. A great social problem will thus be dealt with empirically, not dogmatically. The practice of true experimentation in government will be furthered, and candor and honesty in public life promoted.

Fourth. The election of Smith is a recognition that government is itself an art, one of the subtlest of arts. Government is neither business nor technology, but the art of making men live together in peace with reasonable happiness. Among the instruments for governing are business organization, technological skill and scientific methods. But they are all instruments and not ends. And that is why the art of effective governing is most successfully achieved by men to whom governing is itself a profession. One of the shal-

lowest disdains is the sneer against the "professional politician."
The invidious implication of the phrase is, of course, against those
who pursue self-interest through politics. But too prevalently the
baby is thrown out with the bath. It is forgotten that the most
successful statesmen have been professionals. Pitt, Gladstone, Disraeli, Asquith, and Lloyd George were professional politicians.
Beveridge's new life of Lincoln is a reminder that Lincoln was a
professional politician. Politics was Roosevelt's profession, Wilson
was all his life at least preoccupied with politics, and Calvin
Coolidge, though nominally a lawyer, has had no profession except politics. Canada emphasizes the professionalism of politics by
making the Leader of the Opposition a paid officer of state.

In a democracy, politics is a process of popular education—the
task of adjusting the conflicting interests of diverse groups in the
community, and bending the hostility and suspicion and ignorance
engendered by group interest to the reconciliation of a common
interest and a common understanding. In this sense Governor
Smith is a master of politics. He had proved himself a most successful political educator. In an office second only to that of the
presidency for the complexity of its problems, and in a state with
a population as diversified as that of the United States, Governor
Smith not only brought the instruments of government into practical conformity with the standards of political science, but employed those instruments for the achievement of great social ends.
The clue to his record in New York lies in his extraordinary talent
for accomplishing great reforms not merely *with* popular assent,
but *because* he is able to awaken popular interest in his aims and
to enlist popular understanding of the technical means by which
alone social policies can be realized. In the language of Franklin
D. Roosevelt, he "made the people of the state of New York
think." The reorganization of the government of New York, the
executive budget, scientific standards of administration, were not
original ideas with Governor Smith. What was original was his
passionate belief in such reforms as a program of "practical politics," joined with a power of presentation and persuasion to win
the indifferent and the hostile to such reforms. No man in public

life today so deeply relies upon the expert for achieving reforms, and upon an aroused public interest which alone can give the expert his opportunity. This combination of qualities is indispensable for the adjustment through government of the conflicting economic interests among different sections and different classes in the country.

Governor Smith has revealed these qualities to an extent unique among public men of today, while Mr. Hoover has given not the slightest evidence that he feels politics as an educational process. Mr. Hoover's important accomplishments have been in times of flood, famine, and war, when the coercive powers of great emergencies were on his side. The presidency is a day-by-day and a give-and-take task. It requires, not command, but genial persuasion, not the mining engineer's blue-prints of what can be weighed and measured, but the deft imagination of the social engineer whose instruments and materials are the imponderables. Mr. Hoover's refusal in the campaign to deal with the pressing problems of the future was partly the strategy of evasion, the strategy of relying on inertia. But it was a strategy congenial to a temperament which has no confidence in appeals to the public. He distrusts democratic processes and believes that the well-being of society depends on the direction of the few in key places.

Fifth. Governor Smith's election will give decided momentum to the liberalizing tendencies in American social economy. Happily, Smith has no set, doctrinaire "principles," but possesses a mind free for new experience and responsive to its directions. During his long tenure of political leadership in Albany, he has achieved great things for liberal causes. Above all, he has proved that his temperament and the bent of his mind compel him to the ways of liberalism. He has done very much to improve labor and social economic conditions, particularly for women; under the fiercest tests, he has shown a deep understanding of political liberty; he has infused his government with human sympathy which transcends even tolerance. His mind is fertilized by the concrete event. The impact of specific problems of government leads him to full inquiry, and freedom from obstinate prepossessions, like

Mr. Hoover's passionate fear of government ownership, enables him to go wherever understanding and democratic sympathies may require. This has been true during his eight years as Governor in securing the adoption of a state park system, in the promotion of social legislation, in advancing public education, in a comprehensive grappling with grade-crossing evils, in the protection of the power resources of the state from selfish exploitation. The so-called economic questions of the future are only in part economic. Largely they involve a redistribution of responsibility and power; a more effective share by labor and agriculture in the nation's councils. The emphasis of Mr. Hoover's whole thought is the assumption that increasing industrial efficiency and the mass production of things automatically make for well-being and promote the spiritual quality of life. If Mr. Hoover realizes the moral issues which "prosperity" intensifies and creates and is concerned with their solution, he has not shared his insight with the public. . . .

Sixth. The failure to continue a party in power is a judgment upon its past performances. The election of Governor Smith is a recognition that the sanitation of American politics requires a stern reminder of party responsibility for the most extensive scandals in the history of the national government. If the Republican party is to have credit, as Mr. Hoover would have it, for the lilies in the field and the radios in the home, it must bear blame for the dereliction of its high officials, for the corrupt party management of its chairman, and, above all, for the moral torpor of the leaders of the party in face of the corruption of their associates. Mr. Hoover's complete personal freedom from corruption is irrelevant. He was himself a member of the administration which is tainted with corruption. His failure to dissociate himself explicitly and concretely only emphasizes party responsibility for misdeeds of colleagues and sheds important light on his courage and independence when party associates are involved. That men like Bascom Slemp and Rush Holland and George Lockwood were high in the councils of his campaign challenged the country's judgment, not merely upon Mr. Hoover's personal qualities, but upon the Republican party which Mr. Hoover sponsored. Governor Smith's election gives vitality to party politics by sending into the wilderness a party with so corrupt a record as that of the Republican party since 1921.

Seventh. The election of Governor Smith proves a shrewd unwillingness by the American people to be misled by the parrot cry of "Tammany." Only ignorance or hypocrisy can find Tammany more sinister than the corrupt political machines throughout the country. In the city of New York it is a Democratic machine, in Philadelphia, Pittsburgh, Chicago, Cleveland, and Cincinnati, the corrupt machines are Republican. The argument of "Tammany" is relevant only if thereby is implied that Governor Smith has shown the slightest predilection toward corrupt or self-regarding motives in public office. By his governorship, he must be judged. Those are eight years of maturity and responsibility.

No man's record in politics has ever been placed under a more powerful microscope. His opponents for Governor have been men of vigor and unlimited resources, who would have discovered evidence of wrong-doing or of personal or partisan exploitation of office were discovery possible. Instead, Governor Smith, to a degree unrivaled in the history of the state of New York, has received the praise of the most eminent members of the opposition party. His record is a triumph of character just because he was so long exposed to the temptations of a crude and sordid environment. For the world of politics, Emerson's well-known words find illustration in Al Smith: "It is easy in the world to live after the world's opinion; it is easy in solitude to live after our own; but the great man is he who in the midst of the crowd keeps with perfect sweetness the independence of solitude."

Eighth. Foreign affairs affected the election little, but the result may greatly affect foreign affairs. In preferring Governor Smith over Mr. Hoover, those for whom foreign affairs were important were not confused by the red herring of Mr. Hoover's foreign experience. To be sure, Mr. Hoover is much traveled and knows about countries other than his own. But knowledge of foreign countries is far from being a guaranty of wisdom about their peoples, still less of a broad outlook on foreign relations. That foreign travel and foreign cultivation do not necessarily dislodge excessive nationalism is amply proved by such anti-Europeans in the United States Senate as Lodge, McCormick, and Moses. The feeding of Belgians during the War and of Russians later is no index whatever to Mr. Hoover's attitude toward disarmament, nor ground for confidence in his generous co-operation with Europe. Charity is one thing. The imagination that sees the world in terms of a common brotherhood is quite a different thing. The conduct of foreign relations does not require technical equipment or foreign cultivation. It was the cultivated Seward who tried to push us into war with England, and the untraveled Lincoln who kept us out.

Wise foreign relations require fundamentally not a body that has traveled, but a mind and spirit capable of traveling—a mind that feels the common qualities of men, that values the moral dignity and the love of life implanted in all, and is capable of neighborliness with all sorts and conditions of men however different their accents of speech. The qualities which underlay Governor Smith's success in New York are the best possible sources for foreign policies. His imagination, his generosity, his patient and pacific temperament, his humor, his charm, his flair for reality, his effectiveness in negotiation, are far better guaranties for a wise and tolerant dealing with other peoples than impatience and temper and a dogmatic belief in pre-war economic theories of national self-interest.

Thus, I believe, would Governor's Smith's election be interpreted. They are ends profoundly worth bringing to pass.

Why I Am for Governor Roosevelt

This was a campaign speech which Mr. Frankfurter delivered over radio station WBJ on November 5, 1932.

TUESDAY next will be held what Woodrow Wilson was fond of calling the grand inquest of the nation. The strife of words and partisan excesses during four long months not unnaturally arouse weariness and a sense of futility about the campaign. Surely this is a short-sighted view. Is there not something truly majestic about a people of a hundred and twenty millions scattered over a continent deciding its destiny by debate, by the give-and-take of argument? The only alternative to government by talk is government by force. And violence is not the only form of force; it comes in subtle disguises. We should rejoice that in the midst of disaster and miseries the appeal is still to reason, and that a change in government is contemplated by the uncoerced action of some forty million voters.

A President who offers himself for re-election seeks approval of his first term. We may not escape the duty of examining the record and aptitudes of the President. In doing so, one does not fail of respect for his office. On the contrary, only by choosing a President in the full light of knowledge and criticism do we truly respect the presidential office. In effect, Mr. Hoover asks for the reward of another election although the country finds itself in the third winter of the worst economic and social distress that the people of the United States have ever endured. About the basic situation there can, unhappily, be no difference of opinion—the unemployment of millions, the stagnation of the major industries, the plight of the vast agricultural regions. These tragic facts are recounted not to add gloom nor to undermine hope. But they are

indispensable starting points in any judgment upon President
Hoover's administration. If Mr. Hoover has serious responsibility
for the untoward conditions in which we find ourselves, then
surely it were best for the country to choose a more hopeful leadership. To deny all connection, as Mr. Hoover does, between the
depression and the policies which he has pursued is to make of
politics the emptiest sham. What are politics about if not so to
order and stimulate the economic and social forces of society as to
make for its well-being? No one has questioned the President's
good intentions or his extraordinary energy. No one has doubted
that he has worked without stint. But to say that what Mr.
Hoover has done and what he has left undone have in no wise
affected the course of events is to say that it makes no difference
who is President or what policies he pursues, that depressions will
come no one knows whence and they will go no one knows how.
To assert that Mr. Hoover's direction of affairs is in no wise responsible for the evil days upon which we have fallen, is to deny
the economic and political philosophy of Mr. Hoover himself. In
1928 he asked for and obtained the suffrage of his countrymen
upon the claim that if he were entrusted with the presidency and
were "given a chance to go forward with the policies of the last
eight years"—that is, the policies of Harding and Coolidge—"we
shall soon, with the help of God, be in sight of the day when
poverty will be banished from this nation." Mr. Hoover thus offered the country certain economic policies. These, he promised,
would not only make for continuance of "prosperity" but would
"soon" banish poverty. The American people are good-natured
but not simple-minded. And they cannot be persuaded that political and economic policies are responsible when things go well but
that when things go ill, inscrutable fate and the foreigner are to
blame, but that the head of the nation is wholly blameless.

With all his good intentions, President Hoover must bear a
heavy share of responsibility for our national plight. Of course the
policies of Washington have a good deal to do with the well-
being of the country; and, since this country is the most powerful
nation in the world, the policies at Washington have a good deal

to do with encouraging the forces for good or discouraging the forces for ill throughout the world. There are at work deep forces of transformation in modern economic society due, fundamentally, to our extraordinary material development and its inadequate social control. No man who is aware of these problems would charge the full burden of the depression to Mr. Hoover. But to realize the new economic order, to understand its new problems, to devise ways of dealing with these new problems and not persist in the old ways of an obsolete society—that is the essence of modern statesmanship. The essential question that faces our time is whether we are capable of so organizing production and distribution as to prevent these terrible ups and downs in business, with their consequent moral and economic disaster. More effective participation by labor and agriculture in the nation's councils are needed; more sustained and wider diffusion of the purchasing power on the part of the great masses. This requires an improvement in our standards—better housing, more health, higher levels of education, better and wider uses of leisure. Thus, and thus only, will there be markets for the ever-increasing products of field and factory.

Neither before the depression nor since has Mr. Hoover shown any awareness that we are living in a new economic world. Somehow or other, he thinks, this depression will pass, and then mass production will automatically make for well-being. Certainly Mr. Hoover has not given the slightest indication that he realizes that the "prosperity" the continuance of which he promised in 1928 itself creates the problems which the depression has revealed. And since he does not seem to realize that the industrial inventions of the engineers have in large measure themselves given rise to the perplexities of modern statesmanship, naturally Mr. Hoover has offered not a single solution for their cure. Petty palliatives are not cures. To the President depressions are like the old epidemics, afflictions which come and go. The task of modern statesmanship is to devise social inventions in order to deal with the maladjustments of our economic life in the spirit in which sanitary science has been dealing with epidemics. Such an attitude of mind towards our economic ills is wholly alien to the President. He assumes an economic world which is very real and vivid in his own mind but which is no longer real in fact, no longer true in the real world.

Moreover, President Hoover has demonstrated that he is devoid of the art of governing. However great his talents may be, they do not lie in the field of democratic statesmanship. In a democracy like ours, politics are a continuous process of popular education. With us the task of political leadership is to adjust the conflicting interests of diverse groups in the community and to bend the hostility and suspicion and ignorance engendered by group interest to the reconciliation of a common interest and a common understanding. Mr. Hoover has tragically failed as a political and popular leader because he distrusts the democratic process of reasoning with equals. It is significant that Mr. Hoover's great accomplishments have been in times of flood, famine and war when the coercive powers of great emergencies were on his side, when autocratic authority must be wielded. But the presidency is a day-by-day and give-and-take task. It succeeds, not by command, but by genial persuasion. The equipment for the presidency is not that of a mining engineer who deals with things that can be weighed and measured. The raw materials for a President are human beings, their wants and quirks. To deal with them successfully, to satisfy the varying needs of the diverse sections of a continental nation, requires the common touch, a spontaneously friendly nature, and the great talent of getting on with all sorts and conditions of men.

In Governor Roosevelt's administration of the greatest state in the union, he has shown that he is alive to the problems of the new day, and that he has both the will and the capacity to deal with them in the light of the new day. His financial administration, his early alertness to problems of relief, his refusal to starve social services on the false plea of economy, his reliance on associates like Miss Frances Perkins, the ablest industrial commissioner in the country, all give proof that as President he will endeavor to translate into action that philosophy of government so ably expressed in his speech before the Commonwealth Club of San Francisco and in his address on social justice in Detroit.

His success in wresting wise measures of taxation, power regulation, and unemployment relief from Republican legislatures has demonstrated those qualities of effective persuasion which are the essence of political leadership.

Governor Roosevelt's outlook and achievements and the courage and hope of which his life is a triumph, justify us in following his lead. Supported by the liberal and progressive sentiment of the country, he can help us out of our present moral and material morass and start new ways of thought into new deeds of action. And so his election on Tuesday next may well be the augur of happier days.

What We Confront in American Life

This was the anniversary address delivered before the twentieth annual meeting of the Survey Associates, in 1933. It appeared in the Survey Graphic *for April, 1933.*

IN 1876, the Huxley of our grandfathers ventured some general observations upon America's destiny. ". . . to an Englishman landing upon your shores for the first time," he remarked at the founding of Johns Hopkins University, "traveling for hundreds of miles through strings of great and well-ordered cities, seeing your enormous actual, and almost infinite potential, wealth in all commodities, and in the energy and ability which turns wealth to account, there is something sublime in the vista of the future. Do not suppose that I am pandering to what is commonly understood as national pride. I cannot say that I am in the slightest degree impressed by your bigness, or your material resources, as such. Size is not grandeur, and territory does not make a nation. The great issue, about which hangs a true sublimity and the terror of overhanging fate, is, What are you going to do with all these things? What is to be the end to which these are to be the means?

"You are making a novel experiment in politics on the greatest scale which the world has yet seen. Forty millions at your first centenary, it is reasonably to be expected that at the second these states will be occupied by two hundred millions of English-speaking people, spread over an area as large as that of Europe, and with climates and interests as diverse as those of Spain and Scandinavia, England, and Russia. You and your descendants have to ascertain whether this great mass will hold together under the forms of a republic and the despotic reality of universal suffrage;

whether state rights will hold out against centralization, without separation; whether shifting corruption is better than a permanent bureaucracy; and as population thickens in your great cities and the pressure of want is felt, the gaunt specter of pauperism will stalk among you, and socialism and communism will claim to be heard."

After fifty years of the most feverish preoccupation with material development in the world's history we are face to face with the appalling problems which Huxley foreshadowed in the year of our Centennial. His prescient inquiry, "What are you going to do with all these things?" has become the most exigent and pervasive question of American life.

To be sure, since the nation was born there have been financial crises, panics, and depressions. Indeed we have even been counseled to take comfort in these periodicities of misery. Depressions come we know not whence and go we know not how, but come and go they do, to be endured like the epidemics of old as part of the burden of life. As to epidemics, we have rejected the blindness of such shallow fatalism. Their causes and their sources are pertinaciously explored first to be known and then to be overcome. Even if our present plight were merely a mirror of the past, it is an abdication of reason to rely on time's self-correction. No depression ever stopped of itself. Moreover it is no longer sensational or ignorant to believe that this depression is different. There *are* new periods in history, and *we* are in the midst of *one* of them.

Not that the new era has come overnight. Of spontaneous generation there is little in history. Epochal changes germinate slowly and dates in history are deluding. They mark fruition as much as beginning. To say that even the World War ushered in a new era is to foreshorten events. To be sure, the débâcle of three mighty empires, the Russian Revolution and its violent break with the past, the gigantic dislocation of a world economy, the emergence and resurgence of nationalism, the intensification of technological processes induced by the War, have all loosed economic and social forces far more upsetting to the pre-existing equilibrium than the changes wrought by the French Revolution and the Napoleonic

Wars. But these powerful solvents have only reinforced major influences operating in our national economy. We have been assuming a continuing validity for the economic theories of pioneer America while fact has been steadily undermining theory. The absorption of free land, the steady drift from rural to a predominantly urban society, with the economic consequences of changes in population distribution, the attainment of the saturation point in railroad construction, itself an index of the general shift from the winning of a new country to its maintenance, the implications of technological advances both in industry and agriculture, the enormous extension of leisure among the mass of people, the new areas of foreign industrial and agricultural competition—these were only a few major elements in the making of a new American society when the cataclysmic War broke in upon us. Unfortunately these new forces left substantially untouched the theories of our political action.

Now I shall not attempt to epitomize in a phrase the resulting maladjustments. To speak of poverty amidst plenty and alternating days of feast and famine perhaps hints at the essentials. About the basic situation there can, unhappily, be no differences of opinion; vast agricultural regions in distress, major industries stagnant, twelve millions or more unemployed and several millions, at best, likely to remain so. Deep forces of transformation are at work, due fundamentally to our extraordinary material development and its inadequate social control.

To realize that there is a new economic order and to realize it passionately, not platonically, is the central equipment for modern statesmanship. Only thus shall we be able to understand the new problems and devise ways, however tentative and halting, for dealing with new problems. We cannot carry on upon the old maxims. "Improvement," said John Stuart Mill, "consists in bringing our opinion into clearer agreement with facts; and we shall not be likely to do this while we look at facts only through glasses colored by those very opinions." The governing issue of our time is whether we are capable of so organizing production and distribution as to avert these terrible ups and downs in business, with their disastrous moral and economic consequences.

Technological invention, we all know, has caused an enormous saving of labor; social invention must find ways for a sustained and wider diffusion of purchasing power whereby the great masses can maintain technological society. This implies more than an eventual restoration of the standards of living which have been lost. It demands an advance in standards—more health, better housing, higher levels of education, increasing esthetic development, fruitful uses of ampler leisure. Thus only, in the belief of a growing body of opinion, will we master the machine and not be mastered by it. Thus only, what is equally important, will there be markets for the ever-increasing potentialities of field and factory.

A good part of our past is dead. To hope for its revival is tragic illusion. New circumstances condition the nation's wealth-making; how they are met will determine the national welfare. The road to yesterday's prosperity is largely barred. Recovery, too much pursued by incantation, must deal with factors which in their combination certainly present a new situation. They constitute a decisively different environment, both economic and psychologic, from the slough out of which past depressions have moved. If a mere lawyer ventures to adumbrate some of the factors that predetermine our future economic life, perhaps it is sufficient excuse that even professional economists recognize the existence, if not of a new heaven, at least of a new earth in which they also are groping.

First and foremost, I venture to put the arrest in the rate of increase of our population. Now this marks a break with our whole history. Restriction of immigration has become a settled national policy. An inflow of a million a year before the War has, in the last year, changed to an excess of emigration. No doubt our pre-War immigration raised problems of competition in the labor market. But more important, perhaps, it supplied much consumptive capacity for American production. But a matter of even more far-reaching implications than shutting the door at Ellis Island is the decreasing birthrate. Whatever be the law's attitude towards birth-control, the recent census figures leave no doubt whatever as to the growing prevalence of its practice. I am aware that there is conflict of statistical forecasts as to our future population. But for the present purpose it is immaterial whether our population becomes stationary by 1950 or 1960 or later. The controlling fact is the steady and substantial downward curve. Nor need I labor the point of its bearing upon the prospect of expansion of the domestic market in the light of industrial mechanization.

Equally permeating in its implications is the weight of our debts, public and private. The outstanding indebtedness of the country colors the whole economic situation. It presents perhaps the most serious of all our problems. Here, too, figures are conflicting, but the most optimistic are cheerless. Some say the indebtedness is 162 billions; some, 203 billions. The value of our property was put in 1929 at 396 billions. If that was an approximately correct figure, it cannot be much more than our present debt. Land values were inflated by the expectation of increased population. With the trend towards an arrested population, there must be a heavy shrinkage; and the values of industrial building and equipment, representing in part overcapacity or obsolescence, must likewise be heavily shrunk. To secure a real financial equilibrium, a very substantial cut in both public and private debts appears unavoidable. This process of course is at best painful, though there are *more* or *less* painful ways of doing it. Through their conversion loan the British have taken the lead in doing what must be done; they have also shown how euphemism softens blows. But that the heavy mountain of debts will have to be considerably scaled down is clear, at least to one outside the professional mysteries of finance.

Intimately bound up with our staggering public indebtedness is the increasing burden of taxation. Savings there can be and there must be. Good government demands it as well as our economic plight. But the sum total, I venture to say, will afford relatively little alleviation. To attempt any sizable curtailment of appropriations for the social services would be the blindest misconception of public finance. Under the deceptive slogan of "economy" too many comfortable people preach vicarious asceticism. This is mean and self-defeating. The country cannot become richer by making the quality of its social life poorer. Quite the contrary. Child welfare, health, education, recreation, security for old age, a wider diffusion of esthetic opportunities for the masses, are dictated alike by the amenities of a civilized society and the consumptive needs of modern industry. And in the promotion of these ends the government will have more and not less share; more and not less public funds will be needed for their realization. The debt service, of course, absorbs much more of taxation than the social services. But at the lowest, the debt service will remain enormous. The only opportunities for large saving are spurious veterans' claims and the armed services. Reduced military and naval appropriations imply a pacific temper in the world and a reliance upon that temper far greater than appear immediately dominant.

In the meantime we shall continue to feel the effects of stimulation of European competition against ourselves by our pre-depression export of capital. Related to restriction of our foreign markets is the change in the ratio of luxuries, so-called, to necessities in our economy. With amazing rapidity the whole nation has come to indulge in automobiles and radios and refrigerators. Our heavy industries, it is now plain, have become greatly dependent upon their continuing consumption. Yet the masses can do without these comforts, as they did without them yesterday. But curtailment of these modern luxury trades, unlike the luxury trades of a generation or two ago, dislocates our whole economic life.

Other changes in our economic scene are rendering obsolete its old assumptions and dangerous its old routine. I shall add only one more. The ultimate governing forces of the world are ideas— what men believe in and what they distrust. Do I not report accurately when I note the profoundly important psychological factor of a growing disbelief in the fairness of our capitalistic scheme and even in its capacity to achieve its purposes?

And when we turn and question in suspense
If these things be indeed after our ways,
And what things are to follow after these,
Our fluent men of place and consequence
Fumble and fill their mouths with hollow phrase,
Or for the end-all of deep arguments
Intone their dull commercial liturgies.

.   .   .   .

No gathering could be more appropriate than this twentieth annual meeting of Survey Associates for an attempt to go beneath
the surface of the present situation and to explore dependable
directions for its correction. No group, to my knowledge, is more
disciplined for the long-range view and the resoluteness and re-
sourcefulness, the patience and the good will indispensable for that
reformation and transformation of our society which Sir Arthur
Salter rightly deems necessary, if we are to salvage what we regard
as precious in our civilization. To the country generally, the seemingly sudden reversal of what was considered a securely established order of prosperity came almost like a thief in the night,
like a capricious eruption of malevolent forces unrelated to the
past and therefore unexplained by it. The great body of our
people were, and I am afraid to a considerable extent still are, be-
wildered and baffled by the meaning of it all, largely because
those whom they had been taught to look to for leadership had,
in their recklessness and ignorance and greed, misled and mis-
educated them. During the whole post-War period we were veri-
tably gorged with statistics of material development. With singular
blindness, it was deemed almost disloyal to the Americanism of
the South Sea Bubble era to challenge the meaning of these statistics or even to supplement them with other unpleasanter figures.
Until more recently, the critical inquirer into our social scheme
was looked upon askance; he was characterized as selling America
short. The endeavor to read beyond the ticker and the refusal to
be persuaded by the aurora borealis painted by investment houses
was indeed a very lonely enterprise.

Unyielding, patient, forthright devotion to this uncomfortable enterprise has been the glory of *The Survey* and the achievement of those who make up Survey Associates. For these many years now, *The Survey* has been, as it were, the crow's nest of American society. While the country was drugged into thoughtlessness and indifference, convinced by those in highest authority both in government and finance not only that all was well but that the secret of perpetual well-being had been won, *The Survey*, in its quiet, plodding—some even said dull—way, called attention to the great seams and fissures and faults in the social structure, covered over though they were by a papier-mâché prosperity. And now that the great disillusionments have come, the widespread and growing miseries, mass distress imperiling satisfaction even of the animal wants of man and undermining his sense of security, the public all too widely expects legerdemain and magic to solve its difficulties. Just as these evil days seem to have dropped upon us suddenly out of nowhere, there is still a feeling that "prosperity" will return with miraculous swiftness, in the guise of some new formula or man—some wizard who will restore our happiness, or at least mitigate our misery. Every day we hear and read of new short-cuts; almost daily one receives in his mail some new plan "whereby prosperity can be restored in this country." That is the usual guarantee that is offered. There seems to be the most naïve longing for some three-point program or some five-point or seven-point program, something brief or sententious enough to put in a newspaper "box."

It is not enough for me to compete with these panacea-mongers. Revival or recovery will not come by pulling rabbits out of a hat. There are no tricks that will turn the tide. The way out lies in bold and laborious grappling with the basic forces of our economic situation. But we have been told and are still told, that the path of wisdom cannot be faced and that the hard road of action that we ought to take cannot be taken because public opinion will not support it. I have not believed it in the past and I believe it still less today. The one generalization that can fairly be made about public opinion is that the public responds to truth-telling and courage in high places. Moreover, the function of political leadership is to lead, and not to allow action to be paralyzed because public opinion is confused and distracted. I venture the belief that never have our people been more ripe or more ready to follow determined direction based upon a brave and lucid analysis of our economic forces. I venture to believe that that applies to the international aspects of our national problem no less than to our immediate domestic issues.

Of knowledge we have plenty; of courage to apply what we know there has never been enough. Years ago, in the heyday of post-War prosperity, *The Survey* probed the greatest of our evils, unemployment. It laid bare the dark places midst our vaunted prosperity, it indicated the dangerous trends, the social and economic dislocations that were inevitable, it formulated the objectives for improvement, it gave substantial hints of the inventive efforts by which such objectives could be obtained. But that *Survey Graphic* on unemployment was like suggesting a bleak New England winter to the merrymakers of Palm Beach. The kind of desperate wisdom that is needed in times like these was then lacking. These times have supplied the final insight—that we must dare to act on what we know. Power is given to the man in danger of losing his life to do what he must. We must find that wisdom of courage.

Now the social worker really represents the two major demands on our statesmanship. His immediate concern, of course, has always been relief. It is not open to argument that mass relief has become the primary duty of government and can no longer be left to man's charity for man. Mass relief raises most delicate and complicated problems of administration. And it is important to realize that we must provide, not merely for the backs and bellies of men, but also for their spirits. Ways must be found, and they must be found through governmental lead, to prevent the terrible psychology of idleness and hopelessness from settling upon the unemployed. In diverse forms attempts must be made to turn the enforced idleness of millions of people into opportunities for part-time education and recreation and some constructive economic activity.

Which brings me to the crucial and all-pervasive need. Social workers have long since realized that on the whole relief, charity, is but a poultice and a poultice of short duration. *The Survey* for decades has analyzed our social problems as essentially maladjustments of industry. In season and out of season, it has insisted on what is now plain to all, that industry is not a self-contained economic mechanism, but for good or ill, the way of ordering our society. Hence *The Survey* has perennially emphasized unemployment and irregularity of employment as our greatest social evil. The millions of our unemployed fellow citizens have shown an extraordinarily patient temper. The only way to justify it, indeed the only way to maintain this temper is to make definite progress towards re-employment. This ought not to be merely a pious wish. It is a national "must." Every avenue for feeding men back to jobs must be pursued and vigorously pushed. The problem here has reached such dimensions that there can be no shadow of doubt that governmental intervention in some form or other is necessary. The kind of public-works program which Senator Wagner proposed a year ago seems to me indispensable, except that now we should embark on even a larger, a more ambitious public-works program than he sponsored then. I am not unaware of the various fears that are entertained in regard to such a program. But we cannot get out of the present difficulty by yielding to the fears of men who are too much in the grip of the past and are still guided by economic views that leave out of account the profoundly changing forces of America today.

I venture to say that out of the pages of *The Survey* during the last ten years can be collated a definite, sober, and coherent program for economic revival. We cannot expect such a program to be carried out overnight. But we must start and start quickly upon the execution of a program of re-employment. All else is secondary. The present trend of things must be reversed, and must be reversed at a rather rapid tempo. A change in direction and assurance that new processes are under way are indispensable. Mr. Roosevelt's admirable Tennessee Valley project is an example of what must be done on a large scale. By a well-planned, co-ordinated public-works program of adequate magnitude, quickly entered upon, the United States and the states could, within six months, put to work directly some two million men, and indirectly perhaps two million more. It would set in motion many wheels now idle; it would help transportation, agriculture, manufacture, and merchandising. Such a program would have to be related to a socially sound taxing system. Ultimately it ought to be financed by high estate and income taxes, worked out by the national government in co-operation with the states. Needed permanent investments for the country's welfare would thus be made, and they would not involve competition with private enterprise.

Despite our present plight, we have it more than ever within our power to be masters of our fate, so far as our external lives are concerned, if only we have the will to translate knowledge into action and to gain further knowledge by action. "The Western World," writes John Maynard Keynes, "already has the resources and the technique, if we could create the organization to use them, capable of reducing the economic problem, which now absorbs our moral and material energies to a position of secondary importance. . . . The day is not far off when the economic problem will take the back seat where it belongs and the arena of the heart and head will be occupied, or reoccupied, by our real problems—the problems of life and of human relations, of creation and behavior and religion."

The Shape of Things to Come

This was the address which Mr. Frankfurter delivered at the twenty-fifth anniversary dinner of the Survey Associates in December, 1937. It was published in the Survey Graphic *for January, 1938.*

O N THE occasion of every important celebration there comes to my mind for some strange reason the sentence I heard in my youth in the last fateful speech of President McKinley at Buffalo. "Expositions," he said, "are the timekeepers of progress." What a typical nineteenth-century sentiment. That fortunate, self-deluding age believed in the idea of progress—a wholesome and robust faith, which generates effort toward its attainment and without which cynicism and defeatism all too easily become dominant. But the nineteenth century not merely talked of progress, it fortunately too readily assumed that progress was inevitable. Now we are in a much more chastened mood. We do not speak so glibly of progress, and certainly do not identify the progress of the machine with the progress of man. Not that the nineteenth century was without its warning voices, both here and abroad. But it is significant that today some of the gravest and most penetrating anxieties regarding the gap between the progress of science and the moral health of society are voiced by the great leaders of science itself. No statesman, I believe, today would venture to find in any exposition of material things satisfying proof of the quality of our contemporary civilization. I do not mean to decry things, the material conquests of man. But the vital issue for any society is what we do with them, what they do for us and to us, and on that issue I do not know a more illuminating, balanced and courageous reporter than *The Survey* has been during the last twenty-five years which tonight we celebrate.

With characteristic creative direction Paul Kellogg has sought to give organic unity to the remarks tonight by asking us to evoke the shape of things to come. This is a most salutary goad for the orientation of thought and action, for it is a tonic attempt to shake off the confusions and conflicts of the past and to seek to influence the only thing we can influence, the future. Unfortunately, however, the future is not a clean slate. The life of society, as of the individual, is a palimpsest. What has been, or at least what we think about what has been, may very considerably influence what will be. The shape of things to come depends not a little upon the remembrance of things past. One of the strange paradoxes about man is his disdain of theory as theory and the dominance of theory in practice. William James spoke of "irreducible and stubborn facts." But I think I can summon history to witness that theories are even more stubborn than facts. Men who suggest that no one who has not had to meet a pay roll is entitled to speak on social policy, sometimes seek to meet their pay rolls on theories whose validity they have never critically examined, or whose origin was based on facts which have long since been supplanted. The elder Huxley once said there is nothing more tragic than the murder of a big theory by a little fact. But he hastened to add that nothing is more surprising than the way in which a theory will continue to live long after its brains are knocked out.

The dominant theories concerning the individual and society determine our mental climate, and our mental climate—the intellectual and moral atmosphere which we breathe—determines the outcome of specific issues much more than the so-called intrinsic merits of these issues. It is well, therefore, to disengage ourselves from too much absorption in the immediate present conflicts, and, instead, to examine critically our general outlook and attitude.

Two notions exert powerful and destructive sway over us—the assumption of a Golden Age and the hope of a Utopia: a Golden Age that never was and a Utopia that never will be. These beliefs are powerful because they are rooted in romance, and for the same reason they are destructive. They provide the satisfactions of fairyland, but cloud the mind and debilitate the will in facing the grim realities of an intractable world.

Let me translate these airy generalities into concreteness. Our major domestic issues are phases of a single central problem: namely, the interplay of enterprise and government. Taxation, utility regulation, control of the security markets, labor standards, housing, banking and finance, all these current issues turn essentially on the relation of government to money-making and of money-making to government. This central problem was with us long before the New Deal and will be long after it has passed into history. The controversies which it engenders have at bottom not been differences over details, but as to essential attitudes toward the organic nature of modern, large-scale, industrialized society, and ultimately turn on the conception of the relation of individuals one to another in the circumstances of our society. It is one thing to oppose a specific measure because economically unsound or administratively unworkable or because the cure would be worse than the disease. Quite a different thing is it to oppose some empiric measure aimed at the correction of a specific evil or for the promotion of some concrete public good because such a measure runs counter to what are believed to be eternal verities embodied in slogans or formulas which themselves are merely expressive of the specialized experience of the past. Whatever may be the right or the wrong of Mr. Maynard Keynes's particular economic views, that he is one of the great economic thinkers of the Western world would hardly be gainsaid. And yet he has written a whole book, as part of a struggle of escape from habitual modes of thought and expression, to prove that the so-called classical theory of economic thought in which he was educated, had merely special and not general applicability, and that the characteristics of the special case assumed by the classical theory happened not to be those of the economic society in which we actually live.

But see how a dogmatic position to the contrary—confronting the real problems of society with inherited tags and phrases—operates in a concrete case. Just about the time that the Survey Associates was founded a committee of the United States Senate had before it a bill to raise the weight limit on fourth-class mail from four to eleven pounds, in a word, to extend the services of the United States post offices to include a system of parcel post. The measure was opposed, not by a showing of the probabilities of its economic effects in the light of experience, but "on the broad general grounds that the government should not further engage in competition with its citizens; that our government has already approached the halting line of socialistic and paternalistic legislation." And this in the administration of President Taft! Not only was the favorable European experience not deemed relevant; it proved that the proposal was un-American. Let me read from the record:

"I have just returned," a witness testified, "from Europe, and over there I found conditions exceedingly bad under their system. Why, what they are having now are bread riots in England."

The Chairman: "Due to parcel post?"

The Witness: "Largely due to their system, and parcel post is a part of that system. . . ."

I have read this not for purposes of gaiety but because in the mental attitude that it reveals, widely and sincerely as it is held, we have, I believe, the source of our greatest difficulty, the difficulty of a rigid outlook upon a dynamic world. The grounds of objection to the parcel post bill which I have quoted are not mere historical curiosities. Socialism, alien ideas, dictatorship, bureaucracy, centralization and their like are the recurrent themes encountered in the legislative history of the United States for a full half-century. Not for a moment do I mean to suggest that the more active intervention of government in the affairs of men does not raise serious questions for the proper safeguarding of those individual rights that constitute a fundamental difference between autocracy and democracy. I do not mean, for a moment, to imply that all the laws that have found their way on the statute books during the last fifty years were wisely framed or effectively administered. But I do insist that if every attempt to remove abuses of our system or to promote its avowed ends has encountered the obstruction of abstract notions about government as the enemy of society rather than as its appropriate instrument in appropriate cases, such abstract notions are discredited by the record of history. For it cannot be that half a century of American government— one-third of our whole national existence under the leadership of both parties and the different wings of each party—can consistently have sponsored legislation which deserved to be denounced consistently as alien and un-American.

Would there were time to document this history of federal legislation—and the same story could be told in the sphere of state legislation—beginning with the administration of Grover Cleveland. A few instances—taken at random—must suffice. This year marked the fiftieth anniversary of the first major intervention of the federal government, barring the tariff, into the area of economic enterprise. Today we take the Interstate Commerce Commission as much for granted as we do the post office. Yet some of the most powerful influences in the land opposed the measure, as though it foredoomed the American system. Its very idea was abhorrent. "If this bill shall become law," said Senator Leland Stanford, himself a great railroad figure, "its consequences will be most disastrous . . . to the varied business interests of the country." And, speaking for Massachusetts, Senator Hoar announced that "the passage of this bill will create a panic." Senator Platt of Connecticut found things in the bill that he called "anti-Christian" and expressive of "the old pagan idea," "the old despotic idea." Similar sentiments were expressed by leading members of the House. One of them protested against putting "the commercial and industrial interests of the country into the grasp of a single commission of men," and to another it was "a gigantic stride toward paternal government." One member of the House, however, ventured the prophecy that a later generation would be mystified by these unbridled fears. "The time will come," the then obscure Robert M. La Follette told the House, "when it would be a marvel how such abuses ever arose and why they were so long tolerated; when all parties alike will wonder how the just and simple provisions of this initiatory measure ever created such bitter and uncompromising opposition."

Take another instance. When in 1893 an income tax calculated to yield $30,000,000 a year was passed, both in and out of Congress the measure was assailed as though it could only have emanated from traitors to the republic. According to the New York *Sun*, "Never in the history of this country has so effective a measure been proposed for the creation and maintenance of tramps as the income tax." And the New York *Evening Post* foretold that the country would be ruined by the "accelerating evils of such socialistic legislation." According to Senator David B. Hill, the leader of the fight against the tax, "It was a discriminating, a sectional, a communistic tax." And Senator Sherman of Ohio summed it all up as "socialism, communism, devilism."

And a final instance. It may come as a surprise to those who did not live through the enactment of the Federal Reserve Act of 1913 that it too encountered the traditional abstract objections. According to the then president of the Chase National Bank, it was "socialistic" and sounded the "death knell" of the national banks. The leading bank president of Chicago characterized the Act as "unjust and un-American." And once again the shadow of dictatorship fell across the floors of Congress. "This bill . . . is a confession of dictation and absolutism, the like of which has no parallel in American annals."

Only in the fair perspective of this continuous interplay between government and economic enterprise, for fifty years at least, are the present controversies really intelligible. And the lesson we draw from this history will largely determine the shape of things to come. Surely the social historian of the United States will on the whole judge the course of events since 1887 a great social waste, he will assess the relations between business and government as needless social friction. Needless waste and friction not because opposition to all legislation is not in itself a contributing factor, nor because the specific enactments should not have been opposed in detail and sometimes even been delayed in passage. The social waste has derived from the fact that obvious reforms, now recognized of all men, were unduly delayed, and that in the intransigent opposition to legislation as such, the democratic legislative process was deprived of the indispensable constructive criticism from those with special knowledge even though sometimes also with special interests.

Such an attitude of intransigence, deeply rooted in loyalty to certain abstractions, is at bottom the offspring, not of self-interest, but of self-deception and misconception. What is wrong is not devotion to inherited ideas—they form, as Professor Whitehead has told us, "the tradition of our civilization." But such traditional ideas are never static, "they are either fading into meaningless formulae, or are gaining power by the new lights thrown by a more delicate apprehension. . . . No generation can merely reproduce its ancestors. You may preserve the life in a flux of form, or preserve the form amid an ebb of life."

Now the era of physical expansion after the Civil War was exceptionally favorable to the development of an aggressive and intransigent individualism which imperceptibly but powerfully lent itself to building up an anti-social psychology, and certainly an anti-governmental mentality. In our kind of society there is bound to be a certain degree of conflict between self-interest and social control. We believe in competition, in the excitement of conflict and the testing of man against man in a fair fight. We not only like these things for themselves as the spontaneous expression of personality in a free society; we also depend on them to get things done. At least in our economic system the dynamo is self-interest—a self-interest which may range from mere petty greed to admirable types of self-expression.

We must utilize this powerful drive of self-interest to perform the complex tasks of modern society. But in the circumstances of our time it cannot be trusted to do the whole job by itself. And so various forms of collaborative enterprise, including the largest club to which we all belong, namely, the government, must step in, first, to rein up self-interest where it is doing harm, and secondly to perform those tasks of mutual aid which must be done communally. And in the resistance to these practical,

empiric *ad hoc* interventions of organized society by doctrines
which either have become obsolete or only partially valid because
qualified by counter-doctrines, we find the clue, not only to the
history of the last fifty years, but to the tensions of the future.
Once there is adequate recognition of the intrinsic complexity of
the problems that confront us, and the extremely limited range
of issues that can be settled out of hand by invoking general
formulas, however hallowed, the whole mental climate in which
these problems are worked out and thought out will be changed.
For then it will become manifest that the science of government
is really the most difficult of all the arts, that it is, in the language
of one of the great Justices of the Supreme Court, uttered more
than a hundred years ago, "the science of experimentation."

Once our temper of mind towards the problems that confront
us has changed it ought to be more easy for us than for any other
people, by virtue of our good fortune, to achieve with measurable
success a gracious and civilized society. For were Milton to address
us, the rulers of this land, as he addressed the rulers of England
three hundred years ago, he could justly say:

> Consider what nation it is whereof ye are, and whereof ye are the
> governors; a nation not slow and dull, but of a quick, ingenious and
> piercing spirit, acute to invent, subtle and sinewy to discourse, not be-
> neath the reach of any point, the highest that human capacity can soar
> to.